Dreamwork
Uncovered

Dreamwork Uncovered

How dreams can create inner harmony, peace and joy

Dr. Marina Quattrocchi

INSOMNIAC PRESS

Library and Archives Canada Cataloguing in Publication

Quattrocchi, Marina, 1954-
Dreamwork uncovered : how dreams can create inner
harmony, peace and joy / Marina Quattrocchi.

Includes bibliographical references and index.
ISBN 1-894663-93-4

1. Dream interpretation. 2. Dreams. I. Title.

BF1091.Q33 2005   154.6'3   C2005-903404-1

The publisher gratefully acknowledges the support of the Canada Council, the Ontario Arts Council and the Department of Canadian Heritage through the Book Publishing Industry Development Program.

Printed and bound in Canada

Insomniac Press
192 Spadina Avenue, Suite 403
Toronto, Ontario, Canada, M5T 2C2
www.insomniacpress.com

To Deborah

Table of Contents

Acknowledgements

This is not my book, it is our book—all the people who have been a part of my life, who have shaped and contributed to *Dreamwork Uncovered*. My co-writers have been numerous: my family, friends, workshop participants, academic associates, and, most importantly, the students at St. Augustine. I didn't do this alone.

Without my friend Deborah, this book would never have been possible. Deborah was the person I trusted to edit my doctoral thesis on dreams. She possessed the intelligence to understand this very academic language and the vision to suggest changes. Finishing a doctoral thesis is often compared to giving birth to a baby, and the emptiness afterwards is called "post-doctoral depression." After years of being immersed in dreams I finished my program, went back to teaching high-school English, and was totally depressed. A voice inside kept saying, "Is this it? You finished feeling empty and unfulfilled." When Deborah said, "Why don't you write a book about dreams?" the darkness vanished. I had a purpose again that became ten years of writing, and rewriting and rewriting. What was at first a very academic book became something personal. Throughout my struggles, Deborah was always there to save me. She knew when I needed advice, counsel, and a friend to confide in. We have shared our dreams for years, so I could understand this whole dream thing on a deeper level. Through these insights I was able to change the academic language of a thesis into a book that everyone could understand. Deborah has always been "the wind beneath my wings," and for that I will be eternally grateful.

The teenagers I had the opportunity to teach at St. Augustine have played an enormous part. Dreamwork wasn't part of any curriculum, and most of us believed the average Joe simply couldn't unravel their dreams. My spirit knew anything was possible, but my mind arrogantly said, "These are just kids, they'll never understand dreams as well as you can, you've been reading Jungian psychology for years!" It didn't take long for them to begin teaching me. I was constantly in awe of their dreams and their ability to understand them without all the academic trappings. I began to understand what education could be—a sharing of equals informing each other on mutually exciting topics. I had the opportunity to do dreamwork with eight classes or approximately 240 students. With few exceptions almost every student gave me written permission to use their dreams in my workshops and writings. They were honest enough to tell me that at first they thought I was completely crazy for teaching dreamwork, then gracious enough to share their work. I wish I could name every single student; a special thanks to Kevin Breadner, Melissa Seetaram, Peter Gal, Somer Arthurs, Shane Thomas, and Richard Moura. I look back on those years with tremendous gratitude. Thanks for enlightening me!

Thanks to my principal at St. Augustine, Wayne Marchand, who never considered me a "crazy woman" and supported everything I did. I was sure I would need to send letters home to parents obtaining permission to do dreamwork. Wayne simply said, "No I think what you're doing is really interesting. You don't need to send home letters." I walked away with my mouth open, wondering if this was a dream. Thanks to all those parents who allowed me to learn and experiment and listened to their teenager's dreams, which honoured our classroom work.

The staff at St. Augustine was incredibly supportive with a sense of humour I truly miss. Particularly my department head, Gary Simon, and assistant department head, Brian Serafini, who never acted like I was crazy either when I talked about aliens and inter-dimensional travel. Ian LeMarquand, Lou Bobyk, Kamil Ali, Roman and Irene Galadza, Maria Watts, Kathy Ingleson, Scott Lee, Lois Booth, Dave Martino, Pauline Regan, Teresa Principe, Chris Urso, Carolyn Esvelt, Carrie Lewis, Shirley Cahute, Mary Scamurra, Paul Donovan, Ana Vieira, Genya Woloshyn, and anyone I missed, there were over one hundred staff!

To friends, clients, and workshop participants who have either shared their dreams or have given me permission to use and adapt them over the years; especially Carole Sisto, Sabrina Delgobbo, Nanci Giovinazzo, Melanie Daigle, Nancy McPhee, Paula Ferracuti, Jacquie Lewin, Stephanie Harquail, Shelley Paul, and Allesandra Kelly-Paul. Maria and John Watts for first opening up their home for my dream workshops. Shelley, who has become my "second sister," a gentle and gracious support. To Betty Richardson for reading my first incredibly long and boring manuscript in 1998 and suggesting that this might evolve into several books or workshop manuals. To Maureen Rae for teaching me the wonders of yoga and for giving me an opportunity to blend yoga with dreamwork in classes at her studio. To Mauricio Parra for persevering in getting me to drink white wine and helping uncover my "dark side."

In memory of Annie Jacobson, the Jungian therapist who saved me during the darkest moments of my burnout and migraines. Annie listened to my dreams and guided my understanding. She provided constant encouragement, believing in me when I didn't believe in myself. Her wisdom, intuition, positive attitude, and genuine caring helped me more than any drug, medical doctor, or treatment could have. When she died of cancer on May 17, 2005, at first I wondered how I could possibly survive without her smile and warm support. But at her memorial service I realized she had given me all the tools I needed to survive on my own. And, so, with wine glass raised to the heavens, and all dimensions and dreams, this one is for you Annie.

To my family, starting with my mother who told me her dreams each morning. To my father who never gave me a hard time for living in a dream world. Chris, my sister, who has been my Rock of Gibraltar, and her husband Doug. My brother Frank, who has always opened up his home to me and never complained even when I stayed for a month in the summer and kept accidentally letting the dog loose. To Sitka, Frank's Siberian husky, who opened up a new meditative path for me on our two-hour morning walks. My nephew Frank who is still teaching me not to be afraid of anything in life, and his wife, Debby. To my niece Lisa, who gives the best bear hugs. She has taught me what unconditional love really is and the importance of patience. Although Lisa is mentally challenged, in many ways she has been my greatest teacher. Her dreams are amazing, especially when she dreams in animation with Fred Flintstone and Prince Charming as frequent characters, or her ability to befriend dream dragons that use their fiery breath to make her tea. To my cat, Small Fry, who sleeps with me every night and often accompanies me in dreams!

To my teachers and committee at the University of Toronto who guided me so graciously through my doctoral program; Ardra Cole, my advisor David Hunt, and Jack Miller. David who frequently appeared as a Santa Claus during my dreams has never stopped giving me the gifts of his time and love. A special thanks to Jack Miller who has made dreamwork in education part of his curriculum. Thanks especially for inviting me to speak to your students every year about the possibilities of using dreams in education.

To Mike O'Connor and Maria Aupérin at Insomniac Press who had the faith in this manuscript to publish it. To Dan Varrette for his amazing job editing my manuscript, and everyone at Insomniac Press who are making this possible. A special thanks to Marian Hebb who helped me understand the strange new world of writers' contracts.

And most importantly, to God, for giving us the ability to achieve great things through dreams.

There Is a Light Inside Us

There is a light inside us that has shone for eternity;
A light deep within our core, it's really you and me.
We think we're just a body, but we are so much more;
It's hard to be that body, it can become a chore.
Our body is just a costume that hides away the years,
And it can be a prison that locks our soul in tears.
If we think we're just a body, we never may be free.
No one is insignificant unless we choose to be.
We may think we're here for money, or lots of material things;
We think we just want power and the comfort that it brings.
But we know even billionaires may not find joy or peace;
With poverty of spirit, our problems never cease.
When we strive for joy and harmony, that light inside us grows,
On the journey to enlightenment, we may shed the status quo.
Within the light inside us, there's a force that's greater still,
That's what we've forgotten, but that's what we can will.
We come here with a destiny, to make the world a better place,
Regardless of our status, colour, creed, or race.
We can have earthly riches, but wealth of spirit too;
When we reach this balanced goal, our harmony is true.
To tap into these riches, we need only to believe
There is a joy of spirit, more than we can conceive.
If we can tap into our dreams, that light shows us the way;
If we can meditate and pray, it brightens every day.
We came here for a purpose and our strength is in that light,
And if we let it guide us, then things will work out right.
We're all beings so stupendous, we've just forgotten who we are.
We can shine through any darkness with the brilliance of a star.
There is a light inside us that heals with harmony;
Empowerment is in that light, it's really you and me.

—Marina

Dreamwork Uncovered is my attempt to share the insights and experiences I am passionate about—the things that have given me energy, joy, peace, and truths, which I hope are setting me free. Everyone will find different meanings and insights as they read. I hope whatever you discover adds greater clarity and purpose to your life. Through dreams may you find your wings and fly.

No two paths are alike. As you journey through life, may you grow in the awareness that comes only from connection to spirit. With this awareness we can make a difference in the world. We can light the way for ourselves step by step, then for others, until we collectively are no longer struggling to climb life's mountains because we are soaring in great harmony above their peaks.

In Dreams, We're Free

The unexamined life is not worth living.
—Socrates

For most of my life I've lived in a world of dreams. As a teenager one of my favourite activities was sleeping. I remember being at a rather wild party where everyone was drinking, dancing, generally having a good time, and I was in one of the bedrooms. I'd like to tell you I was passionately making out with my boyfriend. This was the activity of choice at the time. When friends stumbled in to discover my slumbering body, they were aghast and captured this phenomenon on film. However, I always felt I was really on to something in this mystical world of sleep and dreams.

At a party you can consume copious amounts of wine, beer, and liquor, but have you ever considered that in dreams you can drink as much as you want? And in the morning you don't have to apologize for making a fool of yourself and you never have a hangover. In your waking life, you can eat pizza, appetizers, trays of catered food until you're nearly sick, but in dreams you can eat virtually anything you want and never gain a pound. Believe me, there are even unlimited opportunities for healthy sexual encounters in dreams without worries of pregnancy or contracting a sexual disease. While awake, you meet interesting people at parties, but in dreams you can meet people from other dimensions and galaxies. You can talk to your grandmother who just passed away and receive assurance that she's okay. Lovers can have conversations years before they meet, so they don't have to agonize over whether they'll find their soulmate. If you miss friends and relatives because you've moved to a different country, dreams provide nightly opportunities to get together. Mothers can see their babies months before they're born. I've even talked to animals in dreams, which is more exciting than any wildlife show I've seen on television.

To get to a party, people normally take cars, buses, trains, or planes. This can get rather expensive. Consider that in dreams all forms of transportation are free; believe me, the exhilaration of flying in dreams is quite amazing. While you're awake, the music at parties can be fun and uplifting, but if you've ever heard ethereal music—the vibration and singing of angels—nothing on earth quite compares. Besides, anyone who writes music, regardless of the genre, from rock 'n' roll to symphony, received those musical scores first in their dreams.

So I must confess I've slept through many parties because the world of sleep and dreams has been endlessly fascinating. For many years I felt secretly alone with this passion. My first confirmation that I wasn't alone, however, came while reading about Alfred Einstein. Some believe his hair was always so dishevelled in photographs because he often had just risen out of bed. Rumour has it that Einstein would regularly stumble into his office at ten or eleven in the morning after many hours of satisfying sleep. Later, it was consoling to hear a participant at a dream workshop refer to herself as a "sleep slut." She had been journalling her dreams for years because she believed they guided her. When I read in the newspaper that my idol Sophia Loren usually declined all late-night parties, even on Oscar nights, because she liked to be in bed around 9 p.m., I was ecstatic. But the final confirmation came when I went to see the Dalai Lama speak in Toronto. Someone in the audience asked, "Where do you get your energy?" He said he always tried to get a good night's sleep, usually between seven to nine hours every night and sometimes ten. So now I could come out of the closet about my propensity to sleep ten, sometimes eleven, hours a night and to wake up feeling totally invigorated.

There are so many restrictions in this physical world; we pay for everything: food, clothing, shelter, hydro, water, entertainment, holidays, telephones, education. Yet, all of this is free in the dream state, especially education. Understanding a few dreams can give us as much wisdom as years of schooling, counselling, or psychotherapy. In dreams, we're free to discover and enrich our lives with unlimited possibilities. It's a vast exhilarating world that has continued to intrigue me well beyond my teenage years. I've been to some amazing parties in the last thirty years, but, honestly, my dreams are often more fascinating. Hopefully, you'll see what I mean by the end of this book.

Walking Different Dream Paths—
Religion, Spirituality, or Atheism

It can be confusing to know exactly what dreams are or what category they fall into. Is dreamwork a religious path or a spiritual teaching? Does it have any relevance if you've never believed in God at all? The scriptures of most major religions are filled with accounts of dreams. But within each religion there are leaders who openly advocate dreams and others who dismiss dreams as meaningless or irrelevant. I used to teach for a Catholic school board and for several summers I was hired by the coordinator of religious education to teach dream workshops to teachers. One summer the bishop of the diocese visited these classes. Before he entered my classroom, the coordinator explained this workshop was on dreamwork in education. The bishop was completely taken aback and asked, "What do dreams have to do with religion?" Ironically, he entered just as I was explaining that there are more than seventy dreams throughout the Old and New Testament and how these dreams have shaped the course of history.

Recently, dreams have been viewed more as a spiritual pursuit, but some spiritual practises do not advocate dreamwork. And what if you're questioning whether there is a God at all? What if you've been a confirmed atheist for many years, and life is progressing just fine without God? If so, is there any point in delving into this world of dreams and sleep? Unquestionably, I would say *yes*.

Regardless of what we believe, I have no doubt that dreams are there to guide and assist us each night. They exclude no one. It's nightly free therapy for those who want to use it. If you've never believed in God or never intend to, you can still gain insight, help, and comfort from your dreams. And no matter how dark, fragmented, or hopeless our life becomes, dreams can lead us out of this darkness. Even if someone has robbed a bank, stolen a car, or blown up a building, the function of dreams is to lead them out of these messes and restore sanity and balance again. Like music, movement, or dance, dreams speak a universal language; they can be understood and enjoyed for the harmony and goodwill they bring.

So, the intent here is not to promote one religion or path but rather to help us understand the universal truths found within dreams. The intent is to help us have greater clarity with truths found in religions *and* the truths that may not be part of every religion or spiritual path. We do not just seek to understand the mysteries of dreams; we seek to understand the mysteries of life since dreams are meant to inform our lives. To understand this further, let's delve into the similarities, differences, the light side, and the dark side of both spirituality and religion.

At their best, organized religions have many strengths; they promote faith and teach followers to believe in something greater than themselves. Most teach that the purpose of life is not solely for material gain but for personal growth. They advocate leading a good or holy life. Religions are extremely charitable and teach through example; they minister to the poor, sick, disadvantaged, and homeless. Religions can promote a sense of community, a common vision, and set of beliefs. For the lonely, religions can provide a refuge, a home away from home, and a sense of hope. Most religions promote family values. We turn to religions when we want a meaningful service for baptism or birth, rite of passage into adulthood, marriage, and death. Many people feel lost unless they are involved in their religion because it provides a link to their soul or spirit.

But despite teachings that may be rooted in truth, religion has come under great attack. Many argue that although religions were started by enlightened individuals, they've been changed, interpreted, then reinterpreted until we end up with something that is quite different from the truth. In the Christian tradition it is obvious that neither God nor Jesus wrote the Bible. Another criticism is that religions expect followers to adhere to a set of beliefs, dogmas, or rules developed by those within that religion. People feel that many religions do not respect free will; instead, there is an expectation that we follow only their rules. They don't encourage followers to question, probe, explore, and use their mind and intuition; some expect blind obedience to rules and dogmas. Some fundamental religions do not advocate dreamwork or meditation because they believe that in this vulnerable state Satan will affect us. Another criticism is that religions use fear and guilt to ensure their followers comply. For example, they instill the belief that if you don't go to church every Sunday, you'll burn in hell. A huge criticism is that most religions don't believe the validity of other religions. There is little respect or tolerance for different beliefs. Instead, there is a belief that there is only one way to salvation. Consequently, many religions are exclusive of others; you must formally be a member to take part in their rites, sacraments, or rituals. The Catholic Church would not recognize a marriage that took place in a Buddhist temple. Most religions believe you can only be saved if you are a part of that faith. A further barb is that religions have historically competed against each other. Even today, most of our major wars still involve Catholics against Protestants, Christians against Muslims, or Muslims against the Jewish faith. This age-old quest for supremacy and power has fed the egos of many religious leaders. Perhaps the most recent social critique of religions is that they marginalize and exclude members of society, such as women and the gay community.

At its best, spirituality embraces the core truths within all religions and is inclusive in nature. The intent of spirituality is to help each soul learn, evolve, and enlighten, following the truths that resonate within. There is great respect for free will and following one's internal conscience, spirit, or connection to a higher power. Rather than using guilt and fear as a means of control, spirituality attempts to free its followers of these feelings so that they reach a place of personal empowerment. No one is judged or turned away since we all come from the same eternal Source. Each soul is honoured as an aspect of that Source. Most spiritual teachings do not expect blind allegiance. Individuals are respected and encouraged to question, probe, meditate, and reflect until they discover the truths that give them peace. Spiritual truths are not solely seen as black and white; there are many shades of grey. Spirituality helps its followers discern their own truth in ways that honour themselves and others. For example, marriage is usually believed to be a sacred commitment between two people, but if one person becomes physically abusive and refuses to change, it's no longer a union sanctioned by love and it's acceptable to end the marriage.

Most spiritual teachings do not promote physical levels of distinction or competition of any type. This means that "Joe" down the street, who is unemployed, may have more spiritual merit than the priest, bishop, rabbi, pandit, or imam around the corner. It's believed that anyone following a spiritual path doesn't need a saviour or prophet because they can learn the internal wisdom to save themselves. Women are honoured as equals because the process of evolvement requires integration of both masculine and feminine energies. All great spiritual beings were a mixture of the feminine qualities of compassion, tenderness, and love combined with the masculine qualities of strength, focus, and independence. Most spiritual teachings recognize that there is no such thing as a holy war. Wars are perpetuated by fear, anger, ego, and aggression. None of these qualities are aligned with spirit or light. It is because of this that a huge focus in spiritual teachings revolves around helping us dissolve our inflated egos so that the world can return to a place of peace.

Spirituality, however, is not without its criticisms and shortcomings. With spirituality there is always the danger of an inflated ego, feelings of self-importance, or superiority. I've been in workshops where participants complained that their spouse, boyfriend, or girlfriend "wasn't very spiritual." However, this is quite impossible since at our core we're all spiritual beings with the very difficult task of adapting to a human body. While religion has very clear beliefs and boundaries, spirituality has no specific rules or boundaries, so to those who like structure it may seem vague or even flaky. One would ask just what exactly spirituality is since it seems to encompass many different things. From Eastern mysticism, yoga, meditation, and belief in angels, to healing arts, such as reiki, reflexology, and therapeutic touch; it also includes practises that border on the dark arts, such as witchcraft, mind control, and a whole array of practises using potions, charms, and crystals. Since there seems to be no clear rules or boundaries within spirituality, there is always the danger of creating your own spiritual practise that is self-serving, helps no one, and borders on darkness.

Activities such as prayer, meditation, yoga, Tai Chi, chanting, dreamwork, dance, poetry, art, music, or writing can all be religious or spiritual practises. Through these practises we can evolve, even if we choose not to believe there is a Supreme Being. For example, if we choose to follow Buddhism, there is a great focus on meditation, chanting, love, and compassion. But Buddhists do not speak of or worship a god. For some, yoga can be a deeply spiritual experience although it is not a religion. It can, however, open doors to our spiritual nature whether we believe in God, the Goddess or Mother Earth, Krishna, Buddha, Yahweh, Muhammad, the Force, the universe, or no god at all. For others, yoga is a purely physical practise with no spiritual element at all. We choose our own path.

We may choose a spiritual path, make tremendous progress, and arrive at a place of enlightenment and peace. We may also choose the same spiritual path and make no progress at all if we become self-righteous or self-important. We may choose to practise any religion and experience tremendous growth. Or we may be extremely religious and dogmatic but not very loving or compassionate towards others outside that religion. We may be extremely religious or spiritual, but if we have not reached that place of humility, where we treat all beings with respect and compassion, our religion or spirituality has not served us. An example of this is in the movie *The Apostle* in which Robert Duvall plays Sonny, a southern preacher. It appears that Sonny is a man of faith; a man who has devoted his entire life to God and the Bible. But when Sonny hits his son-in-law on the head with a baseball bat, then flees to protect himself, we become aware of his dark side. As the movie progresses, we realize that Sonny is a man with no conscience and an enormous ego who lives through deceit and manipulation all under the guise of religion. Despite his religious fervour, Sonny lost his connection to spirit, having replaced it with a lesser god—his own self-serving ego.

What about atheists? Many atheists are model human beings. They are loving parents who raise families and hold down responsible jobs. They have a code of ethics they live by; they don't lie, cheat, kill, or steal. Although they don't believe in a god, they have a well-defined system of what is right and wrong and they act accordingly. Most importantly, they believe in themselves and their ability to shape their lives and do the right things. A belief in oneself can be the ultimate testament of inner faith. This belief places faith in our essence, that place within us that is spirit whether we acknowledge a god or not.

Regardless of what practise we follow, there's always the possibility of either aligning with light or becoming sidetracked by our dark side. This often has much to do with our original intent—why we joined that religion or spiritual group in the first place. Let's say we decide to go the spiritual route, take several courses, read a lot of books, then begin meditating every morning and evening. During this meditation practise, we would probably begin to receive greater insight into our dreams. If our intent is to purify ourselves, then this meditation practise could make us calmer, more peaceful, energized, and revitalized. This could help us to be more successful, ethical, and responsible at school or work. It could also help us to be wiser and more compassionate.

Aligning with the light always leads to giving back to society. Aligning with our dark side is usually selfish, egotistical, and serves no one. Imagine someone does the same amount of study and reading before beginning their meditation practise, but their intent is to escape society or to appear superior or "more spiritual than thou." They're late for work because they need to meditate. Their baby is crying, but they're meditating. Most conversations are now filled with all the enlightening experiences they're having. But these conversations are really just boosting their ego and making friends feel inferior or not equal to their "enlightened" friend. This is definitely a shadowy side path that is not aligned with light.

Let's say we belong to an organized religion and there's a hurricane in Haiti that has destroyed thousands of lives. People have lost their loved ones, homes, clothing, and all their possessions; they're starving and disease is running rampant. Following the light is always the most loving, pure, compassionate choice. If a group from any religion gets together, gathers emergency supplies, and supports nurses and doctors to help these hurricane survivors, this religion is aligning with the light. The outcome is that all of humanity benefits since we're all connected. But let's say some people belonging to an organized religion have unfortunately been attacked, misunderstood, and persecuted for centuries. In these attacks, they've lost their home, family, and friends, and, most importantly, their sense of security, love, or purpose. There is no opportunity for them to find meaningful work. They're lonely, sick, and filled with despair, then anger, rage, and vengeance. And so in the name of their religion, they agree to be suicide bombers to get revenge on the religion or group of people they hold responsible. This type of action, although sanctioned and encouraged by select members of that religion, is never aligned with the light. In all of these situations, dreams would have been available for guidance.

As we navigate the world of dreams, it is most important to keep an open mind and especially an open heart, respecting the beliefs of others, even if they differ from our own. No matter what our beliefs tell us, dreams attempt to guide us in a just, compassionate manner. Before we come to earth, I believe our soul decides which religion or set of beliefs will best help us evolve or move forward. Maybe we have been overly religious in many past lives until we've actually become unbalanced, fanatical, or out of touch with reality, so we choose parents who are non-religious. Or perhaps we've never been part of any organized religion and so we decide to explore many religions within one lifetime. We also might have been a Christian in many lives who has hated Muslims, so our soul decides the best way to learn compassion is to spend a lifetime as a Muslim to understand how this feels. So religion, spirituality, and atheism all serve a purpose in this world.

Even if we don't believe in God, we still dream; and understanding our dreams will give us great awareness and purpose. However, I believe it matters most that we live our lives with compassion, love, and respect for everyone whether they have chosen to follow a religious path, a spiritual one, or a path with no god at all.

Being Clear on Why We're Here—Full Enlightenment

Every single dream we have is helping us work toward full enlightenment or a state of peace and perfection. Essentially, we're here to wake up to all the illusions in life that trap us. We're not here just to become rich or famous, become successful at a career, be a mother or father, build up a huge pension plan, or travel and have a good time, although many of these situations can help us awaken or become more aware. The real reason we're all here is to clean up our karma, sins, debts, or issues, and to carry out our dharma or destiny—the gifts, assets, and abilities we arrive with. We come to earth because we need to become purified, whole, or holy again. Somewhere in the past our spirit was in this pure state. We were created perfect but were seduced by darkness. The story of Adam and Eve attempts to explain this. Our spirits have become fragmented or disconnected, and we're here to retrieve all those lost pieces that make us peaceful, loving, and joyful. We're here to let go of things like anger, a need for revenge, fear, the inability to forgive, low self-esteem, ego, judgement, denial, and guilt so that we return to our original state of balanced perfection or pure enlightenment. In this form, we possess the wisdom, freedom, light, and grace that we often attribute to angels. Our spirit decides to come to earth essentially because we're incomplete; we come here broken or infected so that we can heal completely. Dreams can provide the medicine and rest we need to promote this healing. It's like we were all once 100-watt light bulbs, but now we're down to only 20 watts, so we come back to the source of our power outage to figure out what went wrong. But when we arrive back on earth, we unfortunately get sidetracked by money, sex, jobs, and parties and we forget why we came here in the first place. We go through life as only a 20-watt bulb, pretty dim-witted, when we have the potential to be a much greater energy source, lighting the way for others.

When we dream, we're in our natural state, which is spirit. Our body stays in bed while our spirit goes out to show us how to find those 80 watts we're missing. We need a body only to house or protect spirit and a brain to help our soul navigate through day-to-day life. It's like astronauts who wear those heavy awkward spacesuits that limit mobility. But if they didn't wear them to the moon, they would float away because there's not enough gravity. Similarly, without our body to anchor us to the realities of earth and our true mission here, our spirits would just float away to more pleasant dimensions.

For most of my life I really had no idea why I was here. I got so caught up in the illusions and dramas of life that it sucked the joy right out of me. I thought my goal was to succeed at a good, high-paying job. But I was never happy because I kept striving for a better job, greater prestige, more money, and a bigger pension plan. Like a rat on a treadmill, I worked really long hours and endlessly took courses believing earthly success was what life was all about. I was never happy because I had completely neglected my soul or spirit. We get so misdirected that we often begin putting all of our energy in places that never really bring us peace. How tranquil or balanced do we feel after we've worked a 12-hour day, or studied for weeks to pass exams? It's been suggested that if we spent as much time every day meditating as we did thinking about food or eating, we'd probably all be enlightened. We eat three times a day but may deprive ourselves of the spiritual food needed to feel balanced, calm, or fulfilled. Our lives may become more meaningful when we realize our purpose for being here is to reach enlightenment, self-realization, or perfection. We're here to perfect ourselves and until we do, we're trapped in an endless chain of misery. We suffer, age, get sick, die, and watch those we love undergo this same painful cycle.

Coming back to earth over and over is like never graduating from high school. High school or "earth school" may be fun and exciting for a while, but it's not our destiny to stay in high school forever. We're better and brighter than that. There are so many opportunities waiting for us after graduation. It's also like being an actor or actress, performing the same role over and over, never realizing there may be endless opportunities beyond that one drama.

If the concept of enlightenment seems plausible, possibly you've never been comfortable with Darwin's theory that we evolved from apes. Before discussing evolution, I want to make it clear that my intent is not to convert anyone. I'm stating my own theories with the humble acknowledgement that I could be wrong. Please feel free to maintain whatever belief system you feel comfortable with. Consider this book like a fourteen-course banquet you've decided to attend. I've prepared all fourteen courses but don't expect you to digest everything. It's my hope that you'll pick and choose only those concepts or dishes that nourish your body, mind, and spirit. If something doesn't taste right, please go on to enjoy the next course. Adopt your own beliefs; to me, the theory of evolution never made sense.

As a child I wondered how we could be created in the image and likeness of God if we were once apes! Did this mean that God was really a big ape like King Kong? My own image of God was something beautiful and majestic. Darwin, like all of us, was searching for answers to the mystery of life and creation. He arrived at his theory after many years of studying how animals adapt to their changing environments. He came up with a scientific explanation since he was a scientist—this was his asset or gift. He got a lot of people thinking and debating. Some adopted his theories wholeheartedly, others strongly disagreed. We've come a long way since Darwin first proposed his theory in 1859. Back then, everyone believed the earth had existed for only six thousand years. Today, we estimate the earth to be over 4.6 billion years old! We've never found the missing link to prove Darwin's theory that apes began walking upright or evolved into humans. Maybe we've never found it because it doesn't exist. We can all probably think of people who seem primitive or Neanderthal. Even "Billy Boy" who passes gas as he drinks beer all morning, shoots birds in the afternoon in his backyard, and delights in his X-rated movie every evening, has tremendous potential for learning and growth. His heart still has the capacity to explore and to love. Believing we evolved from apes takes away our dignity, honour, and, most importantly, prevents us from understanding our past, releasing our karma, and returning to our true state of enlightenment. I believe our true state is as enlightened beings from highly evolved societies; beings that were compassionate, wise, and free.

Most religions are trying to help us reach this wise compassionate state in different ways. Western religions want to save our souls so we don't go to hell. Eastern religions try to help their followers break through the endless cycle of illusion, karma, and reincarnation. There is truth in both teachings. Hell is disconnection from our spirit or light. If we live in karma, debt, or sin, it's hell on earth. If we rob banks for a living, we're never at peace. Our soul vibrates at a lower rate, our world is distorted, and we're not aware of the trap we've fallen into. Life loses its true meaning because we've become susceptible to darkness. We're trapped without having the awareness of how to get out.

I believe, as the Eastern religions teach, that we come back in physical bodies over and over again, until we pay our debts or karma and become completely pure in spirit. This is our ticket out of physical hell, high school, or small-time drama. Dreams help us tremendously in this process. When we reach this place of enlightenment, we're finally free of the endless chain of human suffering and incarnations. We're not subject to death, physical pain, disease, ego, or fear any longer. We're joyful, peaceful, literally light, and we have a greater capacity to serve and sustain other beings, which gives us great purpose and passion.

When we reach enlightenment, the energy (soul) and matter (body) of our DNA alters. This is a long process taking place over countless lifetimes. When we reach enlightenment, we have a lighter body. If someone tried to shoot us with a gun, we could dematerialize or fly away. That bullet couldn't kill us anyway because we have an energetic rather than a physical body. We don't need to eat, go to the bathroom, or sleep a lot because we're more energy or spirit than physical matter. Since we don't have a physical body, we eat more for enjoyment; spirit does not need money or food to sustain it. We're not the same dense, heavy mass any longer. With a lighter body, we have great clarity and awareness. We're not restricted by time and space. We're not subject to physical laws. We don't need to rob a bank because we don't need physical money. We can cross dimensions at will and assist those who have not yet reached enlightenment. We can fly similar to the way our spirit moves in the dream state. We are sustained by the link, energy, or grace we maintain with spirit. We're never forced into anything. We find work that is exciting and personally meaningful—work that sustains and animates all the enlightened souls we are connected to. This is balanced with great periods of rest and relaxation. When we take a holiday, it's to another dimension or galaxy. When we dream, we're using our spiritual rather than physical body. But, unfortunately, after the dream we must return to our physical bodies because we haven't earned enough spiritual merit to be totally free. We're still working through our karma or debts. Our spirit is still trying to inform our body and mind so that we may become fully enlightened. This place of pure enlightenment is what we are all striving for whether we're consciously aware of it or not.

Following What Feels Right

I was not born to be forced. I will breathe after my own fashion.
—Henry David Thoreau

Personal truths are ever changing. It's not my intent to convince anyone to believe everything written here. You may believe we did evolve from apes, or you may not feel comfortable with a belief in karma or reincarnation and that's fine. If you don't, you can still learn to understand your dreams and this process will give you greater awareness. We can approach this like a philosophy or psychology course; some theories will make sense and others may not. When I taught elementry school, the children loved a series of books where they could choose their own adventures. After the book was introduced, they could actually choose a series of different subplots before turning to the ending. Every reader had the freedom to create their own story or experience from many possibilities. Consider this book as the same; we all create our own dream adventures. Accept only the ideas that feel right or help you. The intent is not to put pressure on anyone. Feel free to accept or reject whatever you wish.

I've come to the conclusion that no human being can truly be an expert on dreams since they're part of a vast spiritual domain. Anyone who devotes their lives to working with dreams may hold a great deal of knowledge and insight. We can claim to be passionate, humbled, fascinated, and intrigued by dreamwork. We could be exceedingly grateful for the opportunity to guide people through their dreams, but insisting we're an authority would be like claiming to be an expert on God, the soul, or all dimensions in the solar system. These areas are just too vast and incomprehensible for the human mind. However, I believe each of us holds the wisdom, memories, and insights to be experts of our own dreams; in fact, this is our destiny.

I can't claim that any of my theories are right or perfect because I am human and still evolving. I would have to be fully enlightened to make that claim. And if I was fully enlightened, I wouldn't be living on earth teaching, writing books, and getting colds, headaches, and heartaches! Theories evolve to help us to question, grow, and move forward. Sometimes, after many years, we understand those theories don't apply any longer. I can only tell you that right now, everything I've written has helped me find greater awareness. I find these universal laws exciting; they've answered my big questions such as why I am here and what my purpose is. Ten years from now, I would probably write a much different book because my understandings may have evolved and the world would be different. If we read a book about medicine, psychology, human relations, nutrition, or rocket science written in 1905, we may find it quite amusing. One hundred years from now, people may read this book and feel the same way. I can only tell you that I believe these concepts are true for this time. Some of these theories may be timeless and never change, others may be disregarded as humanity evolves.

Possibly my only credentials are that my life has been characterized by constant physical, emotional, and spiritual pain. In my forties, I began to understand that much of my pain was self-imposed. Before this, I was deluded into believing I was a powerless victim of life. It was even more painful to admit that I held the keys to my own prison. When many dreams helped me become aware of this, I wanted to share what I'd learned. Perhaps we've all created our own prisons in different ways, but it's possible to set ourselves free. The keys to freedom are not that complex or difficult; they're available to anyone who truly seeks them. To help you, I'm teaching everything I'm still learning on this journey. We're in this together, walking hand in hand.

All teachers must humbly admit they don't know everything. No teacher is God on a mountaintop. Our mind may trick us into believing that mountain we're climbing is the final summit of knowledge. We arrive at the top only to discover another mountain in the distance or an undiscovered valley of lost cities and possibilities. Dreams have kept me in a state of awe because they always bring us to higher levels of awareness. It's like getting to the next level in a video game. Once you've cleared away the obstacles and earned the right to a higher level, there are new landscapes and challenges. Just when I think I've figured something out, life throws me a new curve ball, and, humbly, I feel like I'm back in kindergarten. Over and over I must admit just how much I don't know and how much I need to keep changing. Also, I must realize that I need to be open to new experiences. I've been hooked for life because it is humbling yet exciting work.

We All Have the Capacity to Understand Our Dreams

We all have the ability to understand our dreams; it's part of who we are. Although dream experts are knowledgeable, it's not always possible to see them. If we find a dream therapist we connect with, it's a rewarding experience. I had sessions with Jungian analyst Annie Jacobson, who helped me tremendously. I left each session with greater awareness and hope. Annie was a godsend to me at a time when I needed validation and support. I've come to realize that going to a dream expert is a bit like having a personal chauffeur or friend willing to drive you around. At times when we're busy, stressed, or not feeling well, it's better to have someone drive us. But most of the time we can drive ourselves. It's the same with dreams; we all have the innate ability to understand our dreams, but a friend can often help us see things in a different way. Even an expert needs a lot of information about our lives before they can piece together the meaning of a dream. They need to ask questions about our emotions, hopes, challenges, and life experiences. Ultimately, the final decision regarding the meaning of any dream lies inside us. We're the real experts of our lives.

For seven years I did dreamwork in a high school and there wasn't one student who couldn't understand their dreams. These sixteen- and seventeen-year-olds arrived at deep insights that left me in awe. This understanding was never an intellectual exercise; the students with the highest marks weren't gaining deeper insights. As long as their intent was sincere—to arrive at truth—they succeeded. Understanding dreams is not a mental exercise; it's tapping into intuition, or spirit, which is our core. It's really combining reasoning with intuition. We all have the ability to use our intuition and this can be that first step towards enlightenment. Besides, understanding a dream is rewarding and exciting, one of life's natural highs.

Recognize That Dreams Are Just One of Many Tools

Although dreams give us incredible wisdom and insight, dreamwork is one of many methods that can help us evolve. Balance is important on any spiritual path, so if we use only one technique, there is the possibility that down the road we may become unbalanced. There is never an expectation that we must journal our dreams every single night. It's like wanting to get into peak physical shape and believing that the only way to do this is by running. We may be stiff and inflexible because we haven't done enough stretching. If we want to flex our spiritual muscle, understanding dreams is a good place to start. Like running, it can be demanding when we begin, but the payoffs are enormous. As we evolve, we may incorporate several meditative techniques into our life. We may realize the importance of daily prayer. Or we may use dance, music, yoga, photography, painting, art, poetry, writing, gardening, cooking, or reading to help us unfold. As we evolve, we won't focus solely on dreaming; instead we will focus on living and how dreams give balance and clarity to life.

Unlocking Personal Wisdom

Who do you think is the wisest, most insightful, and compassionate being in our universe? This may be someone you know or someone you have never met. It could be an angel, archangel, God, Buddha, Mary, Princess Diana, Jesus, Ghandi, Martin Luther King, or your grandmother. Now imagine there is a passageway from your bedroom to this person. You can talk to this person every night. They will tell you stories in metaphors and symbols that give you guidance and insight. Turning to our dreams is like discovering this passage and consulting this person every day. The opportunity is always there; the passageway is never blocked.

Within each of us lies wisdom and truth waiting to be revealed. This wisdom is not physical; it lies within the emotions, heart, or spirit. Everything we need to know is inside us; we have just lost our set of keys. Dreams give us one key at a time to unlock this wisdom.

Many people believe they don't dream, but the truth is we spend more time dreaming than we do eating, exercising, or having sex! We spend much of our lives looking for answers within the physical environment or through the mind. Without understanding, this can often be the realm of illusion, confusion, pain, and suffering. The mind and all its physical illusions can keep us trapped for an eternity. Truth is found within spirit, which is the landscape of dreams. Once we extract this truth from spirit, we can use our minds to decide how we can best use these truths. When we balance the logic of our mind with the wisdom of spirits, we can be wise, compassionate, and more joyful.

If we want answers to questions like, "Who am I? Why am I here? Why am I confused, sick, or suffering?" the place to find out has always been within spirit. Our soul has all these answers. Our mind will keep us locked in doubt, despair, and confusion since the mind vibrates at a much lower level. The mind is physical. Darkness, doubt, and despair—our personal demons—can seep into and control the mind, leaving us scared and scattered. Dreamwork taps into spirit giving us clarity and insight. Darkness, doubt, and despair do not walk in the domain of spirit. The vibrations there are too high, too bright. It's like the vampire that can only survive in its dark coffin. Doubt and darkness confuse the mind, but dreams help us walk out of this confusion. It is our mind that tricks us into believing that dreams are nonsense with no meaning. It has always been through spirit or soul that we find freedom and peace.

It is a choice. Do we buy into the material world of the mind? Or do we recognize that empowerment lies within our spirit? Do we immerse ourselves totally in the physical world and all its pain or illusions? Or do we allow ourselves time to journal our dreams, meditate, go for long walks, pray for guidance, and observe those meaningful coincidences in our life? Do we doubt? Or do we believe in miracles? Do we follow the masses chained to illusion and suffering? Or do we dare to walk where few have the courage to go? Do we believe we all must die? Or do we believe in the possibility of reaching enlightenment and immortality? Do we allow the physical world to keep us chained forever? Or do we acknowledge that in the world of spirit there are no boundaries, only endless possibilities? Can we think outside of life's boxes?

Each of us leads a double life. We have this physical life we're very aware of, but it's like we're double agents. Every night in dreams we have adventures that are mind boggling, so mind boggling that our conscious minds try to disregard them. Dreams allow us to walk and talk in the dimensions of spirit and to bring back valuable insights. They give us the keys, the codes, the answers to leading a life with joy and meaning. To disregard our dreams is to disregard the life of our spirit. The real you is the being that is free to explore your dreams. The illusion is that we're just a body, meant to grow old, suffer, and die. We are so much more than that, if only we believe.

Chapter One
Karma, Dharma, and Dreams

If you bring forth what is within you what you bring forth will save you. If you do not bring forth what is within you what you do not bring forth will destroy you.
—The Gospel of St. Thomas

Before we become fully enlightened, we have two main tasks to complete. First, we need to work through our issues or karma. Secondly, we need to fulfill our destiny or dharma, the unique contribution we make to the world. So karma is our debt and dharma is often our means of payback or coming clean. If "Joe" were a serious alcoholic, this would be his karma, one of the issues he needs to work through. Let's say Joe goes to Alcoholics Anonymous (AA), learns their twelve-step program, and follows it faithfully for ten years until he's no longer dependent on alcohol. Joe is grateful for the help he's received and decides to be a group leader in AA. He begins teaching classes twice a week, helping others beat their addiction. This giving back or teaching becomes part of Joe's dharma. And who is better qualified to understand the difficulties around alcoholism than someone who has gone through that experience? If Joe had been journaling his dreams, they would definitely have been showing him the self-destructive problems with his drinking. He might have been guided to join AA in a dream. For years, dreams would give him the insight and strength to not fall back into this addiction. Finally, dreams might have nudged Joe towards teaching or volunteering with AA. He might have begun teaching alcoholics in his dreams to give him the practise and confidence to do this in his physical life. In every dream, we're working through either karma and dharma, so to grasp the meaning of our dreams, it's important to understand these underlying principles first.

Without understanding karma and dharma, dreams can seem mysterious or complex. It's complicated to be told there are lucid dreams, prophetic dreams, and waking dreams. We can have dreams where we do the following:
- face our worst fears,
- recognize our shadow side,
- strip down our egos,
- learn not to judge,

- take in new information,
- discard old information,
- problem solve,
- experiment and prepare for new ideas,
- end bitter relationships,
- work on new relationships,
- learn to heal physical problems,
- clear up unfinished business with the deceased,
- clear up messes at work,
- plan any future event,
- gain awareness of our potential,
- prepare for a major change,
- prepare for a holiday, or
- prepare to die

It's simpler to understand that every dream attempts to move us towards enlightenment by helping us work through our karma or carry out our dharma or destiny. Understanding this can put every dream in perspective, except for one major hurdle: most of us don't understand the laws of karma and dharma, especially if we grew up in North America.

If we were born into Eastern religions such as Hinduism or Buddhism, we would understand karma and dharma. Many people don't, however, and this can be what traps us in endless pain and suffering. When we're clear about karma and dharma, we understand what our soul is doing in dreams to move us forward. This awareness has the potential to dramatically alter our lives. If we break down karma and dharma to the most simple Western terms, we could say that karma is sin or debt and that dharma is grace, spiritual merit, or destiny.

The word *karma* comes from the Sanskrit verb *kri*, which means "to do." Karma can be any thought, word, or action that does not contribute to our well-being or to the harmony of the universe. Karma is leading a life without connection to our soul or spirit. It's a universal spiritual law and there is no escaping it. We've all heard people say, "He's gotten away with murder." But do we really know what happens to someone's soul when they die? If we believe in the laws of karma and dharma, we know this simply isn't true. If we don't pay back our debts in this lifetime, we will in another earth incarnation or in another dimension. Since the life of our soul is endless, we have an eternity to pay back our debts. God is extremely patient.

Before we come to earth, our soul determines what debts we will repay. It creates a multi-faceted book or life plan where we script in all the people who were with us in previous lifetimes. Some people will be purely dharmic individuals who will guide, love, and support us. Other people are individuals we've experienced karma with repeatedly. Perhaps Joe has been an alcoholic in countless lifetimes, married to the same woman whom he emotionally abused. Joe scripts in this wife with the intention of giving up alcohol and paying back all the emotional turmoil he's caused her. Each life is an opportunity to wipe the slate clean. If we're sincere, connected, and aware, we take the necessary steps to repay our debts. If we go through life unaware or in denial, we often repeat the same karmic patterns. If we've always been a gossip, it will feel easy and familiar to fall into this trap. It's harder to realize that gossip gives one a false sense of power—that it is a hurtful ego trap. If we're unable to correct our karma then life remains extremely difficult; it's like getting stuck in mud. It's difficult to move forward; we stay in that same dark place and seemingly "unfair" things just keep happening.

Free will and the ability to discern and make different choices can be our greatest assets. We can make the choices that enable us to pay back our debts or wipe the slate clean, but we often choose not to. Instead, we recreate the same scenarios, blame others, believe we're victims, believe life must be hard all the time, or believe life is unfair. When we've paid back much of our karma and are consciously living a more dharmic life, things will begin to flow in a much different way; everything becomes clearer and hopefully more peaceful. Or, simply, bad stuff isn't happening to us *all* the time. The more dharmic our lives become, the greater is our capacity to give back to the world, and this gives us a greater passion and purpose for living. There will always be negativity in the world, but we have a greater capacity to rise above it, rather than become immersed in it. We have the insight to leave many of the unnecessary dramas behind.

Unfortunately, most of us become stuck in karmic patterns and life can be hell. It's like we've dug deep holes for ourselves and don't know how to get out. Most of us are good-intentioned people, but we're often unaware of the traps so we keep following the same patterns. What are some of these karmic patterns that trap us? Usually, these are not obvious things like blowing up a building or robbing a bank. The most insidious traps can be passive things that are not as visible:

- low self-esteem,
- lack of self-honour,
- self-doubt,
- working too much and becoming unbalanced,
- overeating,
- not sleeping enough,
- rarely exercising,
- lack of respect,
- inability to forgive,
- secretly wanting revenge,
- living in fear rather than faith,
- hoarding in fear of not having enough,
- always wanting more material things,
- attachment to physical things,
- getting stuck in depression,
- suppressing our true passions and joys,
- not allowing ourselves to experience joy,
- getting stuck in guilt rather than correcting our behaviour,
- punishing ourselves,
- greed,
- judgement,
- ego,
- silently believing we are better or superior

The list is really endless. What's important to understand is that most of us stay deep in that miserable hole because we're not aware of what keeps us there. Dreams can be the ladders that help us to get out. We often bury our ladders so deeply we can't remember where they are. We say, "I never remember my dreams." Or we think dreams are just random, meaningless brainwaves. Simultaneously, we wonder why our lives seem to be falling apart, why "life is a bitch," or why life is so meaningless, unfair, or cruel. We also believe we have absolutely no control over our lives. We live, suffer, and die. But what kind of a cruel uncompassionate God would design our lives like that? The answer is simple. He or She didn't. Humans did. We have free will and the ability to make informed choices. We can choose to bury the ladder and dig deeper holes of misery and despair for ourselves, or we can climb up that ladder into light.

Understanding the Spiritual Laws

The truth is that we are all here walking around in physical bodies because we have karma, debt, or sin to clean up. But we also have an important destiny or purpose for being here, which is our dharma or path. No one's life is meaningless, unless we choose to make it that way. On some level we're all aware of this, although it may not be conscious. There are so many phrases that explain karma: "He had it coming to him," "You get what you deserve," "Nothing in life is free," "Nothing is the way it seems," "That's when the shit hit the fan," or "All hell broke loose." If it seems all hell is breaking loose, then we are facing our karma. Another way of understanding karma and dharma are the phrases, "What goes around comes around," or the Irish saying, "What is meant for me, won't go by me." Since karma and dharma are universal spiritual laws we can look to the Bible, science, history, even astrology to gain a clearer understanding of these universal laws.

Religion

There is the well-known Biblical phrase that states, "Whatsoever a man soweth, that shall he also reap" (Galatians 6:7). A modern version of Galatians reads like this: "Do not deceive yourselves; no one makes a fool of God. A person will reap exactly what he plants." In other words, whatever we put out is returned to us. Put out hatred and we get hatred back. Put out love and love is returned.

In Western or Christian religions the equivalent of karma would be sin. Eastern religions believe we incarnate carrying karma through from previous lifetimes. Western religions believe we come into the world as sinners or with original sin on our souls. We are simply using different words for the same spiritual laws. Both recognize that we come into the world with karma or sin, and that we can also accrue more karma or sin while we are here. Karma or sin is like accumulating a negative bank debt, credit-card debt, or personal loan. Eventually we have to come clean. We have to pay it off. We can't declare personal bankruptcy in the spiritual world. No being can escape these spiritual laws.

Science

In science we can look to Newton's law of cause and effect to understand karma and dharma. Newton's law states that for every action there is equal and opposite reaction. This is a law of science and a universal spiritual law. There is an effect or consequence for everything we do. Here's how it translates karmically: lie to our neighbour and they will mistrust us; hit a child and they will fear us; don't show up at work repeatedly and our boss will fire us; chain-smoke for twenty years and we develop cancer or lung disease; laugh and belittle a co-worker and they'll resent us; go through life without respecting ourselves and we'll be disrespected; pollute our rivers and we won't be able to swim in them; drink and drive and we lose our license; fail to pay our income taxes and we'll be fined; pile up garbage and create a mess. Cause and effect is impossible to avoid.

History and Astrology

Throughout history there has been the symbol of the scales of justice, settling our score, or balancing our karma and dharma before we enter heaven. Three thousand years ago in Egypt, detailed paintings of judgement scenes showed newly deceased Egyptians appearing before their gods. In the middle of these scenes there is always an enormous scale. The heart of the deceased is placed on one side of the scale while a feather is on the opposite side. It was believed if this soul had unresolved karma at death, their heart would be dark and heavy. This meant the soul would be devoured by an awaiting monster called "the great eater." But if their heart was light, if they had no dark, heavy karmic deeds to weigh down the scale, their spirit or heart would be in complete balance with the feather on the opposite side. Then they would be accepted into the after-world, heaven, or the domain of Osiris, God of the dead. Centuries later, the Romans adopted their own version of this judgement scene. In Roman art, a woman representing justice held a sword and a pair of scales, and the archangel Michael weighed the souls of the dead before Christ.

In ancient Greece there was the symbol of the woman holding the scales, Athena, the patron and protectress of Athens. Athena, like the archangel Michael, is often portrayed brandishing a sword and stepping on the head of a serpent. In her other hand Athena holds up the scales of justice. She is the judge; but her judgement is wise and impartial. No one receives favours; we reap exactly what we sow. To symbolize this impartiality, Athena wears a blindfold representing blind justice. Behind her blindfold, Athena, like her father, Zeus, holds the knowledge of all our karmic and dharmic deeds. Athena's scales weigh our karma against our dharma, and when our karmic debts have been released, we're free at last from the pain and drudgery of the human experience.

In astrology, we have this same symbol of the scales representing the seventh sign of the zodiac, Libra. People born under this sign, like Athena, are said to possess a sense of justice, a desire for harmony, the ability to see both sides of any issue, and, like Ghandi, whose sign was Libra, a yearning for peace and non-violence.

Life is a Huge Reality Series

We can stay trapped in this hole we have dug for ourselves because we want to believe God doesn't see how we lied to our boss, cheated on our income tax, or gossiped at work. But the reality is that God and countless enlightened beings are able to hear every prayer, know every thought, and witness every action we make. Spiritually or energetically, we're never alone. We're like spiritual children who have baby or surveillance monitors on us twenty-four hours a day, seven days a week, until we reach full enlightenment. And these surveillance videos can be replayed any time by enlightened beings. Once recorded, they become part of a vast spiritual library.

If people are not aware of this, they just keep incurring more sins, debt, and karma because they're under the illusion they can "get away with it." Countless movies show villains laughing at their victims, falsely believing they've outwitted them. But when their plans go awry, they wonder why life seems so unfair. The "bad guys" don't understand karma—for every action there is an equal and opposite reaction. They think they get away with things temporarily, but it always catches up with them.

Karmic Traps

We do not always like what is good for us in this world.
—Eleanor Roosevelt

There are four traps we all fall into regarding karma, but awareness can be the ladder leading us out of this darkness.

1. We're often not aware enough to make karmic connections.
2. As we're paying back karma, we're adding new karma and further increasing our debt.
3. We blame God or other people, rather than taking responsibility for karma.
4. We believe *only* doing good deeds erases our karma.

A huge part of the problem with karma is that often we're not aware enough to make connections. We may be burning off karma from several lifetimes ago and so misfortune in our life seems unfair. It's always easier to see the issues or karma of others, so perhaps this can be a way to start before we dig deep down and face our own shadows. I met a man who had an uncontrollable temper. As an adult, he frequently took temper tantrums and terrorized everyone around him. I witnessed his behaviour at an airport when he had missed his flight; he started yelling, screaming, swearing, and he threw his baggage across the terminal—the equivalent of a temper tantrum of a two-year-old. After several years of putting up with this, his wife left him and maintained custody of their children. Because of his violent temper, he was only allowed to see his children while supervised by an approved family member. He also could never keep a job, especially jobs where he had to interact with people because he would get angry, yell, and insult others. He was extremely opinionated and felt he was always right, despite having no specialized training or formal education. In his forties, he was still going from job to job. This individual actually believed he was a victim of life. He believed his wife had treated him unfairly and that every single employer didn't give him a fair chance to prove himself. He rationalized that he was let go because his boss was a jerk, he had the least seniority, or the economy was bad. It never occurred to him for a second that he was creating his own karma, and he had probably carried this violent temper with him from lifetime to lifetime. If he were able to journal his dreams, there would be constant insights helping him become aware how self-destructive this behaviour is. Dreamwork would be difficult, humbling, yet rewarding work. He could begin to make changes, and over time he may unlock that inner harmony and peace that we're all seeking.

A more poignant example could be that perhaps someone was a soldier for Attila the Hun, Julius Caesar, Constantine, or Alexander the Great and he burned down hundreds of huts and left people homeless. Every lifetime afterwards, he lived with the same illusions believing war was just, even noble. Blindly, he followed these types of leaders believing they had great vision. He killed and destroyed for this vision, one of supremacy, ego, and control. He had no respect for the sanctity of life. He believed he was doing the right thing in burning down these homes. With all this self-righteousness, he also felt he was superior to the masses. In this lifetime, he's carried around the same illusions like heavy ammunition. Maybe he's a military commander or a warlord aiding and abetting those who go to war to destroy and burn more homes. Again, he's locked in illusion believing his nation is right, his cause is just, and he's doing the right thing. Except that war is almost always a purely karmic event.

Perhaps for countless lifetimes he's never found the means to repay this debt. So before he incarnated into this lifetime, he agreed to have his house or business burn down to experience the grief and all the emotions that accompany losing one's place of identity. Perhaps his soul realized the most poignant way to end this karmic cycle was to experience first hand this painful loss and destruction. But when his house or business burns down, he becomes angry, bitter, and blames God. It's really easy to blame a Supreme Being. It's emotionally tougher to accept misfortune, be humbled, meditate, pray, or look at one's dreams to get answers. That's why so few people do it. He may blame God, the fire department, the faulty wires, neighbours, or the fire alarm if he's unaware of the laws of karma and dharma. If he were connected to spirit, his dreams would have begun preparing him for this event years before it happened. Although this is an extreme example, it's possible that some souls have chosen to work out karma in this fashion. There are no black and white rules with karma. Every soul is unique and chooses to pay back karma in different ways. If this person was aware, through dreamwork, intuition, visions, meditation, and faith, he would understand on a deep level this is something his soul with its wisdom of all past lifetimes chooses to experience, correct, or pay back. It is never something unfair that has been imposed on any soul.

For most of us this is hard to accept, especially if we've had lots of drama and karma like I did. We've been socialized to believe things like this are "just an accident" or that it's nobody's fault. It's a total shift in awareness that usually needs to be done gradually. The example of a burning house is something I've experienced. Many years ago, I was responsible for a fire that burned down our family cottage at Christmas. I had been cooking with hot oil. The cottage had been winterized, and it was my brother's permanent home at the time. After I had dealt with the shock and guilt of what had happened, I had a deep feeling that this was a huge karmic debt I needed to repay. I'm sure in many previous lives I lived in, it was considered acceptable to burn down houses or burn witches at the stake, and I had played a part in these burnings. I knew this was my soul's way of coming to terms with hundreds, possibly thousands of years of karmic fires.

A second huge problem with karma is that while we're trying to clean up debts from past lives, we often keep incurring more and more present-life karma. It's like people who reach the maximum limit on a credit card, only to apply for a different card, and then apply for a line of credit at a bank; the debt just gets bigger and bigger. Karma keeps us trapped in the hole forever. If we're aligned with our spirit, we won't keep on creating new karma or debts. There's always a way out.

For years I was getting in car accidents and feeling like a complete victim. I believed these were just "accidents" and weren't my fault, even when I was charged. I lived in constant denial. Finally, the company that insured me cancelled my policy because I had two at-fault accidents in one year. For the longest time I was quite angry with the insurance company. I was self-righteous and believed this was a horrible injustice. I told all my friends and created a huge drama in which I was the innocent victim of this horrible company that had been financing my car accidents for years. I kept on like this until a wise man pointed out that I was simply an irresponsible driver. I drove when I had severe migraines, impaired vision, and limited awareness. This was my condition whenever I had an accident. When he told me this I had an awful sick feeling in my stomach. It felt like being struck by a lightning bolt, but I had to admit he was right. I was a lousy driver. I stopped driving completely whenever I had a migraine. I paid huge insurance premiums for four years as a part of my karmic debt but stopped having accidents. Unless we are humbled and look inside for answers, rather than blaming life, we often just continue the same senseless patterns.

The third trap we fall into is blaming God or trying to make God a scapegoat for our actions. We often hear people say, "God must have wanted me fat or He wouldn't have made me this way" or "The Bible says it's okay to spank my children when they're bad" or "I'm exhausted and stressed all the time, but God never gives you more than you can handle." The truth is, it is our soul, not God, that writes our spiritual blueprint or life contract. Imagine how much work it would be for God to create a detailed spiritual blueprint for billions of souls! Imagine how controlling it would be if some greater being predetermined everything for us. God sanctions our contracts before we incarnate, but we design our lives in a way that will enable us to clean up our karma until we reach full enlightenment. God doesn't decide to make us overweight, strict, or overwhelmed in life; we make all those choices ourselves. This tendency to make God responsible for every "bad" thing is so prevalent and ingrained in our minds that we'll examine it in more detail after this section.

We are frequently seduced into a belief system of learned helplessness or victim consciousness. We are not helpless, nor are we victims. Everything that happens to us in life is the result of something we've done. We're all learning to accept responsibility for the past and this can be emotionally painful work. By simply becoming aware, we may unlock the door from lifetimes of pain and hardship, providing great hope for the future. We create our futures by the way we live today.

The final trap is believing that doing good deeds will somehow erase all our karma. A humorous story entitled "Evil bad luck has left me jaded" by Tracy Nesdoly in the *Toronto Star* illustrates this well. She writes, "I have been suffering some very bad luck." What Tracy really means is that her soul decided it's time to face her karmic debts. Tracy says, "Because the bad luck is so extraordinarily bad, so perversely bad, I cannot shake the feeling that something large is at work, that some complex cabal has caught me in its jaws. In a past life or somewhere along the way, I have done that for which I am now paying handsomely." So Tracy does what many intelligent well-intentioned people do: she tries to turn her fate around with good deeds. She continues, "In an attempt to appease the gods or break the pattern of evil, I have been trying to atone for all the bad and semi-bad things I've done. I have been paying it forward as best I can—being kind to people I don't like (this backfires), patting scary dogs, being nice to children . . . Still the badness persists." Tracy is told by a friend that wearing jade jewellery will "balance her karma." Her friend swears that since she started wearing jade nothing bad has happened; she's even had remarkably good luck. So Tracy goes to her local mall and buys a jade ring. She learns, like many of us, that it's not that easy. No piece of jewellery, good luck charm, magic spell, affirmation, or good deed erases our karma or "bad luck." What can bring about this change, however, is serious soul searching, meditation, reflection, and journalling our dreams. Tracy confesses, "Since I've been wearing the ring, a couple of more things have gone terribly wrong—including the sudden work stoppage of virtually every appliance in my home."

Unfortunately, karma just keeps smacking us in the face until we've gained the awareness to clear it up. The funny thing is we don't have to go looking for our karma; it has this brilliant way of finding us no matter how hard we try to hide or how spiritual or religious we claim to be. Priests, saints, and hermits all had to face their dark side.

There is one sure way to know what our karma is. We just ask ourselves questions like, What is really causing me pain in life? What patterns or events keep repeating? What is driving me crazy? What is it that seems unfair? What do I hate to do, admit, or feel? Who are the people that really get under my skin? Chances are, if we can answer these questions honestly, we'll know.

Seeing our own karma is as difficult as seeing that blind spot in our rear-view mirror. We see all those other drivers around us, except that one looming object that can potentially crash into us. As we cruise this highway of life, it's the racing, red Firebird that will probably get a speeding ticket, and it's the bald seventy-year-old man in the Mercedes fondling the eighteen-year-old that may be courting a heart attack, while we fail to notice we're running out of gas. Since it's difficult to see our own karma, yet so entertaining to observe others, we often miss our karma completely or assume if we do good deeds everything will be all right. But even if we pick up a hitchhiker, stop to help an elderly man change his tire, or stop to give someone's battery a boost, this doesn't negate our need to fill up with gas. We can completely run out of gas or energy in life before realizing we're in deep trouble. We can pet a million puppies, give to charities until we're broke, feed hundreds of stray kittens, volunteer until we're exhausted, and smile at every stranger we meet, but if this doesn't address or relate directly to our karmic patterns, we'll be petting puppies for eternity.

Imagine "Charlie" is vice president of a bank, and happily married with two teenage daughters. But he's gone through lifetime after lifetime hating Muslims and committing countless crimes against them. Otherwise, Charlie is a model citizen. He's just won a "Businessman of the Year" award for providing summer jobs to teenagers (like him, all of them are Catholics). He's also won "Volunteer of the Year" for his ceaseless work in raising money for cancer research. But privately, Charlie looks down on Muslims, and he publicly condemns and judges them. He's never hired Muslims in his company and has lectured his two daughters to never associate with them. So guess what happens to Charlie? The house beside him goes up for sale and a large Muslim family moves in. His bank merges with another bank and his new boss is a Muslim. The family that moved in next door has teenaged sons. His eldest daughter secretly begins dating one of these sons, then announces they're in love and will elope if her father can't accept this marriage. Charlie could either wonder why his life is falling apart when he's been such a model citizen, or he could become aware that these are all karmic adventures. This could be a great opportunity for him to be humbled, gain respect for all faiths, and dissolve his hatred into acceptance.

How Could God Do Something So Cruel? He Didn't.

Since our souls or spirits do not originate from earth, they follow spiritual rather than human laws. Every soul comes to earth school to clean up karma, and when the soul has accomplished this, it leaves. Moving on is joyful freedom for the soul, like a genie being released from a bottle that has trapped it for thousands of years. Being able to leave is the reward, not staying on earth. Expecting any soul to stay here forever is like expecting someone to never graduate from high school. There's just no point; it would completely stifle and trap spirit. Each soul leaves when its mission is complete. But since we operate by earthly expectations, we often believe this is the worst fate that could happen to a person.

When we don't understand the laws of karma and dharma, it's easy to blame God if someone we love dies or when anything goes wrong. Rather than trying to understand things from a spiritual perspective, we rely on our minds or we use God as our scapegoat. The logic of rational thought just doesn't work if we want to understand the mysteries of life and death.

When things become karmic in life, we often become bitter and angry. We've lost the ability to make connections and understand why we have things like wars, earthquakes, sniper shootings, suicide bombings, bankruptcies, divorces, cancer, heart attacks, or deaths. We forget these things exist because most human beings are still karmic. We know that people we love will inevitably die, but when it happens we resort to anger and bitterness, rather than seeking the spiritual awareness that brings us comfort. When a child or relative dies, it is common to lose faith. Our minds trick us into believing that physical existence, with all its pain and karmic issues, is the ultimate way to live. We forget that our time on earth was only meant to be temporary. We forget that friends and relatives who have moved on can be better off than we are.

In our anguish we cry out, "Where is God now?" or "How could God allow something so terrible to happen?" If we don't understand the laws of karma and dharma, it's easy to blame God or fall into the illusion that we've been deserted. I believe God weeps at the cruelty and inhumanity that exists more than any other being. Imagine His sorrow at watching suicide bombers kill His children in His name! I also believe God has faith that we'll eventually get it right and clean up our karma. This is why He has given us free will and choices. He believes in us, even though He watches us make the very same mistakes repeatedly.

Many people become disillusioned and blame God when they read about beatings, robberies, rapes, or wars. How could God possibly allow this innocent five-year-old girl to be raped by her uncle? First, we need to understand this little girl and her uncle probably scripted this as a possible choice in their spiritual blueprints. For a myriad of reasons, this painful experience may have been the catalyst for their growth. "Bad things" may occur so we can transcend these experiences and become strong and personally empowered. We can't become fully enlightened if we allow ourselves to be a victim either physically or emotionally. After a rape, someone may choose to shrivel up and die. Alternatively, they may decide to work with their emotions, forgive the rapist, become strong and fearless, and then support other survivors of rape. Many wealthy, compassionate, confident, empowered women were once raped.

The key to understanding all of this is realizing that God doesn't fix our messes because we have the ability to fix them ourselves. God never desired to control us or make us puppets. It's much the same if we think of parent/child relationships on earth. Overbearing, controlling, unloving fathers do not respect their daughters or believe they have the common sense to find a good husband. So they may enforce strict rules and not allow their daughter to date or bring a boyfriend home. A wise benevolent father wants his daughter to find love and happiness, so he sets reasonable rules and allows his teenage daughter to start dating. This father knows his daughter may become hurt or heartbroken, but he believes in his daughter's ability to learn from each relationship and eventually find someone who will make her happy. A good father watches, supports, gives guidance when asked, but does not interfere. All parents know that their children may be involved in a car accident. They know that if they learn to drive, they may be seriously injured or even killed. But most parents let their children drive because it brings freedom and greater responsibility.

Another example is a father whose child has been sentenced to time in jail for robbery. Parents know they must follow the rules, especially civil and criminal law. They know this jail sentence is the karma, debt, or payback their child must endure. Few parents enjoy seeing their children in jail, but they allow this process to occur, hoping the sentence will allow their child to realize the severity of their actions and not repeat past mistakes. Most parents honour and abide by the judicial system. They don't try to break their children out of jail. It's the same with God. He watches us complete our karmic time on earth, but He can't intervene. Even God follows the rules. He wants us to understand and come clean on our own. He respects us as intelligent autonomous beings and believes in our ability to mature and reach enlightenment. Like a human father, He doesn't control us because we are respected and loved.

Somehow our vision of God has become terribly distorted. We forget that the One True God is a being of purity, compassion, forgiveness, and truth. Instead, we've been tricked into believing in this unpredictable Old Testament deity who takes delight in playing cruel games. God doesn't wake up in the morning and decide to create a war in the Middle East, AIDS in Africa, earthquakes in Italy, tornadoes, or tsunamis. Throughout history, humans have done cruel barbaric things to each other, God did not. Perhaps it is the unbalanced, subversive, controlling, greedy, helpless, or chaotic energies of the people living in that area that causes the earth to heave and break apart. Perhaps it is disturbances from other galaxies we have yet to understand; right now, it is beyond our minds' comprehension. Quite possibly, it is darkness, not God or light, that creates many of the natural disasters that wreak havoc on earth. Maybe God cannot fix or counterbalance the work of darkness without disrupting the earth's natural harmony and creating a worse disaster. This would be like God trying to stop the earth from spinning on its axis to avert a hurricane in Chile. We possibly would never see an earthquake, volcano, tornado, flood, or typhoon in any place where enlightened or awakened people live in absolute harmony, love, and truth. I don't believe we will ever eradicate earthquakes, snipers, cancer, or war by blaming God. We can only begin to lessen all these things if globally we begin understanding, taking responsibility, and having faith. It's easy to blame a cruel self-righteous God that blows up buildings and slaughters children. This makes God the bad guy and we the noble victims. It's far more painful to look deep within ourselves at the anger, bitterness, jealousy, or desire for money and power that are the seeds of global injustice. Because of this, karma runs rampant on earth. But it's possible for all of us to grow up, enlighten, and stop blaming God. It's more than possible; it's our destiny.

God Does Not Punish—Our Soul Strives to Correct

Let everyone sweep in front of his or her own door, and the whole world will be clean.
—Goethe

We are not victims of life as our mind leads us to believe; we are subject to our own karma or debt. When we have completely paid back this debt, we are free of all the pain and suffering of the human condition. Paying off this debt is a correction of karma, not a punishment. God does not punish; this is one of our biggest illusions. God gives us a means to correct our karma or come clean. Our soul decides how we can best do this before we incarnate into a physical body. We are never forced to come here. We are never told how we are going to pay back our debt. Our spirit, in consultation with many enlightened beings, decides this before we incarnate. Unfortunately, when we come to earth, all of our past memories are erased. It would be terribly traumatic to remember we were thrown to the lions in a Roman coliseum, hung by the neck for treason, or blown apart in World War II. We come without these horrific memories of the past as a form of emotional protection. It's like being part of a witness protection program. We're given a different place to live and a new identity so that we can make a fresh start.

If someone borrows $10,000 from their Aunt Jenny and it takes them ten years to pay this back, this payment is not a punishment; it's setting things right. If someone gets really drunk, drives a car through a neighbour's front window, and it takes three years to repay the damage, this isn't punishment; it's taking responsibility and wiping the slate clean. If a family is Catholic, and a Jewish family whom they distrust moves next door, this isn't a punishment. Perhaps they've been Catholics who have hated Jewish people lifetime after lifetime. This is an opportunity to release their distrust, hatred, and fears and realize they may even like the same things and share the same interests.

Karma is an opportunity for us to return to our greatness, and earth is the place designated for this. It's like an opportunity to do several years of community service, rather than being locked in prison. Like those people who opt for community service, we're essentially free, but we're watched. God knows exactly what we're doing and He prefers giving us this more compassionate route. Through our community service to others, we may grow, evolve, and become more compassionate and caring. Hopefully, we literally become different people—the type of person God originally creat-ed—wondrous beings in His image and likeness.

There was a time on earth when humans were not walking around experiencing the pain of karma. In prehistory, and while Atlantis existed, there were enlightened beings free of karma. We were like gods and goddesses—pure in spirit. It was from this time that many of our Greek myths evolved with beings that could perform wondrous things. Our bodies did not break down and die. We did not grow old and suffer because there was no need to. If our lives are eternal, why would God want us to keep on suffering, experience pain, and die? What would be the point of all that death and suffering?

The Biblical stories of Adam and Eve attempt to explain a time when men and women lived without karma. It was a Garden of Eden—a place with no physical suffering. When Eve eats the apple this is a metaphor for turning away from God and choosing darkness. To simplify, humans became infected with ego and all its illusions; we fell into darkness and became trapped. It was like a beautiful garden party where everything was in perfect harmony. Then some shady dark characters arrived, they seduced the naive people, everyone got drunk, and everything started to fall apart. The stories of Noah and the great flood attempt to explain a similar time in history. We're told that there were few "good" people left on earth, except Noah and his family. These pure people vibrated at a level of purity, love, peace, compassion, service, and insight. When great numbers of people turned to the dark side, the vibration became lower until earth became a denser darker place to live. Over time as people became seduced by the ways of darkness, anger, hatred, jealousy, competition, and betrayal, our bodies literally changed. This didn't happen overnight, but we went from light beings with great abilities to denser physical beings trapped in karmic patterns on earth.

A wise compassionate God never punishes. After these great falls, God, the compassionate parent, needed a way for humans to return to grace. But this method of returning needed to be just, true, and fair. He couldn't just wave a magic wand and return things to the way they were before. We may make the same mistakes or naively become seduced by those clever dark characters again. The forces of darkness are extremely intelligent. We needed to acquire the wisdom to see through their illusions. We had to understand deep within our hearts that what we had done was not in alignment with spirit or our true nature. We needed to understand how darkness had seduced, trapped, and infected us. We had to understand this on such a deep emotional level that we wouldn't repeat the same karmic patterns. So God created the laws of karma on earth.

Karma is not something we understand or can rationalize because darkness can work through the lower vibrations of the physical mind. Karma is something we know, pay back, and correct through our emotions, heart, and soul. Only our spirits can bring us to that place of sorrow or humility where we begin taking responsibility for every thought, word, or action. To correct karma, it's not good enough to understand that at a mental level it was wrong. We all know it's wrong to gossip or tell a lie, but we keep doing it. Most bank robbers know it's wrong to rob a bank, but after they get out of jail they often rob another bank. We know what a horrible karmic situation war is, but there is rarely a time on earth when several wars are not going on. In order for karma to be paid back or corrected, we need to feel in our heart that this action does not serve us. We need to experience genuine sorrow and remorse. We need to understand and acknowledge the pain we have caused others. Our soul, emotional body, or spirit needs to feel such a deep sorrow that we don't repeat this action because we understand it is not in alignment with our true nature or spirit. We need to understand these actions will never bring us peace. We need to feel the sorrow so deeply that we correct our karma and return to grace, which is really an altered lighter vibration. This is our spirit's purpose for being here. It's our greatest wish, whether we're consciously aware of it or not.

Karma Isn't About Revenge

One of the most misunderstood concepts in the world today is the Biblical notion of an eye for an eye. This initial concept of serving justice has been amplified and distorted so that we have become a society bent on revenge. Revenge is not the way of the One True God of light. Compassion, understanding, and returning to a state of balance is. So when we accumulate karma, we absolutely need to work through it. We need to foster compassion to understand why our actions were wrong in the first place.

If we kill someone, we need to come back and work through our karma with that person. We need to come to an understanding that life is sacred. We need to respect one another, rather than kill one another. If we don't work through this karma, we keep repeating senseless lives of coming back killing and being killed. Hopefully, in one life we make a decision to stop killing and clean up our karma. When we reach this level of awareness, experience genuine sorrow, and decide to never kill again, we have worked through our shadow side and erased our karma. God rejoices. He doesn't make us come back dozens of times to be killed for the lives we took over many centuries as a soldier, judge, or Roman gladiator. There's no point because we've reached a critical awareness that prevents us from ever killing again. Perhaps we become a nurse, doctor, medical researcher, firefighter, paramedic, or ambulance driver and begin saving those same lives we once took.

If we never reach that critical awareness of understanding, that killing locks us in an endless cycle of karmic pain; some sell their soul to the dark side. Now they're under the illusion of having all kinds of power. But in turning to the dark side, like joining the Mafia, we lose our free will. Like a puppet, we must now perform the bidding of the dark side or become destroyed and swallowed up by it. We essentially have two choices: we can remain controlled by darkness and continue killing, deceiving, and manipulating—all karmic deeds—or we can return to the light and ask God for the opportunity to clean up our karma. No easy task, but not impossible. Cleaning up karma means breaking through all the illusions that bind us so that we can begin to lead lives of greater joy and purpose. God does not want revenge. He does not operate under a petty system of an eye for an eye, a tooth for a tooth. Instead, He has devised a system where we can become aware and purified through insight, awareness, clarity, meditation, and dreams.

From a Soldier in Atlantis to a Police Officer in Canada

Imagine being a soldier of Atlantis twelve thousand years ago. During this time, darkness is trying to infect the enlightened beings and take over. You are entrusted with the sacred responsibility of guarding a temple where many high priests and priestesses work. You're seduced into drinking on duty by dark characters that promise you gold if you leave for just an hour. While you're gone, a group of dark magicians murders a great priestess named Diana. You didn't live up to your responsibility, but you lie, plead innocence, and aren't condemned. You're demoted and feel really sorry for yourself, rather than feeling the deepest sorrow for this great priestess who was murdered. You blame the dark characters that orchestrated the murder. You never take full responsibility for the part you played and live in denial. You try to enjoy the money you were given but never acknowledge where it came from. After you die, you agree to enact a similar situation in your next life so that you can take responsibility for your actions and correct this karma.

It's the year 1072, and now you're a soldier entrusted with the important task of guarding the duchess of Cornwall. But you start drinking and playing cards with the other soldiers as someone steals into the castle and murders her while she sleeps. Again, you're demoted and once more you feel sorry for yourself, rather than feeling the deepest sorrow for the loss of the duchess. Again, you blame this "filthy murderer," rather than acknowledge that you could have prevented this if you weren't drunk.

Now it's the year 2005, and you have repeated this same karma over and over and have never fully taken responsibility for your actions. The priestess/duchess incarnates as your artist girlfriend. You're not a soldier in this lifetime; you're a police officer. Your responsibility remains to protect others. You're drunk, speeding, driving carelessly, and there is a serious accident. Your girlfriend is killed, but you survive suffering several broken bones. You plunge into the greatest despair and sorrow, but this time you allow yourself to feel this way for your *actions*, rather than just feeling sorry for yourself. You take complete responsibility for your actions, something you have never done before. There were several accidents that winter night due to the reduced visibility and black ice caused by freezing rain, so you're not charged, but you go to the girl's family to admit your mistakes and beg forgiveness. Your girlfriend was an aspiring painter, so you start a trust fund for emerging artists in her name. You manage this fund and put much of your own money and energy into it. Then you tirelessly crusade for the remainder of your life against drunk driving. You experienced the deepest sorrow for what you did, rather than blame anyone or feel like a victim. However, you don't stay trapped in depression and sorrow forever. This is never the wish of spirit. You move through it so you can channel your time and energy into dharmic actions that will help others. Finally, in this life, you've cleaned up your debt.

A different scenario is during World War I and you are a soldier who kills ten people. Spirit is never cruel; it doesn't always make us enact scenarios with all ten of these people. It recognizes that the consciousness at that time believed this war was the noble thing to do. You incarnate with one of these people, "Harry Johnson," who is your neighbour. Harry has a serious heart condition and needs a heart transplant. You're dying of cancer and have about six months to live. Even though you don't agree with organ transplants, you sign the papers to donate your heart to Harry. Then you will yourself to die in eight weeks so you can give life back to this friend. Donating your heart was the means to correct this karma. In Western religions, paying off our debt or correcting our karma is the same as earning grace, eternal life, wisdom, or spiritual merit. All of these things in Eastern religions translate into dharma. Both recognize this as spirit's desire and the ultimate goal of all human beings.

Karma Doesn't Need to Control Us

The future is made of the same stuff as the present.
—Simone Weil

We have far more power than we realize. We're not just pawns who jump into the game of living. Nothing in life is an accident. We create it. To think we have no control over our lives is another great illusion that deceives us. As long as we believe we have no control, we won't take the steps necessary to become empowered. Buddha once said, "What you are is what you have been, what you will be is what you do now."

There is a story that has circulated on the Internet called "The 90/10 Secret to Happier Daily Life." It's quite good because it gives us practical ideas for leading a dharmic life. The story says we're responsible for 90% of the things that happen to us. But it contends that we're not responsible for the remaining 10%—the minor things like being cut off in traffic, having our daughter spill coffee on our shirt, or being on a plane that arrives late throwing off our entire schedule. I believe we've agreed to 100% of everything that happens to us. If all of these things happen to someone the same day, they may be working through issues of patience, not blaming others, controlling their temper, and living in the moment. These issues will keep repeating until they've mastered them.

How many times have we listened to people relate stories of woe, followed by that familiar phrase, "What can you do?" In these cases, they're usually locked into the belief that nothing can be changed or altered because they're victims: "I have a terrible teacher who doesn't like me. There's nothing I can do." The truth is, a responsible student can learn and excel no matter how karmic their teacher/student relationship is. We could always try to put ourselves in that person's shoes to understand why he or she may be acting a certain way. We can ask that teacher, parents, relatives, or peers for help. We can try a tutor. We can believe in ourselves and not give up. We can meditate on why this may be happening and whether it is a pattern.

"I think my husband is fooling around, but he gets mad if I try to even bring it up. What can you do?" Lots. Stand up to him, go to marriage counselling, and/or have the courage to leave him if he refuses to change.

"My metabolism is slowing down as I'm getting older, I've put on twenty pounds, but what can you do?" We can change our eating habits, see a nutritionist, balance diet with exercise, and honour ourselves just as we are.

"My kids don't want to visit me any more; their lives are so busy. I miss them, but what can you do?" We can take up new hobbies, visit old friends, volunteer, travel, and be grateful for these children.

"I'm just too tired to go anywhere; my job is so demanding. I work 60-hour weeks, but it pays well, so what can you do?" We can work fewer hours, begin looking for a less demanding job, attempt to balance our life, and/or take some time off and enjoy some of our money.

It's important to understand that our karma is not fixed, so our future is not fixed. We're not helplessly locked into karma for the rest of our lives. It's a choice. We can keep on being locked in fear and feel we're not good enough to apply for a new job. This means we are trapped in karma. Or we can believe in our abilities, face our fears, and start applying for that position we've always wanted. Karma transcended into dharma. When we truly understand the laws of karma and dharma, we no longer buy into the faulty belief system that life isn't fair. We're no longer bitter or angry for what happens to us in life. Most importantly, we stop blaming others and we take greater responsibility for our actions. We understand that everything that happens is a result of either karma or dharma. Whatever we have sowed, we will reap.

When people start taking responsibility for their lives, they stop being a victim. We're not victims of life. We aren't thrown into life and controlled unless we allow others to control us. We choose our lives. We have actually chosen and created our own spiritual blueprint; we're masters over our destiny.

We can all actively make choices each day that allow us to either take responsibility for our actions or create more karma. If everyone is gossiping at work, we can join in or choose to walk away. The power of dreams is that they show us that we can't control other people, nor do we have a right to. Trying to control others can become very karmic. We can, however, control ourselves. We can control our thoughts, deeds, and emotions. We can always change the way we deal with every situation. Since dreams work with our intuition, they can teach us to be masters of our destiny, rather than victims of life.

There are certain things in life we simply cannot change. We can't stop an earthquake from happening in California. We may not be able to stop our sister from eloping and stepping into a karmic marriage. If our best friend is moving, there is little we can do. However, we can change our lives—we can erase our karma and begin to live more dharmically. The insight found in dreams enables us to do this. This is, perhaps, when the beginning of Reinhold Niebuhr's "Serenity Prayer" comes in handy: "God grant me the serenity to accept the things I cannot change, the courage to change the things I can, and the wisdom to know the difference."

Turning Karma into Dharma

The wise are never arbitrary when leading others into harmony with the truth. Wise, they are guarded by truth, for they act in accord with the Dharma.
—The Buddha

We can struggle unconsciously to become aware of karmic patterns and to turn them into dharma or grace. Or we can become aware of our dreams and dig up the ladder that bridges the physical and the spiritual. Let's imagine "Jason" is working for a legal firm that often represents unscrupulous characters—people who pay his boss under the table, then go out and re-offend. His boss is egocentric and verbally abusive, but Jason stays there for years because he doesn't believe in himself. He's under the illusion he can't get a job elsewhere. He's rapidly losing any semblance of self-esteem. Meanwhile, he has a vision of opening his own legal aid firm.

If opening this legal aid office is Jason's destiny, he may receive guidance in dreams for years. His dreams would help him clean up karma while he sleeps. It's karmic for Jason to remain at that legal firm because he's being undervalued and exploited. His dreams may begin by showing him it's karmic to work at this law firm. He may have dreams where he is being manipulated or battered by clients, mirroring what is occurring in his physical life. He may go forward in time and witness an illegal deal his boss makes. He may have a dream where his boss is partying with dark underworld characters so that he can understand the karmic nature of this law firm. Then his dreams may help him rehearse standing up for himself, confronting his boss, and challenging corrupt decisions. Dreams could even help him practise his resignation speech.

Once he breaks this karmic cycle, dreams would begin moving Jason in more dharmic directions. They may take him to a building for his legal aid firm that would be available in two months, so he recognizes it immediately in his physical life. He may test run everything he needs to set up this new business in the dream state, before he enacts it physically. This is the power and function of dreams. We all have the ability to go forward in the dream state to pay off our karmic debts without the restrictions of time and space. In the dream state, we can gain new insights and change karmic situations into dharmic adventures.

We Create Our Future Destiny

It is by no means an irrational fancy that, in a future existence, we shall look upon what we think our present existence, as a dream.
—Edgar Allan Poe

In ancient teachings, we learn of a man called Thoth the Atlantean. There are many different legends of Thoth; he is believed to be the god of all learning and knowledge. Ancient Egyptians believed that he founded record keeping, writing, mathematics, astronomy, and medicine. Legends say he was the king of mythical Atlantis. To the Greeks, he was their winged god Hermes. Jewish mystics believe he was Seth, the second son of Adam, who wrote the Emerald Tablets, the esoteric spiritual laws for humanity.

The twelfth emerald tablet explains the laws of cause and effect. Thoth tells us the future is an open book that anyone can read. Everything we do right now will bring forth effects. The future is not fixed or stable, it varies according to what we do now. So if we examine our lives today, we know what the future will bring. Thoth says,

"Be sure the effects that ye bring forth are ever causes or more perfect effects. Know ye the future is never in fixation, but follows man's free will as it moves through the movements of time-space toward the goal where a new time begins." In essence we create our future by what we do today.

If we understand karma and dharma, we can alter our destinies. We are creating the future by our thoughts, words, and deeds. We are creating the type of world we live in each and every day, affecting the quality of our lives for tomorrow. If we say life isn't fair, we're still living in illusion because we have the ability to create every detail of our lives.

Life becomes what we make it, and we are actually creating the world future generations will live in. If we create a world of disharmony, irresponsibility, pollution, and war, this becomes karma until we correct or change it. We see this in war-torn countries where people hold onto injustices or karmic events that happened hundreds of years ago. They're raised to never forget a battle where thousands of their ancestors were killed. If they can't let go of their anger, that anger continues to destroy them. The bitterness, hatred, and mistrust of the past become poisons that infect each new generation. But it doesn't need to be this way. It's a choice. If we create a world of forgiveness, harmony, responsible action, environmental sustainability, and peace, we create a dharmic world for the children of tomorrow. Through our combined efforts and beliefs we can create a Garden of Eden or heaven on earth again; or we can fall from grace and watch as our planet self-destructs as it did in the time of Atlantis.

Dharma or Destiny

Those who see worldly life as an obstacle to Dharma see no Dharma in everyday actions; they have not yet discovered that there are no everyday actions outside of Dharma.
—Zen Master Dogen, thirteenth century

There isn't a precise English equivalent for the original word *dharma*; it's derived from a Sanskrit root word meaning "to hold." Dharma is any action, behaviour, or understanding that holds us back or protects us from hardship, pain, and suffering. We can think of dharma as our ultimate path—the way of purity and truth or living in grace. For example, it's karmic to steal your sister's diary and love letters; it's dharmic to return these letters, apologize, and work to understand what motivated these actions in the first place. As we pay back our spiritual debts, life becomes more dharmic. A dharmic lifestyle means we are aligned with our spirit or the light of the One True God. We go to work each day and perform our job honourably. We don't gossip. We're not late for work. We don't cheat our boss. We interact with everyone in a compassionate respectful manner. We treat cashiers, waiters, and waitresses the same way we would presidents or prime ministers. We follow the speed limit on the way to work. We don't drive recklessly and put others in danger. We don't pollute. We respect, honour, and love friends and family.

Most of us are a combination of karmic and dharmic experiences simultaneously. We do things that are karmic and then things that are dharmic all in the same day—often in the same hour! Our lives are rarely just black and white.

The more our life becomes dharmic, the more opportunity we have to help or assist others; and we feel better about ourselves. Eventually, we're not performing a job just to get a paycheque. We're not doing a job for selfish gain, to better our position in life, or to boost our ego. As we evolve, we understand that all work is meant to provide a service to the rest of humanity. We may be presidents, or we may work with mentally challenged children. We may pick up garbage, or we may work in a recycling plant. We may serve coffee in a donut shop, or we may bake bread. It doesn't matter how great or noble our work is. There are so many needed services. It's the *intent* that matters. We choose this work because we recognize it's our contribution to the world and it brings us joy and satisfaction.

Dharma and Intent

When you work you are a flute through whole heart the whispering of the hours turns to music. To love life through labour is to be intimate with life's inmost secret. All work is empty save when there is love, for work is love made visible.
—Kahlil Gibran

Understanding the importance of intent can be the key that unlocks our spirit from centuries of karma. Let's say you understand your destiny and dharma is to be a yoga teacher and to open up a studio. If you're teaching yoga because you love it, that's an honourable intent. If you honestly believe in what you're doing, this too is honourable. And if you're teaching yoga because you believe it's providing a valuable service to others, this type of intent is in alignment with spirit. Perhaps you see people coming into your studio who are worn out, stressed, physically stiff, and searching for answers. You see that with each class, they become more flexible physically and spiritually. They become calmer, stiller, better able to focus, and you find this tremendously rewarding. This energizes you, confirms you're on the right track, and makes you want to teach yoga even more. You're not expecting miracles. You're not trying to convince everyone they should be doing yoga. You realize yoga isn't part of everyone's path. But you're doing something you know is an important service in our harried world. We're all here to provide a service to others, and we all have something unique and important to contribute, provided our intent does not become muddied or arrogant.

Now let's examine the same scenario with a different intent. Imagine being a yoga teacher operating a studio. You believe you're the best yoga teacher in this area and you therefore have the best studio. Only your yoga is the true form, all other types of yoga are incomplete, ignorant of truth, or these other teachers just don't have your experience. You know better, you're superior, and you must therefore educate your students who will never have your knowledge or expertise. You may even be successful and pull in lots of money. But our services become karmic, rather than dharmic, if we carry out that service only to make a lot of money or to appear important and superior.

Doing anything with the sole intention of making lots of money can become a trap because we all need money to survive. There was a time in our society when every job was essential because it provided a service. We needed shoemakers, teachers, shopkeepers, farmers, and midwives to provide these services. Everybody's job was essential. Slowly and insidiously in the nineteenth century our mindset toward work changed from service to others to making money. A hundred years ago every shopkeeper knew that if they shut down, people wouldn't have the food they needed. Now we have shopkeepers competing with each other, all in an attempt to make the most money. We also have people going into jobs not because they love what they're doing, not because they know inside that these jobs are an expression of who they are and what they believe is important, but because these jobs are trendy, fashionable, or provide opportunities to make the most money. If we did a survey and asked people why they're a salesperson, business owner, banker, or teacher they may say, "You've got to make a living," "It pays the bills," "I've got a family to support," or "I need to work to pay the mortgage." These people have forgotten the core reason for all types of work—service to others—and, most importantly, that working with the intent to serve others is meant to be a joyful uplifting experience, not day-to-day drudgery.

Arrogance or ego is another huge trap, particularly if someone is extremely talented or if they become famous. Many souls write fame into their spiritual contract because they've been famous before but allowed their ego rather than their spirit to guide them. It's so difficult to become rich or to gain world recognition yet remain humble. These all become mental traps even for people who could be providing a real service. And since we're all teachers in many jobs we can apply this type of karmic arrogance or ego to many professions. Many politicians, priests, bankers, teachers, and salespeople sincerely believe their way is better or superior and therefore should impress their way on others. They forget we're all here on individual paths.

It's important to understand why we've chosen our type of work. And often it's okay to recognize the need for making money. An eighteen-year-old may decide to paint white lines on the highway as a summer job, so they can pursue their real passion of being a veterinarian. Each day, as they go to work, they could remember, "Without these lines on the highway, roads would become unsafe, and so I'm providing an important service. This links me with the thousands of people who may drive this highway in the future."

It's also important to understand that we don't have to be in a paying job to carry out our dharma. Children, teenagers, stay-at-home parents, volunteers, senior citizens, people between jobs, the unemployed, sick, and disabled all make enormous contributions to society. Sometimes they can be our greatest assets and teachers.

When our life is dharmic, we're aware of the intent and consequences of our actions. If given a choice between painting lines on a highway and working in a factory that manufactured rifles, we'd happily paint those white lines. When our life becomes dharmic, we feel a greater connection to nature, animals, and all the people we happily serve. We see the interrelationship in everything. We feel and experience beauty at deeper and more meaningful levels. We may weep at the beauty of a piece of artwork, a song, or a sunset. We are often overwhelmed by tears of joy or deep emotion. Life flows. We're more peaceful. We know the bliss of unconditional love. We do things not for recognition or glory, but because we know inside it's the right thing to do. A dharmic lifestyle is never a ticket to an easy or blissful life, but we do leave the pain and turmoil of our karmic existence behind. If we consider people like Terry Fox, Mother Teresa, Princess Diana, Pierre Trudeau, Nelson Mandela, Mohandas Ghandi, or Martin Luther King, they didn't have easy lives. But they also experienced joy, peace, and awareness, and were of great benefit to humanity. They continue to inspire many, and the world became a better place because of them. They made a difference. There is a saying, "Live your life in such a way that when you die, the world will cry; and you rejoice!" When we live a dharmic life, we affect others in positive ways. We uplift and inspire, and the contribution we make becomes timeless. Any dharmic action always stands the test of time—from white lines on the highway to heartfelt teaching that inspires; from poetry and music to any art that's done from the heart.

Karma and Dharma Playing Out in Life

The future belongs to those who believe in the beauty of their dreams.
—Eleanor Roosevelt

Now that we've delved into the universal laws of karma and dharma, let's look at people reported in the news to understand how dharma and karma played out in their lives. We'll look at Timothy McVeigh, the notorious Oklahoma bomber, who believed he could escape karma or get away with it. We'll move to an unknown man, a principal named Richard Gallagher, whose sexual exploits with young boys eventually caught up with him. And finally, we'll look at Toronto police officer Laura Ellis who died in the line of duty leaving behind a young daughter and husband. In Laura's case we'll hopefully understand that some souls have chosen a shorter time on earth. She came to be of service, provided this service to her community as a police officer, and gave her husband a daughter to love and cherish. With this dharma complete, perhaps her mission on earth was accomplished.

Timothy McVeigh

Perhaps one of the best examples of how karma operates is the story of Timothy McVeigh, the Oklahoma bomber. In 1995, his act of terrorism took 168 lives when he blew up a federal building to protest the policies of the United States government. Many family members of those who died in the bombing felt they could never be at peace until McVeigh was executed. When this execution took place six years later, his killing was on the front page of every newspaper and was the lead story of every newscast. It seemed we had regressed to the days of public hangings or Roman gladiators—public killings to appease the masses. The only difference was that in 2001, we had the illusion of civilized sophistication—simple lethal injection. We have replaced the coliseum with closed-circuit viewing rooms and countless television, newspaper, and magazine reports. When Timothy McVeigh was executed, many complained bitterly it was "too easy for him," "he did not suffer enough," or that it was "unfair that he should just go to sleep." When it was all over, some families realized that McVeigh's death had not given them the much-needed peace they were seeking. Perhaps this is because whatever karmic emotions we put out, we get back—the law of cause and effect. If the families put out hatred, bitterness, anger, and resentment for six solid years leading up to the execution, a single needle doesn't erase these emotions. Peace is something we earn through heightened awareness, right action, compassion, and love as we move toward a more dharmic life. If society understood the laws of karma and dharma, we would know with absolute conviction that Timothy McVeigh will pay back his debt. God sees to that. If we don't believe in God's wisdom we feel we must take things into our own hands and play god to make things right. This usually creates even more karma. It's less complicated and far wiser to have faith and to understand that justice is *always* carried out. As a society, we probably had an obligation to make sure that Timothy McVeigh was behind bars and to attempt to rehabilitate him, understand the root causes of his actions, and take measures so that this type of karmic action was not repeated. Beyond that we can never be sure.

The murder of 168 people does not go unnoticed by God. Timothy McVeigh's final media statement contained the last two lines of the poem "Invictus" by William Henley, "I am the master of my fate: I am the captain of my soul." Yes, we're all captains of our souls because we have free will. We can go around killing people for eons, but that doesn't excuse us from paying back our debts. In McVeigh's case, being captain of his soul could mean he spends eternity living a hellish existence. He can never escape it. A thousand years from now Timothy McVeigh may lose his home and family in a town that is bombed by terrorists. This may occur again and again until he understands the sanctity of human life and relinquishes his need to kill. McVeigh's dreams would never lead him to blow up a building. His dreams played no part in his final media statement, "I am the captain of my soul." This was the work of an ego-led mind, totally disconnected from spirit. If he doesn't begin to understand the laws of karma, he will forever walk around saying how unfair, cruel, and bitter his life is. The only way for McVeigh to truly become the captain of his soul is to do some serious soul searching. In his next incarnation it will be his dreams, not his mind or ego, that has the wisdom and the power to lead him out of this darkness.

Richard Gallagher

Another story that shows the laws of dharma and karma at work is the case of a retired Brampton schoolteacher and principal, Richard Gallagher. The story first appeared in the *Toronto Star* on February 24 2002, in an article written by Kerry Gillespie entitled "Family bereft as abuse cases die." For years, there had been rumours of sexual impropriety in his life, but they remained only rumours. Gallagher had an impeccable reputation. Gillespie writes, "He was respected and trusted by parents. He was a teacher, a regular at church, a sophisticated world traveller, and a caring man who was ready to lend a supportive hand." We're all a combination of karma and dharma, so Gallagher's teaching, leadership, and administrative abilities were possibly part of his dharma—what he gave back to the world. If he had an impeccable reputation, chances are he did accumulate spiritual merit. But dharma and karma can become intertwined. Gillespie writes, "He was also popular with boys. His Muskoka cottage was on the lake and his Brampton home had a swimming pool. He enjoyed their games and listened to them." One of his early transgressions was with a sixteen-year-old Muskoka resident who moved in with Gallagher, so he could play a higher level of hockey than was available in his hometown.

For years, Gallagher miraculously avoided all the allegations of sexual misconduct. Over a period of twenty-two years, at least twelve boys came forward and claimed Gallagher had sexually abused them. One of the allegations came from the eleven-year-old son of a police officer, the only case that actually made it to court. But even in this case, which went to court twice, a deal was struck between the lawyers. Gallagher agreed to get counselling, and technically he was free without a criminal record.

Things reached a peak in 1999 when three brothers confessed

they had all been sexually abused by Gallagher. One of these boys was the hockey player from Muskoka. Each brother thought they had been the only one and never came forward with the truth. When the family went to the police, twelve sexual-assault-related cases were laid against Gallagher. The case never made it to court, however, because Gallagher's lawyers obtained a series of delays and adjournments. News of the legal allegations set off a chain reaction in which many boys came forth claiming Gallagher had abused them too.

A year later, Gallagher developed severe prostate cancer. The prostate gland secretes a fluid that is the major ingredient of semen. Justice or karma may have been playing itself out. Gallagher required surgery and several rounds of painful chemotherapy. The doctor hired by the Brampton courts determined that clearly Gallagher had less than six months to live. Based on the doctor's report, the Brampton Superior Court's Mr. Justice Ronald Thomas stayed the case. He said, "The family must take focus and understand that the administration of justice must be tempered with mercy and understanding." But these families could feel no mercy or understanding. They were angry, bitter, and outraged that Gallagher, a dying sixty-year-old man was not being brought to "justice."

In Bracebridge, a short time later, where Gallagher was also up on sexual misconduct, Mr. Justice Robert Weekes also granted a stay. A doctor's note stated that Gallagher was too ill to travel to court. Again, the families were angry, frustrated, and emotional. However, this time the judge showed compassion. When the lawyers left, he sat at a table with family members and allowed them to talk so they could begin the process of healing. "Weekes listened as the family told him of poor grades, lost university years waiting for trials, failed relationships, of drug and alcohol abuse trying to deal with what had happened to them, depression and thoughts of suicide." We're told in the article that the "50 minutes of compassion shown by Weekes went a long way to balancing three years of pain believing that no one in Ontario's court system cared." The final words in this story, a quote from Mr. Justice Weekes says it all: "I know you're a religious family. There is a greater justice out there than this court can deliver."

It would appear from this newspaper article that Mr. Gallagher's past or karma caught up with him. However, it's important that we don't point a finger and judge. If we do this, we all fall into our own karmic traps. I believe it's better to exercise the same type of compassion that Judge Weekes showed. Rather than judging, condemning, or becoming angry at another individual, this may help us understand there is a universal system of fairness, justice, and compassion that no one escapes.

Laura Ellis and the Illusion of Physical Death

The death of Toronto police constable Laura Ellis in February 2002 is perhaps a story difficult to understand with the limited awareness of our minds. While Laura was responding to a robbery, her police cruiser was involved in a fatal crash and she was pronounced dead at the scene. Two other men were involved in the accident: a fellow constable who was driving the police cruiser and the driver of another car—both survived. Laura, who was thirty-one years old, had just returned from maternity leave a month earlier. Ironically, this was to be her last shift with the Toronto Police Service. She had decided to transfer to Durham Region to be closer to home and her family. She left behind her husband, Tim, also a police officer and a one-year-old daughter, Paige. One of the police chaplains appointed to console her fellow officers that morning could make no sense of the accident. In the *Toronto Star* newspaper article by Keith Howell entitled "Reaching out a hand in comfort" the chaplain is quoted to have said, "How could a God who is merciful and loving allow that to happen to a mom and a police officer? What is the meaning of life?"

The answers are there, yet sometimes they allude even our priests, ministers, and chaplains. God did not suddenly take the life of Laura Ellis. The soul of Laura Ellis had predetermined this as the time she would leave. It was part of her soul's karmic and dharmic contract. Laura's soul had probably also decided to die quickly and perhaps painlessly in a car accident. It was not a senseless death; it only seems that way if we're locked into a physical belief system. God was not controlling Laura's life. Laura's soul decided this was the most auspicious way to leave earth. The event of death often means we've completed our karmic experience and it's time to leave. We come here to clean up karma and death is often the release or reward. But when we deeply love someone, this is difficult to grasp. It's natural to feel the deepest grief and despair when we lose a loved one. But it is also natural to understand that death is the movement of the soul; that love is the strongest force in the universe and this force of love reunites souls in other dimensions. In her book *Until Today*, Iyanla Vanzant explains:

People never really die. They leave their bodies. They end

their physical existence in order to continue their spiritual journey in another form, on another plane. A person who has entered the realm of existence we call *death* is never beyond your love. The thing we call death is not a cold or a dark or a frightening and cruel existence. It is an essential part of life that teaches us to believe in what we cannot see. Once you know a person, you will always know a person. Once you have loved a person, your love will keep them alive.

Laura's soul did not die; it moved on because its contract on earth was completed. On a soul level, Laura's daughter and husband would also have agreed to this before they incarnated. It is our conscious minds that do not understand or lack the awareness of these emotionally difficult agreements.

What possible reasons could there be for a mother to leave a one-year-old daughter and a grieving husband behind? The reasons are all spiritual in nature, reasons that enabled the souls of Laura, her daughter, husband, and fellow police officers to evolve from the experience. Maybe her daughter needed to know what it's like to be strong without a mother. Her daughter might have needed to learn independence. Possibly she needed to know how to hold her energy and stay grounded and focused without the nurturing of a mother. Maybe she needed to work out her karma with men so she needed to be raised only by her father. Maybe the husband needed to know what it was like to lose love but also to show love and compassion to a child. Possibly, the husband needed to understand the natural rhythms of life and death on a deeper level without feeling resentful. Maybe that family and the fellow police officers needed to know that human laws do not govern the universe. Human laws do not determine life and death on earth. There's a greater law than the physical law that everyone has to abide by, even new moms and police officers. This was possibly an opportunity for all her fellow officers to begin understanding the laws of dharma and karma that Laura abided by. Maybe this was an opportunity for everyone involved to turn inside to prayer, meditation, and dreamwork to find answers and peace. Maybe Laura had finished her time on earth school and needed to leave her legacy behind in a child. Perhaps her soul had determined she would go out quickly and painlessly in a blaze of glory, to be remembered as an example for others.

There is a strong possibility that the dreams of both Laura and her husband began preparing them for this car accident, although their conscious minds did not hold this awareness. It is also possible that weeks, months, or years later, Laura could visit her family members in the dream state to let them know she is okay. For every event there is a reason that surpasses the limited awareness of our minds. Understanding the spiritual laws of karma and dharma are so important to enable each soul to graduate from earth school. While we're here, even the most basic understanding of these laws can be a constant source of insight, clarity, and peace.

Focusing on Our Own Karma and Dharma

Once I began realizing how the laws of karma and dharma worked, I began looking at other people if they had a serious illness, their marriage was breaking up, or they'd lost their job. I believed if I understood these laws that somehow I should have all the answers. I would know why that person had an incapacitating illness or why they lost their job. I viewed life as one big karmic/dharmic jigsaw puzzle that I should be able to put together. But karma and dharma are so complex, involving so many people over so many lifetimes. The possibilities of working it through are so diverse we can never understand the karma or dharma of another human being—nor do we have the right to—unless, of course, we're God.

I realized this was yet another ego trap. It would be really easy to point a finger at "Aunt Mabel" and say she died of cancer because she refused to attend her lesbian daughter's wedding. Or smugly believing "Mrs. Crosbie" across the street had her new car break down because she yelled at me every time my cat harmlessly made paw prints on her windshield.

Hopefully, the information here will give you a better understanding of how karma and dharma works, so that you can apply it in your own life. We may have theories about Aunt Mabel, Laura Ellis, or Richard Gallagher, but they will always be incomplete theories of unenlightened souls. Their stories were presented to illuminate the possibilities and to give a framework for understanding how these laws could play out.

I realized the more I was shifting my attention on others, the less I was really examining and taking responsibility for my own karma. It's always easier to see the shortcomings of others. It is exceedingly difficult to muster up the courage to face our own shadows. Perhaps an important part of our combined destinies is to honour anyone with the tough job of working through karma, while remaining supportive and compassionate. As we walk our individual paths, it's essential to keep our focus and determination inward. It's important to work through our own karma and not become sidetracked by the drama of others. One by one, we are capable of making an enormous difference.

Dreamwork Can Be Tough

The laws of karma and dharma are not something we completely understand after attending one workshop or reading one book. Rather, it is something we grow into, something that unfolds, as we are open to its wisdom. We begin listening and observing others and ourselves with a new awareness. Once we understand karma and dharma, our reactions and impressions of world news shift dramatically. We don't listen to the news or read a newspaper with the same reactions or beliefs that we did before. Our outer life changes; bitterness, anxiety, fear, and self-doubt melt away as we realize its futility. All these karmic emotions are replaced with greater clarity. Understanding karma and dharma can change and transform our lives.

As we make this transformation, recognizing karma in dreams can be tough work. That is why we call this dreamwork. Looking at our dreams is like examining our life in the mirror without any illusions or distortions. Often this is a painful process. If one of our issues is that we're always late for work, dreams will show us these karmic qualities. If we're afraid of anything, we'll face these fears in dreams. If we're going to change jobs, dreams will help us prepare for this. If someone close to us is preparing to die, we may become aware of this in the dream state. Dreams also allow us to rehearse situations. Sometimes we test out possibilities only to discover that they don't feel good, and we wake up feeling unsettled and not knowing why. Working through karma in dreams is working on anything that prevents us from living in alignment with spirit. When we are aligned with spirit, there is no fear; instead, there is great faith in a power our minds cannot fathom. Dreamwork may be the toughest work we ever do, but the most exciting, meaningful, and rewarding. I still decline some party invitations just to get a good night's sleep.

Chapter Two
What Is a Dream?

Row, row, row your boat gently down the stream,
Merrily, merrily, merrily, life is but a dream.

Dreams Are Spirit Informing the Mind

There have been three stages in my life where I struggled to understand dreams. In the first stage, I was locked into a rational view of dreams. I thought dreams could be analyzed and interpreted using psychological theories and knowledge of symbols. So I studied these believing dreamwork was an intellectual pursuit. I really wanted to believe all this intellectual probing would make me an expert. But I was wrong. Understanding dreams has little to do with intellect—it's mostly intuitive. I could read every book that's ever been written on dreams and still have difficulty understanding their messages if I wasn't tapped into my intuition.

Dreams are not an intellectual exercise, they're a journey of spirit. All dreams cannot necessarily be analyzed or interpreted. Some dreams are straightforward and don't require any analysis. And symbols in dreams don't always have a deep hidden meaning. Even Sigmund Freud who believed that everything shaped like a rod, pole, stick, or cylinder was a sexual or phallic symbol, once said, "Sometimes a cigar is just a cigar."

If our grandmother died and appeared in a dream driving a car into white clouds, wearing a blue dress, waving goodbye, and saying, "I love you, don't worry about me," there's nothing to interpret. We don't need to look up grandmother, car, driving, clouds, blue dress, or waving in a dream dictionary. She appeared in a dream to say goodbye because she loves us. We can't always analyze or interpret every dream since many help us prepare, plan, or pave the way for the future. But we can become aware of what our spirit is trying to show us. We can begin building informed bridges between our mind and spirit.

In stage two, while I did my doctoral work in dreams, I thought dreams were spiritual messages from the soul that guided us each night. I was locked in this way of thinking for a long time. I could understand some of my dreams but not completely. I was trying to put dreams in boxes—rational academic boxes, or spiritual mystical boxes. I finally got over this way of thinking, but it took real mental gymnastics. It took a long time for my mind to break out of the boundaries laid out in the boxes I'd been building for years.

In stage three, I realized that dreams are spirit informing the mind. For the first time, I understood the childhood nursery rhyme, "life is but a dream." If we think physical life is the ultimate reality, that's the trap that keeps us stuck in karmic patterns. Dreams are the real thing, not illusions. We won't always have this physical earthly body, but we will have a soul for eternity that travels in other dimensions. Our soul shows us things every night, so that we can return to the drama or dream on earth to get things right. There was never meant to be a separation between the physical world and the spiritual world. The purpose of dreams is to have experiences in other dimensions so that spirit can inform the mind. If we try to operate in life with only our mind, we will have a very limited level of awareness. It's our soul and its work in the dream state that enables our mind to be wise and informed. Without the wisdom of the soul, the mind can become lost, disconnected, depressed, or delusional. When the mind and the soul work together in harmony, we are grounded, balanced, creative, and joyful. The soul enables the mind to become whole or holy. It informs and enhances the mind's limited awareness. If we believe there's a separation between our spirit and mind, we may remain stuck in rational patterns that limit our potential.

Each night, as our soul travels in other dimensions, it's informing our mind whether we're consciously aware of it or not. Perhaps that's why we hear people say "let me sleep on it" before making an important decision. These people know that in the morning, they're able to make a better decision after a good night's sleep. Most of the time they can't tell you what they've dreamed, but they do have a clearer sense of how to handle that problem.

Let's say our soul goes forward in time and shows us a huge fatal accident. There's a transport trailer overturned on the highway we take to work. In the dream, we also see several cars involved in this deadly accident. If we wake up and remember the dream, we will probably take another route to work. But let's say we wake up and have no conscious memory of the dream. We've overslept, so we scramble to get out the door for work. But as we get into our car, we have this funny feeling or intuitive nudge to take a different highway. We can't logically explain why, but we take a different route. That afternoon while listening to the news, we discover intuition may have saved our life. If we had taken our usual route to work, we could have been involved in a serious and possibly fatal traffic collision. This accident occurred around 8:15 a.m., the time we use this highway to get to work. The soul is always trying to inform and guide the mind. When we bring this guidance into conscious awareness, integrating mind and spirit, we are truly aware.

We were never meant to put our body and mind in one box and our spirit in another as I did for so many years. The whole point of discovering spirituality is to meld spirit into our being to allow our minds to become aware. Spirit is the core of who we are and it contains our truth. Dreams allow us to walk in the real world. Often, we do our spiritual things then believe it's necessary to go back to our physical world. But the real world is our spiritual existence. This physical life is the illusion—the dream. Life is a huge drama school designed to help us evolve. We're in a physical body temporarily so we can clean up karma and be set free to live in the dimensions of spirit or return to our true home. These dimensions are similar to what we travel in when we sleep and dream.

Buddha taught that the physical world is an illusion. That does not diminish in any way the importance of our time here. It's still important to honour the physical world and live with compassion and integrity. We all have important roles to play. But we pass through this physical reality the way actors and actresses move from movie to movie, play to play, drama to drama. We're here primarily to clean up karma and to have experiences that help us evolve. The physical world is always subject to change. Our time on earth is part of a passing show. It's like a giant movie set or costume party where we get to wear various costumes and masks. But our goal is not to stay at the ball forever. Our goal is to evolve, self-realize, become enlightened. One of the best ways to become enlightened is to understand our dreams.

What Happens When We Dream?

Why does the eye see a thing more clearly in dreams than the mind while awake?
—Leonardo Da Vinci

While we're dreaming, we don't have the boundaries of the physical body and that's important because the physical body is very limiting. In dreams, we can fly! We don't have the boundaries of linear time in dreams, so we're freer to explore and act out human situations without limitations. We can transcend time as we travel in the world of spirit. When we dream, our body goes into a chamber or frozen state and is allowed to rejuvenate, rest, and replenish, while our real body—our soul or spirit—goes ahead and does more work. It's something like science fiction movies where we see astronauts or people in a state of suspended animation. Working with dreams really helps us click into the fact that there is another world happening simultaneously and it's very real.

This work frequently helps us prepare for the future. Dreams prepare our paths. That is basically what dreams are, preparation of the future without the restrictions of linear time and without the restrictions of the body. Without these restrictions, we are able to cross dimensions. In dreams, our soul is truly free to enact its wisdom and prepare our path. We test out scenarios. We test run situations. We experiment and grow.

So we're not simply going to sleep only to have our mind roam. Our body is in suspended animation so our soul can cross dimensions and prepare our path. We aren't going to sleep and getting spiritual interpretations. We're going to sleep and allowing our soul to show us many things. We're getting wisdom and insight from our soul, which is an aspect of spirit and therefore true genius. Our soul is not learning anything; it's already informed. It already knows what our mind does not understand; it's enacting situations that show our mind the way. When we dream, our soul goes ahead to another dimension and helps us work through karmic issues. In these other dimensions, our soul tests things out. It examines and explores possibilities. We visit the future, rehearse, get ready, and try things out. Sometimes we're preparing for that same day. In other dreams, we may be preparing for the following day, week, month, year, or several years into the future.

Imagine how disastrous it would be if you were a movie producer who tried to film a major motion picture without any rehearsals or preparations. You had never talked to any of the actors, actresses, the camera crew, or anyone working with costumes, props, or sets. It's the same way with our lives—without the real preparatory work we do in the dream state, life would be a walking disaster.

I once spoke to a pregnant woman who was eight days away from her due date. Although this was her first baby, she had absolutely no fears; instead, you could feel her excitement. She seemed remarkably calm, relaxed, and emotionally prepared. Part of her calmness, perhaps, could be attributed to the fact that she had remembered many dreams throughout her pregnancy. As her pregnancy progressed, her dreams became more vivid. In one dream, her water broke, so she was able to rehearse and feel the emotions associated with this important event. In another dream, she was a third person in an operating room, observing a baby about to be delivered. A month later, with no problems or complications, she gave birth to a baby boy named Michael. With everything in life, from birth to death, dreams allow us to explore every possible emotion, scenario, or obstacle so that we're ready when the time arrives.

Moving from France to Canada

Pretend we live in France and are planning a move to Canada. We're an expert in solar power and have been hired to work in Canada as a consultant for two years. Before the move, there's a lot we need to prepare. We travel to Canada and spend a month visiting our new workplace, making friends, exploring neighbourhoods, finding schools, fitness clubs, and activities we may want to join. This is exactly what we do when we're dreaming, only we don't have the barriers of time and space.

Imagine that before we went to Canada, we kept having a vivid dream of walking around in a red brick home. We even know the address: 23 Maple Drive. We walk around the kitchen and remember its curved bay windows and sunflowers on the wallpaper. There were three silver maple trees in the backyard around a circular pond. In the dream, we felt a real connection to this home.

We go to Canada three months after the dream and one of the houses we look at is exactly the house we've been dreaming about. When we walk into the backyard and see three silver maple trees, we know instantly this is where we want to live. The first time we had this dream in France it would be difficult to interpret or understand. We were just walking around a house and it felt comfortable. So the dream doesn't *mean* anything. The dream is making us aware of a future possibility, getting us ready, preparing, so that when we see this house in Canada, we'll instinctively know it's the right place.

If we realize this, we understand that dreams don't have meaning in the way many people think. Dreams can't always be interpreted, but they can be understood. They help us become aware of the work our soul is doing in other dimensions to prepare our path. They heighten our awareness, enabling us to bring this insight back to our waking life. They navigate us through life's challenges, so that we don't get stuck in endless karma or problems. Dreams bring us a sense of mystery and awe and help us realize we're all part of something large and miraculous.

Dreams As Movies in Other Dimensions

A dream is a theatre in which the dreamer himself is the scene, the player, the prompter, the producer, the author, the public, and the critic.
—Carl Jung

There is a hermeneutic phrase that states, "As above, so below." It means for everything that takes place in the spirit worlds, there is always a direct analogy on earth. On earth, one of the most effective ways to learn and grow is through movies, theatre, or television. Consider how powerful movies have become in shaping human awareness. They can be effective teachers awakening new ideas, emotions, and insights.

Let's look at the movie *Chocolat* as an example. The plot centres on Vianne, a mysterious woman who arrives in a French town to open a chocolate shop. When she appears, everyone's in church because the entire town is extremely devout. We learn that since it is Lent, Vianne's shop will not be busy because everyone has been told by their priest that chocolate is a temptation of the devil. When Vianne announces she doesn't attend church, the parishioners ostracize her. The most influential man in the village, the Comte (Count) De Reynaud, writes a sermon for the town's young priest, condemning her chocolate shop. However, Vianne's chocolate shop is the place where she ministers to those with broken spirits. Since money is not her primary goal, we see her giving away much of her chocolate. She touches hearts and begins to work miracles. Vianne rekindles romance between a husband and wife, gives a woman shelter from her abusive husband, softens an ornery grandmother dying of diabetes, then unites this grandmother with her only grandson. Vianne accepts everyone without judgement, including a band of gypsies the churchgoers despise.

In the end, Vianne wins over the town. We understand that although she is the only villager who doesn't attend church, she is wise and compassionate. She heals many in the village of their hypocrisy and mean-spiritedness. This movie could get people thinking about whether they foolishly give up things they enjoy. Some may begin reflecting on whether they judge others, particularly if they are different in any way. Others may realize the importance of love and compassion, treating everyone with respect and following your heart even when others don't understand.

There is, however, one important distinction between dreams and movies. Movies are often contrived, and dreams are not. We may watch a movie, but it may not provide the key insights we need at the time. Dreams are *always* designed by the soul to move us forward so that we grow and evolve. They provide the experiences we need to help us make critical decisions in our waking life.

In dreams, the soul or unconscious produces personally meaningful movies. The soul writes scripts, produces, directs, and acts in these movies. We travel with friends—some known, some unknown—and go to the most appropriate movie set or dimension. Some sets are very similar to earth and others are extremely different or "out of this world." The most challenging work of the soul, perhaps, is to act in these movies. For example, we may take part in movie after movie where we can integrate the struggles, emotions, and triumphs of leaving an abusive relationship. We become the main characters in a movie where an abusive spouse, boss, or friend is exploiting us. We experience in the dream state how terrible this feels. It becomes a mirror to examine and understand what is taking place in the physical dimension. When we're ready, we play the part of someone who stands up to the abuse for the first time. This may happen in the dream state months before it happens on earth. Our roles in the next few movies may involve experiencing the pain and fear of the actual separation. They may examine the challenges of living independently—packing and throwing away old possessions, trying on new clothes, hunting for a new place to live, and moving to a new house and unpacking. Finally, soul concludes the series through several roles where we experiment with new opportunities in life.

Every movie is acted out in dreams, either simultaneously as they are happening on earth, or well before the events on earth actually transpire. This allows us to take these new insights back to the physical dimension so that we can work through karma. It never feels good to be endlessly embroiled in the dramas of life. Being master of our soul doesn't mean we spend an eternity acting in movies where we try to face our fears or learn to be more tolerant. Being master of our soul means we have worked through karma and earned the wisdom to direct our life with greater compassion, clarity, and awareness.

Dreams As Plays within the Play of Life

We can also think of dreams as plays we actually watch or take part in every night while we simultaneously go about our seemingly real-life drama or play on earth. I've had dreams where I was actually on stage acting out an identical role to one I was playing in life. But most frequently, my spirit devises clever scenarios with slight plot twists and characters that experience the exact same issues, emotions, and insecurities that I'm dealing with.

Shakespeare was a master of this literary technique of using a play within a play. One of the best known examples is *Hamlet*. In this play, Hamlet is the young melancholy prince of Denmark. Hamlet is deeply depressed at the death of his father, the former king of Denmark. He becomes sullen and bitter when his uncle, Claudius, quickly marries Hamlet's mother, Gertrude, and is crowned the king of Denmark. In the play's first act, the ghost of the former king appears to his son and demands that Hamlet seek revenge for his murder. The ghost reveals that Claudius and Gertrude were having an affair before his death and that he didn't die from a snakebite as everyone was told. Claudius killed him while he was sleeping in the orchard by pouring poison into his ear.

After the appearance of his father's ghost, Hamlet devises a clever plan, a "mousetrap" for his uncle. A group of travelling actors are visiting the court. Hamlet convinces them to add sixteen lines to a play they are performing, which involves a murder, and changes the title to *The Murder of Gonzago*. In Hamlet's revised version, the duke Gonzago is murdered when poison is poured in his ear. Hamlet's plan is to watch his uncle Claudius during the play to see his reaction. The play obviously strikes a guilty chord with King Claudius. As soon as this murder scene occurs, he rises from his seat, orders the lights to be turned on, and the play is stopped. Claudius is upset and shaken, but Hamlet is ecstatic, believing his uncle's tempter tantrum has proven his guilt.

So Shakespeare's *Hamlet* demonstrates how dreams can often mirror events that have transpired in our lives. As in *Hamlet*, names and situations in dreams may vary slightly, but when we remember the dream, there will be an uncanny resemblance to our physical lives. When our dreams have recreated a play that is similar, just like Claudius, we often have a strong emotional reaction. Dreams cleverly play their part in helping us see things clearly.

Dreams As Simulations

We've all seen those computer simulations that allow us to experience what it really feels like to fly a plane or chase villains through tunnels and mazes. Dreams work the same way. Imagine "David" is a seventeen-year-old living with his parents and attending high school. He has two younger sisters. He's going through a tough time because he feels his parents are too controlling and he doesn't want to follow their rules. He battles with his father over his school grades and the amount of time he spends with his girlfriend. David feels like a prisoner in his home, wants to escape, but needs a plan. So while David sleeps he simulates or tests out all of his options. The first night he vents his anger and frustration. He may have a dream where he yells and screams at his parents telling them that none of his friends have to be in by 11 p.m. He may have several dreams where he actually runs away from home. In the first dream, he goes to live with his grandparents. Even though this seems like an easy way out, his grandparents have more stringent rules, and in this dream he feels completely stifled. He misses his bedroom and his mom's cooking. In the second dream, he lives with his best friend but feels uncomfortable and alienated because they speak Chinese, which he barely understands. In the third dream, he tries a shelter for runaway teens, but this is even more isolating and depressing. Then he has a vivid dream, where he tells his parents he doesn't want to be part of the family because they've never tried to understand or support him. This time, he empties his bank account and gets his own apartment. He also discovers that it's financially impossible to support himself and finish school. He misses his younger sisters, feels depressed, and when he tries to cook he burns everything.

After these dreams, David knows there isn't another place at the moment where he'd feel comfortable living. He realizes that he's not emotionally ready to leave home yet. In the dream state, he rants and raves at his parents, lets all his anger and frustration surface, and experiments with several places to live rather than actually running away in his physical life. These dreams enable him to work through his emotions, figure out what he can and can't do, and come to terms with his living arrangements.

In many of our dreams, we're exploring, testing, trying things on for size, which saves us incredible amounts of time, money, and energy in our physical life. In David's case, just because he dreamed he was going to live with his grandparents, doesn't mean he actually will. It means his spirit is allowing him to safely explore this possibility so that he can eliminate it from his list. The dream and especially the accompanying emotions help David understand whether this is something he really wants. Since David felt lonely, depressed, and isolated in every dream simulation, his spirit is helping him understand these are not options that will nurture him.

Every dreamer is unique. Perhaps David's classmate "Jennifer" is living in a home where she is physically and sexually abused. Jennifer desperately wants to leave for different reasons, but she's afraid to even try. While she dreams, she may experiment with the same simulations as David. She may try living with her best friend, going to a shelter, getting her own apartment, or moving in with relatives. Perhaps her grandmother lives alone and is willing to take her in. Jennifer may spend several weeks or months acting out scenarios where she sneaks out of her house in the middle of the night and runs to her grandmother's home. In the first few dreams, she may be terrified to leave her house, so she uses these dreams to work through her fears. In each occurrence, when she arrives at her grandmother's, it always feels secure. She has long conversations with her grandmother in these dreams and is assured she'll be safe and cared for. Jennifer may rehearse in her dreams until she has the courage to secretly pack her bags and leave.

Every night, we go through these simulations or dramas until we have decided exactly what we will do in our physical life. These scenarios will often take months, even years before we have tested out all the alternatives and have arrived at a plan we're comfortable with. Just think of all the time, energy, and money we save by doing this while we sleep!

Chapter Three
Déjà Vu—Crossing Time Dimensions

The reason birds fly, and we can't, is simply that they have perfect faith,
for to have perfect faith is to have wings.
—Sir James M. Barrie

"Twinkle, twinkle little star, how I wonder what you are." Most children have a fascination with stars because this is the dimension we come from. They know it's real. Try to remember the last time you looked up at the stars on a clear night and were filled with awe at their beauty and vastness. We reside in the Milky Way galaxy— a solar system comprised of roughly one hundred billion stars. It's even more mind boggling to consider there may be more than fifty billion galaxies in the universe, each with billions of stars. The universe extends farther than we can see or comprehend with our mind's limited awareness, making earth seem as tiny as a grain of sand on a vast beach. On some level, we all know we're part of something bigger. We have little trouble believing that Peter Pan or other such characters were transported through galaxies and dimensions while they slept. But we have difficulty translating this into our physical lives. We're all Peter Pans when we sleep, and the realm and possibilities of these nightly adventures are enormous.

We can't navigate in these other dimensions with our mind, but we can with our spirit or soul. Our soul knows exactly where we need to go to work through karma and dharma because home for the soul is not the physical dimension. In dreams, our soul takes us to the dimensions it knows. Just like in the television series *Star Trek*, it knows how to beam us down to the right coordinates. This is pure science for the soul. It knows exactly where to travel to help us become more aware and informed. We're all experienced dimensional travellers. Imagine how enlightening these journeys can be if we bring them into conscious awareness.

We Can't Change the Past, So We Go Forward in Dreams

As Peter Pans having these nightly adventures, our spirit not only chooses which play, simulation, movie set, or dimension will best help us, there is also another critical choice it must make: Where do we go in dimensions of time—to the past, present, or future? I can't honestly tell you I've ever remembered journalling a past-life dream or a dream where I went back in time and relived something that happened in this life. Years after I was badly burned in a fire, I remember a nurse who did counselling asking me if I had nightmares about it. I didn't. But before the fire, I did have dreams where I went forward in time to emotionally prepare me for this huge karmic event of being burned. I never ever relived this experience in my dreams because I honestly believe there was no point. We can't change, alter, or undo the past. And it can be traumatic and stressful to relive these experiences. Reliving a trauma doesn't help us grow. Experimenting with options and possibilities after the trauma does. With very few exceptions, every single dream is preparing us for the future. Every night, we take out our Peter Pan wings in the dream state to test out future possibilities. For example, a student in her last year of high school may not be able to decide whether she wants to be a computer programmer or a veterinarian. So in dreams, for months or years, she may go forward in time to try out both these possibilities to determine which one feels right.

We're all experienced in crossing dimensions, travelling in other galaxies, and going forward in time. This is why we've all experienced déjà vu—that feeling that something is eerily familiar—that we've heard those words spoken before, or we've already been in this very situation. Every time we have a déjà-vu experience, it's confirmation that we've gone forward in time while we slept, and now we're remembering that experience. This is why sometimes we just feel uneasy about something we're about to do. Other times, we may have a strong sense that everything will be okay or we may feel elated and not understand why. In both cases, we've probably witnessed or rehearsed something in a dream.

Déjà vu is remembering segments of our dreams or nightly journeys. It may be a few words we said to a friend or it could be a major experience. Perhaps we dreamed of an actual funeral in great detail before it happened to help us emotionally prepare. We may have visited our future college or university, and we remember only a few words of a class we attended. When we begin journaling our dreams we realize how often we go forward in time. We begin to really see there's no reason for going back in time. We can't change the past, but we can prepare for what is to come by working through future possibilities. We all travel through time. Each night, we go forward to prepare, then come back to fit this experience into our waking lives.

My friend Jacquie had a vivid dream that helped her face fears and insecurities and, perhaps, to realize part of her destiny. She had been doing yoga for several years and had just completed a teacher's training program at a studio. Although the owner of the studio, Maureen, was willing to hire her, Jacquie felt insecure about her teaching abilities and told Maureen she'd decided not to teach. One of her recurring themes in life was feeling that she simply couldn't measure up. Like many of us, Jacquie was experiencing that classic "I'm not good enough" syndrome, even though she was completely competent. Whenever we're holding back, fearful of our destiny, dreams will bring us forward in time to help us practise, rehearse, or experiment until we've gained the confidence we need.

The same week Jacquie had decided she wouldn't be teaching at the studio, she woke up with a vivid dream. In the dream, she was teaching a yoga class but was interrupted by several people who arrived late. She said it seemed like a very unorthodox class and there were many students who intimidated her. She felt "terribly anxious because the energy of this class was very unusual. Some people were doing what I wanted and others seemed to be doing their own thing. It brought up all my fears about doing a good job." Maureen was in the dream for support and that assured her to "just keep to what you're doing." Although she initially was a bundle of nerves, Jacquie said her voice was strong and she managed to teach the entire class.

In the morning, the dream was etched in her memory. Reflecting on it, she thought, "Wow, that was intense! I was definitely puzzled. I knew the dream had relevance, that there was an importance to it. I lay there thinking about it, replaying it over in my mind. There was a deep nudging in me." It was Sunday morning. Normally she attended an 11 a.m. yoga class at the studio but had overnight guests, so she decided not to go. In the middle of making everyone breakfast, she felt a strong urge to attend the class. She told her partner to finish with the breakfast and raced out the door. When she arrived, people were waiting because the teacher wasn't there. This was unusual since the studio opens half an hour before every class. They waited and waited, then finally realized there wasn't going to be a class. Since Jacquie was an intern, she had keys and told everyone she'd be willing to teach. She unlocked the door and without time to be nervous started the class.

Everything went smoothly; Jacquie's students were supportive and appreciative. Now she completely understood what her dream was all about. Although our conscious minds have absolutely no idea what each day will unfold, our soul knows everything. Jacquie's spirit knew there would be an opportunity for her to teach, so it prepared her the night before. It took her through all the moves with a challenging class to boost her confidence. When it was over, she said, "I felt that everything was clear, that it all came together. Teaching the class was the final piece of the puzzle. I felt exuberant." Thanks to this dream, she no longer felt inadequate. She taught another class the next day with a greater sense of confidence. Her fears and insecurities had been replaced by a sense of "I can do this."

Like Jacquie, we're all psychics in dreams. The entire human population is psychic in their dreams, but we're often not aware of this. Every night we spend seven or eight hours being our own personal psychic. What is a psychic? Someone who can access information from the spirit realm or other dimensions and bring it back to the physical world. Isn't that exactly what we do when we dream? The only difference is that most of the time we don't bring this psychic or soul information back with us after the dream is finished. We don't allow the wisdom of spirit to inform our minds, so we often miss those nudges toward our potential for greatness. Our soul longs to bring us those experiences that help us work through all our fears, insecurities, and personal demons. When the journey is over, we may experience exuberance, a deeper understanding of the power of dreams, and, like Jacquie, the knowledge that "I can do this."

Dreams That Helped Me Prepare

Nothing happens unless first a dream.
—Carl Sandburg

Teaching

In my own life, there are three major déjà-vu experiences that were clearly helping me prepare. Sometimes, dreams or déjà-vu experiences can be intense emotions without any visual memory or story. The first major experience occurred in 1980, when I was working as a photographer at the University of Western Ontario. This was around the time when I first started keeping a dream journal. I woke up quite late one morning, with no memory of having dreamed anything; but my emotions were soaring. I was ecstatic, floating, euphoric—a mixture of emotions I had never experienced with such intensity. Along with these emotions, I awoke knowing with absolute certainty that I would apply to teacher's college, get accepted, and have no problem finding a job. I can't rationally or visually explain how I knew; I just knew at the deepest level possible, and this certainty was intoxicating. I also felt that my body was so light that I could fly. It was a wonderful feeling that stayed with me for several hours. The flip side was that none of this seemed very logical. From a sane, logical perspective, this seemed unlikely because I had just really established myself as a photojournalist after years of hard work. I wasn't sure if the type of degree I had would even be accepted at a teacher's college. I had never worked with children before in my life or even felt a desire to. At that time in Ontario, we were subject to wage and price controls, and no one was hiring teachers. Most new teachers faced several years of unemployment, and I hadn't saved any money to enable me to return to school full time.

But the emotions I woke up with that morning were so strong; none of this seemed to matter. I did all the necessary things, filled out the applications, and soon learned I was accepted at every place I had applied. I was able to afford it; things just worked out. I learned the university had been putting money into a pension fund for me that I could draw on. Around the same time, I learned I had a second cousin Dale who was living in London, Ontario. Our grandfathers were Sicilian brothers who died not speaking to each other, and so I'd never met her. She was also attending teacher's college that year so we met and decided to live together. Dale found us an affordable apartment that I loved.

On the first day of classes, all my rational fears surfaced and totally deflated me. We were sitting at a round table and everyone was doing introductions, explaining why they wanted to teach and outlining previous work experiences. Everyone had been working with children their entire lives: summer camps, YMCAs, volunteering in schools, day cares, coaching, you name it. Their qualifications were impressive. I was the only person who hadn't worked with children. When it was my turn, I felt totally inadequate. I wanted a trap door to open and swallow me up. I said I had been a photographer and my favourite subjects were children and senior citizens because they had no egos and therefore could be natural and spontaneous in front of a camera. But as I was saying this, my mind was telling me this was a really stupid thing to say. I must be crazy. I didn't belong here. I was way out of my league. Who was I trying to kid? I didn't have what it takes to ever be a teacher!

On the third day of classes, I received news that my mother died of colon cancer. It seemed like the worst possible timing because I wasn't sure, emotionally, if I'd be able to get through the year. I flew home and missed the next week of classes. When I returned, I was always grateful there were soundproof music rooms for students at the faculty of education building. For the rest of the semester, I visited those rooms daily to cry and attempt to deal with the loss of my mother. My mother really wanted me to become a teacher, so I poured my heart into everything I did that year. I didn't stop believing since the morning that I woke up knowing I would be a teacher, although I had never told anyone about it.

Halfway through the year, when it was time to start applying for jobs, I had a vivid dream telling me exactly which school board to apply to. But there was a dilemma because I had two Saturday-morning interviews that were scheduled around the same time. One interview was in London and the other was in Mississauga, so I had to make a decision. The interviews couldn't be rescheduled, and it was impossible to attend both. In the dream, I was trying to ride my bike to the London interview, but I kept hitting dead ends. It seemed a frustrating losing battle, and I couldn't make progress. But when I tried to bike to Mississauga, it was smooth riding. After this dream, I talked to one of my instructors. I told him about my biking dreams and he didn't try to dismiss them as figments of my imagination. He said, "It's obvious you have to go to the job interview in Mississauga." I took his advice, cancelled the appointment in London, and drove to the Mississauga interview. While driving there, I had the sensation that my car was flying. It seemed like it had lifted off the highway. It was a kind of other-dimensional euphoria I had never spoken about—the same kind of "high" feeling I had the day I woke up knowing I would be a teacher. The interview went extremely well. Three days later, I was hired.

Despite the fact I had never worked with children, I was the first person in my class to get a teaching job. In fact, I had a job in February, well before the school year ended. I also received a position in the grade levels I had secretly wanted—grades one and two. I was given a split one/two posting in an idyllic country school surrounded by rolling hills and cornfields. The nine years I spent at that school were perhaps the happiest of my life. It's now obvious to me what happened that night of my initial euphoric dream when I woke up knowing my vocation. I'm sure I went forward in time and was shown everything: a new life that I would love. In physical life, I've always been afraid of major changes—I'm definitely not a risk taker. But thanks to our ability to go forward in time, that one night of dreaming literally changed my life.

The Fire

The second major déjà-vu experience took place in December 1985. I was wrapping Christmas presents and preparing to stay with my brother for the holiday. Since my family lived about four hours away, I usually tried to get all of the wrapping, packing, and preparation done so I could leave right away. I loved going home to be with my family and counted the seconds like a child. I was always filled with anticipation and excitement, so the sooner I got home the better. But wrapping the presents seemed to be taking a long time. I had this foreboding feeling that I didn't want to leave, but I didn't understand why. I knew I was stalling, but there was no rational reason. The day after I arrived, I was severely burned in a house fire. My entire body caught on fire, and I survived only because I was able to run outside and roll in fresh snow. My brother's house burned to the ground, and it was a miracle I survived. I went through five years of emotional and physical pain, skin grafts, and wore a protective bodysuit for two years. Deep inside I knew something like this would happen; I had received hints locked into my unconscious mind, which translated into uneasiness before the actual fire.

Spirit is never cruel. It knew being in this fire would be difficult, and so in dreams it began emotionally preparing me for years. Looking back, I realize it would have been too traumatic to have vivid recall of any of these dreams. When I reviewed my dream journal years later, there were dreams of burning houses, but I didn't seem to have any emotional connection or strong recollections of those dreams. I'd completely forgotten them and was amazed reading them. I believe years in advance, my spirit revealed as much as it could to cushion me emotionally. I knew something was coming, but if my mind had full awareness I probably wouldn't have driven home for Christmas or I wouldn't have gotten out of bed that morning. Throughout this whole experience, there was knowledge deep inside me. I knew this was a huge karmic debt I had to repay, and there was never any question in my mind that I would survive it.

Thesis Defence

A third intense déjà-vu episode took place ten years later in 1995 when I again awoke with absolute euphoria. (This waking up with euphoria has only happened twice in my life.) It was the day I was to defend my doctoral thesis in educational psychology. I thought I would be a nervous wreck and doubted I would sleep at all the night before. But I slept like a baby and had vivid dreams where I was running through electrified rainbows. In another dream a mystical raven landed in my lap and spoke to me. When I awoke, I knew with absolute certainty there would be no problem with my oral defence. I wasn't nervous, intimidated, or doubtful. I just knew the defence would go well.

Defending a doctoral thesis can seem like a make-it-or-break-it proposition. Every doctoral candidate has heard horror stories of students who studied for years only to fail their oral defence. I'd invested seven years on this project and it had become my life. An expert from another university had been flown in to join a committee of five other experts—all of them distinguished university professors. So I sat before this panel of six esteemed individuals discussing why I had done a doctoral thesis on teenagers and dreams. No one had done this before, which made the whole procedure dubious; I was treading new ground. Fortunately, however, dreams had guided me the entire time. Whenever I got stuck writing my thesis, I would dream literally every word of the next few pages. When I woke up, I often couldn't write fast enough. And so I talked about the work I'd done with a calmness I don't usually have. For seven years, I'd been going forward in time preparing for this day, and my spirit already knew the outcome. When my defence was concluded, I was instructed to leave the room and wait outside while the committee decided my fate. This may involve many hours of waiting if the committee isn't sure whether your work measures up. I think I waited about ten minutes. My thesis advisor, David Hunt, opened the door with a huge smile on his face and said, "Congratulations, Dr. Quattrocchi." It turned out to be one of the happiest and most rewarding days of my life. All my dreams did come true.

Chapter Four
Working with Our Dreams

I shut my eyes in order to see.
—Paul Gauguin

Dreamwork is a unique experience for everyone. No two people will ever dream the same because we each have different backgrounds, karma, and destinies. So it's fruitless to compare our dreams to someone else's, to believe our dreams aren't exciting, or to think that other people are having better experiences. Every dream is a piece of gold we bring back to the physical world. They are sacred and worthy of respect, whether we're being chased by monsters or flying over mystical lands. I've had people tell me they feared something was wrong with them because their dreams all seemed dark and depressing. It's funny how most people love stories of horror, mystery, and suspense, but when these stories become intensely personal, we fear them.

Since dreams offer us potential for growth, even scary dreams where we're confronting our personal demons hold enormous possibilities. It's one less monster we have to conquer—one less battle to fight—a personal victory on the road to enlightenment. After we've fought our battles, conquered personal demons, and become more aware, we've opened the door to unlimited potential. Who knows what lies ahead after we've kissed that frog or confronted an ogre? So it's healthier to accept our dreams—the good, bad, and the ugly—with awe, fascination, and gratitude. That doesn't mean every dream will be dark and depressing. Once we start journalling dreams, we soon realize they're similar to titles in a video store. Some will be surreal fantasies with intense colours and fascinating landscapes; others resemble science fiction; some will be tragedies, but many will be dramas that stir your emotions and comedies that keep you laughing for years.

In this chapter, we will receive the tools needed to begin mining our personal gold. First, we'll examine why so few people remember dreams even though these messages are so important. Then we'll look at tried and true techniques for remembering dreams even if you swear on a stack of Bibles you've never recalled a dream before. I used this list with high school students and it worked for everyone. For most people, it takes about two or three weeks before they begin remembering. Like many things, dream recall is a skill; the more we do it, the easier it becomes. Most of us remembered our dreams as children. Then as teenagers or adults with many responsibilities, we started to forget what we already knew. And living in a society that didn't honour or understand dreams didn't help. We already have this skill or ability; it's innate, a part of who we are. It's very natural or normal to remember our dreams, and perhaps very "abnormal" or counterproductive not to. It's like riding that bike again that's been sitting in your garage for years. A little scary at first, but really not that difficult. Surprisingly, you don't fall and it's quite exhilarating once you get the hang of it again.

What Prevents Dream Recall?

1. We don't believe that dreams are valuable sources of insight. Over time, most of us have been socialized to believe dreams are weird or nonsense. Dream recall is a natural healthy process that our conscious mind slowly filters out or shuts down. That's why most children can recall their dreams every morning. It's our true state.

2. We may be involved in so many things, thoughts, or distractions each morning that make relaxation and taking the time to let dreams resurface difficult.

3. We may be scared or not ready to face issues, so dream content may be blocked until they're ready. Our conscious mind acts as a censor. Sometimes people who have been abused or traumatized will work through their trauma while they sleep. So consciously remembering the dream isn't necessary. It's enough that they're working through this issue while they sleep.

4. We may be emotionally overloaded or too emotionally vulnerable to engage in dreamwork. Sometimes, if we're desperately struggling to hold together our outer world, we won't recall our inner world. Working with dreams requires courage and strength.

5. We may experience events that will happen far into the future. We could go one to ten years into the future to work through karmic situations to make them easier to deal with.

So there's no point in remembering them because they haven't happened yet. We remember them when we need to. We may begin to remember them when we start experiencing or dealing with those situations in physical life. This is often when people have déjà-vu experiences.

6. We've listened to the messages in our dreams and are actively working to understand, change, or balance our lives. Our recall of dreams isn't as vivid or as often because we've already "gotten it."

• Dreams are more vivid and memorable during periods of change, transition, or crisis.

• We often dream in waves or patterns. It's not uncommon to have an intense period of dream recall followed by a period with little or no recall. A period of strong recall is bringing up issues that are important for us to understand. This is often followed by a period with little or no recall so we have an opportunity to work through those issues.

Techniques for Remembering Dreams

...seek and you will find; knock and the door will be opened to you.
—Matthew 7:7

Remembering dreams can take patience and perseverance in the beginning. We're reprogramming our mind to start remembering something it's been programmed to forget for a lifetime. Most of us have been told repeatedly: "forget it, it's only a dream." These techniques will help you begin remembering, but this may not happen overnight. Some may remember a dream the first night; for others, it may take a week or two. I've never worked with anyone who couldn't remember their dreams using these techniques. A good time to begin may be on a holiday or weekend when you're more relaxed and not as pressured for time.

1. Tell yourself at least five or six times (silently or out loud) that you want to remember your dreams. You may do this during the

day or just before going to sleep. You can say something like: "Tonight, I will remember my dreams," "I am remembering my dreams," or "I want to remember my dreams."

2. Have a notebook beside the bed. This gives a clear signal to your spirit that you're ready to honour your dreams. Having this notebook ready is important because approximately 5 minutes after the dream is finished, half the content is forgotten; in 10 minutes, 90% is forgotten. If you don't have time to write down your dream, you can use a tape recorder. You can record what you remember, then transcribe it when you have more time.

3. Keep your eyes closed when you wake up and just lay there silently. If you open your eyes to outside stimuli you may lose the dream. If you have woken up to a clock radio or alarm, turn it off temporarily. We need to temporarily drift back to that relaxed alpha state of lowered brainwaves. External stimuli will prevent that.

4. Don't force recall, just relax. Like everything in life, if you try too hard, it won't happen.

5. If you don't remember anything, with your eyes still closed try shifting to a different position or turning to the other side. This helps some people.

6. Talk about dreams with friends and family members. This stimulates greater recall and understanding. Again, it's honouring the dream state. Often when you start talking about a dream, you'll remember something new, or the meaning will suddenly become clear.

7. Treat dreams with respect and appreciation. Believe and act as if they contain valuable and important insights and keys to awareness.

8. Meditate. Try each day to clear your mind of any negative thoughts, ideas, or stresses you may be experiencing. Meditation enables you to have greater awareness. When you

meditate, you lower your brainwaves to the alpha state, which is the realm of dreams. This allows greater insight to come through. Daily meditators often report dreams with greater clarity. Any solitary activity where you're able to quiet your mind and focus can be a form of meditation. So it's possible that you will remember a dream while you take a bath or shower, walk your dog, ride a bike, garden, wash dishes, sit in front of a fireplace, or watch an aquarium!

9. Have faith. Believe that you will remember your dreams and you will, and, most importantly, pray/meditate/ask for clarity, guidance, insight, and wisdom. Then it's almost impossible not to be grateful for the insights you receive.

Keeping a Dream Journal

There is no *one* correct way to journal dreams. Everyone finds a way that suits his or her personality. If you're artistic, you may decide to sketch or draw your dreams. If you're a dancer you may dance through the emotions. If you like music you may turn the images and emotions found in your dreams into a song. These are all suggestions that will, hopefully, provide a starting point to stimulate your imagination further.

• Recording just one or two dreams a week will begin to give you incredible awareness. If you record one dream every night, that's more than adequate. It's probably easiest to remember the last dream you have before you wake up. Most dreams are working through the same or related issues. You can still have great clarity if you record only one or two dreams a week.

• If you wake up in the middle of the night and realize you've just had an important dream, try to run all the details of the dream through your mind once or twice. Often, when people start recording dreams for the first time, they start losing sleep over it. If they have a dream at two o'clock in the morning, they turn on the light and write it down. This isn't necessary. Instead, we can tell ourselves we're going to write down this dream in the morning. This is almost like scanning the dream so we can retrieve it a few hours later without losing sleep. In the morning we can usually remember the dream in great detail. You'll be surprised how well this works. With a little practise, you may be able to retrieve two or three dreams in one night.

• Record everything and anything you remember. Never dismiss dreams as silly or unimportant. Often these are the most telling dreams. Our ego (conscious mind) may be fighting against this like an overprotective parent hiding us from the truth! Sometimes we just remember a fragment or piece of dream, but it's still worthwhile to write it down.

• Write down your dreams without censoring or editing. Include images, reactions, actions, thoughts, attitudes, feelings, impressions, conversations, and character descriptions— anything you can recall. Write quickly without worrying about spelling, grammar, or punctuation. You may find that as you start writing, this will stimulate and enhance greater recall. Sometimes memories will come back so quickly, you can't write fast enough. We often become aware what the dream is telling us while we're writing it down.

• Express the main emotion or emotions you felt during the dream. This is always key to the dream's meaning. There may be one predominant emotion throughout the dream—fear, for example. Or the emotion may change and evolve; it may start as fear, then change to amazement, and then become a feeling of safety. *Emotions in dreams always communicate our core truths*; they never lie.

• You may want to include what was going on in your life when the dream occurred. What are your current emotions, issues, challenges, fears, frustrations, goals, or aspirations? There is always a direct relationship between our present life and the dream. Did something that day upset you? Did you go someplace, do something, watch something, or talk to someone that might have triggered the dream?

• You may decide to circle, highlight, or underline key words, symbols or important phrases in the dream. This is not necessary, but many people find it helpful.

• It is also optional to record the date the dream took place. You may want to do this so that you can make connections between when the dream occurred and what was taking place in your life. This is also helpful if you go back after a period of time and review your dreams. Sometimes the date will help you make connections.

• You can give the dream a title if you wish. This often helps you summarize what took place, but, again, this is optional. What is most important is that you're aware of what the dream is showing you!

• Once you've kept a dream journal for a while, it's quite revealing to go back and review your dreams. This can be done during any time interval: a month, four months, six months, or a year. If you have the opportunity to do this you'll become aware of symbols and themes that repeat over time. You'll also become aware of your own personal symbols and what they mean. This also helps you become aware of your growth and progress.

Asking for Guidance in Your Dream Journal

As a final tool, we'll examine the technique of asking for guidance in a dream journal. This is like going to a very wise guru or swami with a question. If you want to know whether to break up with a boyfriend or girlfriend, sell your house, or change careers, dreams can provide important insights. Simply repeat the question silently or out loud before you go to sleep, asking that an answer be revealed in a dream. Or you can write the question in your dream journal before you fall asleep. If you're using this technique, there are a few important things to understand.

First, you must trust and have faith in the clarity and wisdom of your dreams.

Second, you need to be patient. Sometimes the answer doesn't come right away. Although you may believe the question you asked is the most urgent matter in your life right now, your spirit may not agree. It may send you other messages first until the timing is right. Or you may think you haven't gotten an answer when, in fact, you have. The answers may be hidden in symbols you're not ready to understand, or it may not be the answer you wanted, so you simply dismiss it.

Third, the answer sometimes doesn't come in dreams, but in our waking life. Several years ago, I wondered whether I should see Jungian dream analyst Annie Jacobson. For months in my dream journal, I kept asking whether I should see this person. I didn't receive clues in a dream, but in my waking life I was repeatedly getting answers. A good friend told me she had seen Annie and felt she was extremely helpful. A few weeks later, I picked up a magazine and the first page I turned to was an article written by Annie Jacobson, and a few weeks after that, the same friend repeated her praise of how great she was. She then gave me a pamphlet advertising Annie's writing workshops. The following week, when a different friend gave me the same pamphlet, I finally realized I just wasn't getting the message. I kept thinking the answer had to come through a dream.

It's also important to understand that we won't get answers that don't involve our spiritual growth. Although it says in the Bible, "ask and you shall receive," it's obvious these words can't be taken literally. If this were true, we'd all look like supermodels. We'd also be millionaires who never got sick, grew old, or had problems. It's only in matters of personal growth, cleaning up karma, or discovering dharma that we receive answers. We'll wait an eternity if we ask for the winning numbers of next week's lottery. We'll never be shown how to cheat on an exam or rob a bank in a dream. But if we ask a question that helps us move forward spiritually, then we will truly receive.

Sample Dream Journal Entry

The Frustrated Frog — *Eleventh-grade female student*

This was a very peculiar dream I had that took place in the forest located in my backyard. In the forest the most important detail that I focussed on was the little river or creek that runs through it. At first the forest looked peaceful and gentle, and the little creek was running smoothly. However, the forest started to change and soon became very lifeless. The little creek turned murky and the water ran rougher. In one section of the creek, there was a little frog lying just beneath the surface of the water. As the water flowed it just remained in its place.

Then certain objects like twigs and branches started accumulating around the frog and they kept adding up. The most bizarre part of the dream occurred when the arms and legs of the frog started being stretched out. They kept extending out as the water became more rapid. Eventually, the bits and pieces of branches that had gathered around the frog were taken away with the water. The creek became calm once again and the limbs of the frog returned back to normal.

At the beginning of the dream I felt relaxed, but as the forest and creek started turning murky I felt upset. I felt sorry for the little frog just laying there and when the twigs started accumulating around it I felt angry. A feeling of frustration came over me when the limbs of the frog were being stretched. After things returned back to normal and I awoke I was filled with a feeling of relief.

At first I considered this dream very bizarre and thought it has no relevance in my life, however it turned out to be the most symbolic dream. The forest and creek symbolizes my life. At first it was very calm and peaceful but then it became very hectic, just as the water became more rapid. At this point in my life I am under a lot of pressure especially with school. With the year ending soon I have been bombarded with work such as essays, projects and assignments. Also, exams are coming up and I am under extreme pressure because of that too. In this dream, I think the frog symbolizes me. The twigs and branches that accumulate around it probably reflect the work and assignments I am trying to finish. As the water gets rougher the frog still struggles and remains in its place which is what I am doing. The fact that the frog did not get washed away, shows how I am not giving up and am still holding on. The peculiar part of the dream which includes the limbs of the frog being stretched could symbolize how I am being stretched or pulled into many different directions.

The mood in my dream parallels that in my life because I have been very angry and frustrated with all the work that has been building up. The fact that the frog and creek returns back to normal could foreshadow that soon my life will turn back to how it was, and this probably will happen after exams.

Chapter Five
Famous Dreamers

Dreams have inspired writers, inventors, composers, singers, scientists, saints, politicians, and peace activists to improve the human condition. We can safely say that anything of real genius, creativity, or vision began in a dream. Each of these famous people understood their dharma or destiny through dreams. Reading through this list of famous dreamers will hopefully help us understand that in dreams we not only plan our own path, but we work for the benefit of all humanity.

René Descartes is referred to as the father of modern philosophy. He was also a brilliant mathematician who made important contributions to the field of algebra and is also considered the father of analytical geometry. He coined the famous phrase: *cogito, ergo sum,* "I think, therefore I am." He was a rationalist, convinced that we arrive at truth only through reason and the mind, but, ironically, Descartes's major theories came through his dreams! Perhaps he could have said, "I dream therefore I am." He believed in priming his mind before sleeping to promote meaningful dreams. Descartes was able to blend his spirit and mind so effectively that he struggled to find a clear distinction between his dreams and waking experiences. He once said, "When I consider this carefully, I find not a single property which with certainty separates the waking state from the dream . . . Even if I were asleep, everything that appears evident to my mind is absolutely true." Moreover, he once asked, "How can you be certain that your whole life is not a dream?"

Harriet Tubman's routes leading from the southern United States to various spots in the northern states and in Canada came to be known as the Underground Railway. This railway was actually a series of safe houses, different methods of transportation, and links to conductors or sympathizers who helped lead slaves to safety. Harriet, one of the main conductors, was called "Black Moses" because of the nineteen trips she made to lead hundreds of slaves to freedom. When the war was over, she founded schools for these former slaves. She was considered a wanted woman and $40,000 was offered for her capture. Harriet was never caught even though she was vigorously pursued by slave hunting patrols. Why? Harriet said dreams always guided her to safe escape routes.

Thomas Edison, who invented the light bulb, understood the

power of dreams. He kept a small cot in his office. Whenever he needed inspiration, he would focus on the problem, then take a catnap to arrive at a solution. He was also famous for another creative technique. Edison would focus on the problem and hold a small ball in each of his hands while he sat in his rocking chair, moving back and forth. When he fell asleep and started dreaming, the balls would drop to the floor and wake him up. This allowed Edison to remember his dreams—usually the next step he needed for an invention he was working on. During his lifetime, Edison patented a record 1,093 inventions despite his propensity to survive on only four hours of sleep each night. This, of course, did not include his frequent naps or the time he spent rocking in his chair.

Elias Howe was a humble watchmaker until a terrifying dream led to his invention of the sewing machine. He would watch his wife work long into the night sewing clothes by hand for their family. His skill with watches motivated him to develop a machine that would take the long hours and drudgery out of sewing. But he was not alone; during the 1830s, many others had their minds set on the same invention. Howe tried to perfect a machine with two needles—one that moved up and down and another that moved across simultaneously. But he couldn't get his idea to work because he was putting the eye of the needle at the top. This was the same position as those needles that he had watched his wife use each night.

One night, Howe dreamed he was captured by savages and dragged to their king. The king declared that if he couldn't produce a sewing machine, he'd be put to death. Howe was given a deadline for this project that was impossible to meet. As the savages began spearing him to death, he realized the spears had eye-shaped holes in their tips. He woke up realizing these spears represented the needles he had been endlessly labouring over. Placing the eye in the tip or point of the needle led to the first successful sewing machine.

The following is an example of how insight from dreams produces a ripple effect. The father of Elias Howe's friend Charles Goodyear, Jr. had invented a process that made rubber flexible in all temperatures. The elder Charles did this by heating sulphur and applying it to the rubber. He called this process vulcanization after Vulcan, the Roman god of fire and volcanoes. When Howe told his friend that his new sewing machine had a strong needle capable of sewing leather strips together to make shoes, it triggered Charles Goodyear, Jr.'s imagination. He decided to experiment with a new type of shoe containing a canvas top sewn to a rubber bottom. This shoe remained relatively lightweight with the added benefit of keeping people's feet dry. In 1870, using Elias Howe's sewing machine, the first pair of running shoes walked into history.

James Watt was repeatedly awakened by a recurring dream of being in a storm of heavy lead pellets. Eventually, he hit upon the idea that if molten lead was dropped from a great height it would form into small spheres. Testing this theory led to his invention of ball bearings.

Fredrick A. von Kekule, a chemistry professor in Belgium, discovered the molecular structure of benzene, the benzene ring, in a dream. This discovery is said to have revolutionized organic chemistry. In his dream, he saw atoms forming different patterns and structures. Gradually, long rows of atoms began to form and twist like a snake. Finally, he saw one snake hold its tail and continue to whirl in a circle or ring. When he described his dream at a scientific convention, he said, "Let us learn to dream, gentlemen, and then perhaps we shall learn the truth."

It was through a dream that professional golfer Jack Nicklaus learned how to adjust his swing, bringing him out of a long career slump. In 1964, a story in the *San Francisco Chronicle* reported him saying:

> I was hitting them pretty good in the dream and all at once I realized I wasn't holding the club the way I've actually been holding it lately. I've been having trouble collapsing my right arm taking the club head away from the ball, but I was doing it perfectly in my sleep. So when I came to the course yesterday morning, I tried it in the way I did in my dream and it worked. I shot a 68 yesterday and a 65 today and believe me it's a lot more fun this way. I feel kind of foolish admitting it, but it really happened in a dream. All I had to do was change my grip just a little.

Diaries, journals, and letters of numerous writers credit dreams as a major source of inspiration. Poet Samuel Taylor Coleridge dreamed his entire poem "Kubla Khan." In a letter to a friend, D. H. Lawrence wrote, "I can never decide whether my dreams are the result of my thoughts, or my thoughts the result of my dreams. But my dreams make conclusions for me. They decide things finally. I dream a decision. Sleep seems to hammer out for me the logical conclusions of my vague days, and offer them as dreams."

Poet and visual artist William Blake once said, "I am not ashamed to tell you what ought to be told—that I am under the direction of messengers from heaven, daily and nightly." According to Blake, all his artistic genius came to him through angels.

In his autobiographical *Across the Plains*, Robert Louis Stevenson includes "A Chapter on Dreams" where he describes how the "Little People" helped him materialize story ideas: "And for the Little People, what shall I say they are but just my Brownies, God bless them! who do one-half my work for me while I am fast asleep . . . the whole of my published fiction should be the single-handed product of some Brownie, some Familiar, some unseen collaborator, whom I keep locked in a back garret." Each night, his dreams would continue stories where they had left off the night before. He once dreamed about a criminal who drank a potion that changed his appearance. This became his famous novel *The Strange Case of Dr. Jekyll and Mr. Hyde*.

It was through a dream that Mary Shelley received her inspiration for the classic novel *Frankenstein*. One evening, she and a group of friends sat up late telling ghost stories at Lord Byron's villa. Before going to bed, Byron challenged his guests to write a horror story. That night, Mary Shelley had vivid dreams, which became the basis for her novel:

> My imagination, unbidden, possessed and guided me, gifting the successive images that arose in my mind with a vividness far beyond the usual bounds of reveries . . . I saw the pale student of unhallowed arts kneeling beside the thing he had put together—I saw the hideous phantasm of a man stretched out, and then, on the working of some powerful engine, show signs of life, and stir with an uneasy, half-vital motion . . . Swift as light and cheering was the idea that broke in up upon me. "I have found it! What terrified me will terrify others; and I need only describe the spectre which had haunted my midnight pillow." On the morrow I announced that I had thought of the story.

Painter Salvador Dali is well known for his surreal dream-like paintings. He used to wake himself up and immediately begin to paint what he had just been dreaming. Both Beethoven and Mozart woke up with symphonies playing in their heads. Who knows how many of the world's great pieces of music originated in dreams? Harpist and composer Hilary Stagg was an electrician until he attended an

Andreas Vollenweider concert when he was in his mid-twenties. Hilary was so enthralled with this style of music that he decided to buy a small harp. Using his knowledge as an electrician he amplified his harp creating his own custom sound. He tried taking formal music lessons but decided to learn on his own probably because he'd been a lucid dreamer for years. Since he was fully aware when he was in the dream state, Hilary began composing music in his sleep. He set up a recording studio in his living room to fine-tune these songs from his dreams. In time, he became an accomplished harpist developing a powerful yet enchanting sound. Hilary's dreams resulted in seven titles for his recording company New Music before he died suddenly in 1998. One of his albums is appropriately entitled *Dream Spiral*.

In the episode entitled "The Creative Spark" on the Discovery Channel's television series *The Power of Dreams*, singer and songwriter Billy Joel said in an interview, "All the music I've composed had come from a dream." He often dreams sounds: angelic choruses, complete musical arrangements, and solos. "I say to people if you only could have heard what I dreamt. If you only could have been there." Despite his musical success, he admits it is difficult to bring music from the dream worlds into physical reality. "What I'm producing is a poor substitute for what I dream." One morning he awoke actually singing the lyrics to his famous song "River of Dreams." He explains, "All your life you learn how to control things and how to edit things and how to craft and how to hone and shape and refine. When I'm asleep all that goes out the window. I'm a barbarian. I think I go back to the primeval artist who is at the core of me."

Gandhi was guided through a dream to bring freedom to his people. India was experiencing harsh domination from England at the time. He was instructed to encourage his people to spend twenty-four hours in prayer and fasting and to halt their usual business activities. This resulted in the non-violent mass strikes (hartals) of 1919, which were instrumental in achieving liberation for India.

In a series of dreams beginning when he was nine years old, Giovanni Bosco was encouraged to care for young boys. In his initial dream, he saw himself in a field with many boys who were laughing and playing. But several of these boys were cursing. Young Giovanni was so shocked at this language he jumped into the middle of the crowd and began swinging his fists wildly and shouting at them to stop. At that moment, a man appeared. He was dressed in white, and his face radiated so much light that Giovanni could not look directly at him. He told Giovanni, "You will have to win these friends of yours not with blows but with gentleness and kindness. So begin right now to show them that sin is ugly and virtue beautiful."

Then a glowing woman appeared. She took his hand and showed him that all the children had been replaced by a variety of animals: cats, dogs, bears, and goats. The woman said, "This is your field; this is where you must work. Make yourself humble, steadfast, and strong. And what you will see happen to these animals you will have to do for my children." The animals were transformed into gentle lambs. Giovanni began crying and begged the woman to explain the dream's meaning. He was told, "In due time everything will be clear to you."

This dream recurred over a period of eighteen years, always with different variations. Giovanni Bosco eventually became a priest, founding the Salesian order of monks who cared for homeless children. For over sixty years, he continued to have remarkable visionary dreams often leaving him exhausted in the morning but providing indisputable insight and direction.

St. Patrick was not Irish as most people think; he was the son of a Roman-British army officer stationed in Britain. His real name was Maewyn Succat. He changed his name to Patrick only when he studied to become a priest. Although his father was a town councillor and deacon, and his grandfather a priest, young Patrick wasn't particularly devout.

His life changed drastically at the age of sixteen when Irish Druids captured him from his farm and sold him into slavery in Ireland. Patrick's head was shaved to signify his loss of freedom; he was given a slave's sheepskin tunic and was forced to work as a shepherd on the slopes of Mount Slemish. Years later, he spoke of his hunger and nakedness and remembered being "chastened exceedingly every day." This period of oppression had a tremendous effect on young Patrick who longed to bring his Christian faith to the Irish people.

Finally, six years into his captivity Patrick had a dream telling him he would soon return home. Shortly afterwards, he managed to escape, walking two hundred miles through unknown country. Exhausted, he arrived at the seaport of Brittany where he convinced a captain to give him free passage. Patrick made it home, studied to become a priest, and then a bishop. In a dream he heard "the voice of the Irish" calling him back. He eventually returned to Northern Ireland where he was instrumental in converting much of the country to Christianity.

A few days before he was murdered, Abraham Lincoln said he was impressed by the number of prophetic dreams in the Bible. When his wife asked him why he had brought this up, Lincoln related a dream he just had: he was wandering through the halls of the White House trying to find out where the sound of weeping people was coming from. His search led him to the East Room where he saw a coffin lying on a platform, guarded by soldiers and surrounded by a throng of mourners. "Who is dead?" he asked in the dream. "The president, killed by an assassin," was the answer. The loud grieving sobs of mourners finally awoke Lincoln from this dream. Lincoln's former law partner Ward Lamon described this dream in great detail in his biography of the president. He said, "To him it was a thing of deadly import, and certainly no vision was ever fashioned more exactly like a dread reality. . . . After worrying over it for some days, Mr. Lincoln seemed no longer able to keep the secret."

The night before his assassination, Julius Caesar dreamed he was soaring above the clouds and shaking hands with the Roman god Jupiter. Jupiter (Zeus in Greek mythology) then welcomed Caesar into heaven. That same night, Caesar's wife Calpurnia dreamed of seeing her husband's body after he had been stabbed to death. Her bedroom door burst open on its own as the dream jolted her into consciousness. Calpurnia begged her husband not to attend the senate that day. After much persuasion from Brutus, Caesar went. Both dreams became prophecies.

In her book entitled *Wake Up to Your Dreams*, Sandra Collier discusses how dreaming affected Albert Einstein. He is said to have slept an average of ten hours each night. It was during these nocturnal meanderings that his theory of relativity took form. As a young man, Einstein was a dismal failure to his parents. His shy placid nature set him aside from the other children. Einstein's parents feared their son was mentally challenged because he spoke haltingly until the age of nine and then would only respond to questions after a long period of silence. Teachers considered him a misfit. Albert had very few friends and avoided their games. His idea of fun was composing religious hymns on the piano and humming them while he walked. When Albert failed math, his parents wanted him to give up academic studies to become a plumber. During this difficult time Einstein had this dream:

> I was sledding with my friends at night. I started to slide down
> the hill, but my sled started going faster and faster. I was going
> so fast that I realized I was approaching the speed of light. I
> looked up at that point and I saw the stars. They were being

refracted into colours I had never seen before. I was filled with a sense of awe. I understood in some way that I was looking at the most important meaning in my life.

Years later, Einstein said, "I knew I had to understand that dream and you could say, and I would say, that my entire scientific career has been a meditation on my dream."

Chapter Six
The History of Dreams

We come to this earth to live is untrue: We come but to sleep, to dream.
—Aztec Poem

As long as human beings have lived on earth we have dreamed. And so the history of dreams, particularly in ancient times, is well recorded. As you read about dream lore of the last four thousand years, history will hopefully speak for itself. Rather than providing a detailed account of the history of dreams, the attempt here is to show how dreams have gone from being revered for their wisdom and sacredness to being reviled as the work of darkness. Perhaps now the tide is turning. And like our ancestors, we'll turn to dreams for understanding, hope, solace, and the vision for creating a more enlightened tomorrow.

• Biblical dreams are perhaps the best known dreams of antiquity. There are *seventy* accounts of dreams in the Bible, most of which appear in the Old Testament, along with numerous visions, trances, and appearances of angels.

• In his book *The Forgotten Language: An Introduction to the Understanding of Dreams, Fairy Tales and Myths*, psychoanalyst Erich Fromm explains that for both great Eastern and Western peoples of the past, myths and dreams "were among the most significant expressions of the mind, and failure to understand them would have amounted to illiteracy."

• John Sanford in *Dreams: God's Forgotten Language* tells us that in both the Old Testament and the New Testament, dreams and visions were regarded as revelations from Spirit—that the entire Bible can be seen as "God's breakthrough into the human conscious mind via the unconscious."

• Although dreams are not as frequent in the New Testament, their role is critical in the life and death of Jesus. While Joseph and Mary were first together an angel appeared to Joseph in a dream with this message: "Joseph . . . do not be afraid to take

Mary to be your wife. For it is by the Holy Spirit that she has conceived. She will have a son, and you will name him Jesus—because he will save his people from their sins." (Matthew 1:20–21).

• The three wise men, after being guided by a star or vision to the stable where Jesus was born, are "warned in a dream not to return to Herod" (Matthew 2:12). Joseph is then warned in a dream that "Herod will be looking for the child in order to kill him. So get up, take the child and his mother and escape to Egypt, and stay there until I tell you to leave" (Matthew 2:13). Joseph remained in Egypt until he received these instructions from an angel in a dream: "Get up, take the child and his mother, and go back to the land of Israel, because those who tried to kill the child are dead" (Matthew 2:20). Thirty years later, while Pilate was contemplating the fate of Jesus he receives this message from his wife, "Have nothing to do with that just man, for I have suffered many things in a dream today because of him" (Matthew 27:19).

• The British Museum holds the Chester Beatty papyrus originating from Thebes, Egypt that contains dream material from 2000 B.C.! Much of this material is still relevant today.

• The concept of dream incubation, which eventually spread to Greece and other parts of Europe, originated in Egypt. The early Egyptians believed gods revealed themselves in dreams. They used various methods—divine inspiration, ritual incantations, and special potions or ointments—to contact these invisible spirits. Contact with the spirit world could offer important warnings and advice, bring success in love, aid recovery from illness, or bring pleasurable experiences. Several serapeums or temples were constructed throughout Egypt for the Egyptian god of dreams, Serapis. The history of these serapeums dates back to 3000 B.C. Professional dream interpreters, or oracles, known as Learned Men of the Magic Library practised in these temples. A sign found at the entrance of one serapeum read, "I interpret dreams, having the gods' mandate to do so; good luck; the interpreter present here is Cretan."

• Ancient Greeks believed dreams were visits by gods or ghosts who entered through a keyhole, stood at the foot of the dreamer's bed, delivered their message, then made their exit through the same keyhole. During the fifth century B.C. it was believed the soul could leave the dreaming body to take trips or converse with the gods. The most fascinating contribution of the Greeks, beginning around this time, was the process of dream incubation. By the second century B.C., there were more than three hundred active incubation temples in Greece and the Roman Empire. These temples were dedicated to Aesculapius, the god of healing and medicine, who lived during the eleventh century B.C. His symbol became the serpent, symbolizing strength, tradition, fertility, and health. Today, the medical association still retains this symbol of Aesculapius, a single serpent wrapped around a staff.

Greek dream-incubation temples could actually be considered our first hospitals. Incubation meant sleeping in a special sanctuary with the intention of receiving a dream-reply to a question asked of a god or goddess. Before this occurred, the dreamer performed rituals in which they were bathed and abstained from sex, alcohol, and food. Offerings were made to the deity or god they wished to evoke. Often they were led into a subterranean room containing harmless snakes since they were believed to have great wisdom. After a night of sleep, they were asked to relate the content of their dreams in the morning. It was believed these dreams contained the information needed to cure their illness.

• Parts of the Islamic religion and the Koran, the sacred book of the Muslims, were revealed to Muhammad by the angel Gabriel in 1610 A.D. through a series of dreams and visions. Understanding dreams was greatly revered by early Muslims. They considered it a noble science taught to Adam. Adam then passed it to Seth, then Seth to Noah, until it reached Muhammad. In his famous writing *Nocturnal Journey*, Muhammad describes his dream experiences.

Gabriel took Muhammad on many journeys in the dream state. They rode a white horse Borak, which Gabriel guided through seven celestial realms. Together, they viewed majestic gardens, rivers, oceans of light, and thousands of angels singing before a great throne. Muhammad is instructed in these dreams to pray every day.

After these experiences, Muhammad began discussing his dreams each morning with his disciples. He also listened to his disciples' dreams and offered insights. Muhammad began the Muslim practise of adhan, the daily call to prayer, after listening to a disciple's dreams.

• The Babylonian or Jewish Talmud devotes four chapters and 217 references to dreams. A popular statement on dreams belongs to Rabbi Hisda: "A dream not interpreted is like a letter unopened."

• Before the arrival of other cultures, Native Americans cherished the world of the dream. They depended on dreams, waking visions, and trances to shape every aspect of tribal life. Every Native American tribe believed that dreams were the source of spirituality. This world was so real that a Native American bitten by a snake in a dream would seek out a medicine man's healing advice in the morning.

• Perhaps the most fascinating dreamers were the Senoi, a large tribe of approximately twelve thousand members who lived in the mountain jungles of Pacific Malaysia. Anthropologist and psychologist Herbert Noone first studied the Senoi in the 1930s. Two features made the Senoi particularly unique. Firstly, dreams were the most central aspect of their lives. Secondly, although a seemingly primitive tribe, they were psychologically sophisticated—there had been no accounts of violent crime for over two hundred years! The Senoi were described as cooperative, individualistic, and creative. They maintained this peacefulness despite nearby warring tribes who were fearful of the Senoi's mystical powers. Although researchers are unable to establish a definite link between the Senoi's dreamwork and psychological well-being, it certainly seems dreamwork had only positive effects.

In *Altered States of Consciousness*, Kilton Stewart states that the Senoi were so astonishing "they might have come from another planet." The most important question in their culture was, what did you dream last night? Each morning at breakfast, every family member discussed his or her dreams. Young children were involved in this process as soon as they were able to talk. Older family members gave children advice on how to deal with their dreams. Once each family's dream session was complete, many of the family members went to the village council where serious dream discussion continued. The Senoi shaped all daily activities from their dreams. Friendships were formed based on dreams, as well as decisions for tribes to move to more fertile ground. Adults spent much of their day helping children turn dream images into artistic or mechanical creations. Other adults created costumes, sang songs, or worked on paintings and dances inspired by dreams. The Senoi believed everyone had the ability to master their universe through guidance from dreams.

Dreams Fall from Grace

Go confidently in the direction of your dreams.
—Henry David Thoreau

Historically, dreams were always regarded as sacred, but they slowly lost the reverence and respect they once held. Since this change occurred over hundreds of years, it's difficult to trace exactly how this happened. It seems three factors contributed to this downfall:

1. St. Jerome's mistranslation of the Bible around the year 382 A.D.

2. When printing presses became popular in the fifteenth century, sacred dream material became mixed up with the dark arts and superstitious beliefs.

3. Over the next few centuries, many began to mistrust organized religion. Rather than turning inward to spiritual pursuits such as meditation or dreams, we placed our faith in the external world hoping it would provide answers.

St. Jerome's Mistranslation

St. Jerome was a highly respected biblical scholar who lived during the third and fourth centuries A.D. He came from a wealthy Christian family, travelled widely, and studied in Rome. Jerome loved to read and collected a library of classic literature that were his coveted treasures. He loved the smooth sophisticated style of Cicero, the famous political orator, and Plautus, a comic playwright who influenced even Shakespeare and Molière. Jerome found the writing of Biblical scholars rough or crude in comparison. Unfortunately, his books were considered "pagan" classics by the Catholic Church. As a Christian, he probably had to read them in great secrecy. This could have been a source of repressed conflict, guilt, and shame for him.

When Jerome was a young man he became ill and had this nightmare that had a profound effect on him for the rest of his life:

> Suddenly, I was caught up in the Spirit and dragged before the Judgement Seat. The light was so bright there, and those standing around the Seat were so radiant, that I threw myself to the ground and dared not to look up.
>
> A voice asked me who and what I was.
>
> "I am a Christian," I replied.
>
> "You are lying," said the Judge. "You are a follower of Cicero, not of Christ. For where your treasure is, there also is your heart."
>
> Instantly, I became dumb. He ordered me to be scourged and, along with the strokes of the lash, I was tortured more harshly by the fire of conscience . . .
>
> I began to cry and wail, "Have mercy on me, O Lord, have mercy on me." My cry could be heard amid the sound of the lash.
>
> At last, the bystanders fell down at the knees of the Judge and asked him to have pity on my youth, and give me a chance to repent. The Judge may still inflict torture on me, they insisted, should I ever again read the works of the pagans . . .
>
> Accordingly, I swore an oath calling upon God's name: "Lord, if ever again I possess worldly books, or if ever again I read such, I have denied you!"
>
> On taking this oath I was dismissed.

When Jerome woke from this dream, his eyes were drenched with tears. He said his shoulders were black and blue from the dream and that he felt the bruises for some time. After his nightmare, he lived as a hermit in the desert and continued his Biblical studies. He was afraid of dreaming and sided with the Old Testament prophet

Jeremiah who clearly denounced dreams. Jeremiah (23:32) says, "I am against the prophets who tell their dreams that are full of lies. They tell these dreams and lead my people astray with their lies and their boasting." Jerome agreed dreams could be the work of our soul, but he also believed that some people manipulated or twisted dreams for their own self-serving needs. He decided God could not be found through pagan practises such as dream incubation. For the rest of his life, he was deeply afraid of having demonic attacks in dreams.

What Really Happened to St. Jerome?

St. Jerome's dream was definitely the work of demons. Any dream that leaves us this terrified is never the domain of God or spirit. Unfortunately, he became subjected to these fears, which is exactly what these dark forces in his dream desired. Jerome, like many Biblical scholars, believed that dreams were *only* messages from spirit. He didn't understand that dreams are actually dimensional travel, and while our soul is travelling, it may be seduced into entering frightening places. Our soul can be tricked by dark forces into entering dimensions of darkness rather than dimensions of light. This is similar to thinking we're driving to a friend's house, but end up in a dark seamy neighbourhood that terrifies us. This is exactly what happened to Jerome; he believed the frightening, vengeful character in his dream was God punishing him. But this is never the way the One True God works.

There is no horror, fear, or trepidation within the dimensions of God or spirit. If we encounter an aspect of spirit in a dream—a saint, angel, archangel, or enlightened guide—we would probably feel peace, love, joy, contentment, or awe. The One True God is a being of peace, love, and compassion, not an angry punishing deity. In fact, God allows us to examine, rehearse, test out, and experiment with issues in dreams so we will not be afraid. Dreams help us dissolve our fears so that we're empowered. The true function of dreams is never to terrorize or immobilize. That is not how a compassionate omniscient being wishes us to evolve.

This dream was an elaborate drama designed to terrify Jerome so much that he became fearful of dreams. The being or judge sitting at the judgement seat surrounded by intense light was a lesser god, trying to impersonate the One True God. There are many beings in other dimensions that have great powers. Just because they have great powers, it doesn't mean they use these powers wisely, well, or with compassion. They are masters of trickery and illusion. They also know our weak spots, fears, sources of guilt, or feelings of inadequacy because they can access or infiltrate our minds. They can't penetrate our spirits because its frequency is too high for them, so they work with our minds. They always attack where we're most vulnerable. In Jerome's case, the vulnerability was his love of classic literature that the Catholic Church did not approve of. Awareness is always the key. If we understand how these dark beings operate, they will not be able to trick us.

Fortunately, most people never encounter this type of dream experience. Jerome understood how horrifying a nightmare could be, but he failed to recognize the positive aspects of dreams. He never understood that the function of dreams is to move us out of darkness. He wasn't aware that he'd been seduced, manipulated, and tricked by a clever dark being. Darkness knew that Jerome would soon be asked to translate a Bible that honoured the power of dreams. So darkness seduced Jerome and used clever illusions. Jerome was filled with so much fear about his dreams that he never understood they could be a source of enlightenment and peace.

In 382 A.D., Jerome was called to Rome by Pope Damasus I and was given the task of translating the Bible from Hebrew into Latin. There were few scholars like Jerome who understood Greek, Hebrew, and Latin. At that time, the Hebrew word *anan* had very negative connotations. It was associated with sorcerers, snake charmers, black magicians, wizards, soothsayers, and witches. Jerome deliberately mistranslated the Hebrew to the Latin words *observo somnia* or "observing dreams." So Leviticus (19:26) was changed from, "You shall not practise augury or witchcraft" to "You shall not practise augury nor observe your dreams." In their book *Dreams and Spiritual Growth: A Judeo-Christian Way of Dreamwork*, Savery, Berne and Williams explain: Seven times Jerome translated *anan* correctly as *witchcraft* . . . But the other three times, where the Hebrew and Greek texts are condemning witchcraft, Jerome translated it as observing dreams . . . Many of the Church leaders born in the sixth century and afterward knew only Jerome's Latin Vulgate, and used his new translation as a prohibition to keep people from turning to their dreams for insight, consolation, and hope. Sadly, the Christian tradition of relating to God through dreams and visions had come to an end . . .

In *God Dreams and Revelation: A Christian Interpretation of Dreams*, Morton Kelsey concludes that Jerome's mistranslation might have been deliberate, possibly due to his terrifying dream years earlier. Kelsey believes it is highly unusual given Jerome's scholarly expertise that he would correctly interpret *anan* seven times, then revert to a completely different translation for the other three. Unfortunately, Jerome's translation, the Latin Vulgate, has remained until this century.

Within two centuries, Gregory the Great, a Roman known as the teacher of the Middle Ages, would cite the mistranslated passages to discourage Christians from paying attention to dreams. Then in the thirteenth century, St. Thomas Aquinas, considered the church's greatest theologian, issued warnings about possible demonic invocation through dreams. Although Aquinas conceded that some dreams were sacred or prophetic in nature, he warned Christians that the majority of dreams originated from the devil, false ideas, or bodily conditions.

Aquinas also believed he was modernizing the church by writing Christian theology in Aristotle's language. According to Aristotle the true way to discover reality was through rational thought and logic. This theory left little hope for developing intuition, clarity, or inner vision through dreams. Following Aristotle's beliefs, Aquinas wrote the *Summa Theologica*, which became the authoritative text in Christian teachings until the second Vatican Council in the mid-1960s. In reference to dreams, Aquinas cited Deuteronomy (18:10), which had been mistranslated by Jerome, "Let there not be found among you, him who observes dreams."

Like Jerome, Aquinas too appeared to be strongly affected by both dreams and visions. Although writing sections of *Summa Theologica* was often a struggle, one particular morning he dictated it with considerable ease. He told his scribe that in a dream he had conversed with the apostles Peter and Paul, and they told him what to say. Then in December 1273, Aquinas suddenly quit working on *Summa Theologica* and abandoned other writings and his daily routine. He said, "I can do no more. Such things have been revealed to me that all I have written seems like straw, and I now await the end of my life." Experts believe Aquinas probably had a dream or visionary experience that shattered his rational way of perceiving the world. From this point on, any important decisions he made acknowledged the sanctity of dreams and visions.

Aquinas was on a short journey in the Austrian Alps just before his death. During this trip, he hit his head on a tree branch and was knocked off his donkey. While he was recovering that evening in a nearby monastery, the monks persuaded him to say a few words. Acquinas decided to read the Biblical *Song of Songs*, or *Canticle of*

Canticles, a passionate proclamation of love between a man and woman, believed to represent God's love for His people. While he was explaining lines 7:12, "Come my beloved, let us go forth into the field—" He died suddenly. Perhaps it is telling that a man, who devoted his life to reason and logic, uttered a love song in his final breath. But despite his obvious change of heart, what influenced Christians were not Aquinas's personal revelations at the end of his life. Unfortunately, what lived on were his books advocating a rational, logical approach to God.

The Popularity of Printing Presses

Perhaps the greatest shift in thought occurred during the Middle Ages with the invention of the printing press. During the fifteenth century, alchemy, astrologers, fortune tellers, occultists, magicians, magic spells, potions, and witchcraft were extremely popular. Shakespeare's *Macbeth*, with its frequent references to witches and black magic, is a good example. During the Renaissance, superstitious ideas, dreams, and magical practises were common with the upper class and in intellectual circles. Sacred wisdom such as dreams became mixed with the dark arts or black magic. (This is similar to our new age movement with its revival of sacred practises such as dreams, yoga, meditation, and angels, mixed up with dark arts such as witchcraft, spells, charms, and fortune tellers. Another comparison is the Internet, which contains excellent information and sites along with what many people consider garbage, trash, or spam.) Over time, intellectuals felt that dreams were the nonsense of the uneducated and superstitious young girls. As printing presses flourished, cheaply printed pamphlets were circulated in London with titles like *The Old Egyptian Fortune Teller's Last Legacy* and *The Royal Dream Book*. Titles included the words *palmistry*, *moles*, *lucky numbers*, *lucky colours*, *birth stones*, and *fortune telling* along with *dreams* to make them more appealing. As the years passed, dreams lost the spiritual or sacred meaning they once held.

The Birth of Scientific Reason

To understand the present perspective on dreams, it's helpful to walk back through time. During the Middle Ages, there was no large middle class like we have today; people were either peasants or aristocrats. Kings and queens were believed to be God's representatives on earth. Spiritual growth was considered more important than material growth. Since peasants had very little money and no real opportunities for gaining wealth, their goal in life was not to become rich—they were more concerned with richness of spirit or saving their souls.

But this medieval world view began to fall apart during the fourteenth and fifteenth centuries. Clergy and government officials were often corrupt and violated their positions. Rebellion resulted, and in 1517, Martin Luther advocated a complete break from papal authority and began building alternate churches. Distrust for papal and royal authority was everywhere. By the early 1600s, Galileo was proving that the sun and stars did not revolve around the earth as the church had always proclaimed. People realized many religious teachings were misleading. This dramatic shift of consciousness from the spiritual to the temporal is evident in the emerging art of that period. Painting was no longer dominated by angels, saints, and the life of Christ. With all our foundations eroding, we turned to science to give us the answers that religion seemed unable to provide.

In the eighteenth century, in reaction to the political and religious tensions in Europe, the Age of Enlightenment began. Its purpose was to shed the light of reason upon the darkness and superstition of the past. There was a tremendous thirst for knowledge particularly in the field of science. The eighteenth century measure of progress was the study and advancement of science and technology. The practise of applied science became dominant. Alchemy became the science of modern chemistry. An era of power-driven machinery was unleashed by James Watt's application of steam power in industry. We were illuminated with the discovery of electric currents by Italian Alexander Volta.

By the nineteenth century, the full impact of these industrial and technical changes were everywhere. We eventually embraced a world of telegraphs, telephones, air travel, radios, televisions, telecommunications, computers, VCRs, satellites, and space travel—all benefits of science and technology. Everyone believed this age of enlightenment was serving us well. True knowledge or scientific advancement was the product of serious testing and re-testing. Great advances in science, medicine, and technology brought increasing integrity to this method. Hard facts, solid numbers, and tested results were revered because it was believed they did not lie or deceive. Quantitative research using numbers was regarded as the superior method. If something couldn't be measured or proven scientifically it would rarely become fact.

Scientific and mathematical truth replaced inner truth. We worshipped at the altars of science and technology, but in the process we began losing our souls. This type of reasoning left scant credibility for mystical knowledge such as dreams.

Until the 1950s, we had no scientific methods to prove that dreams even existed. We had made great scientific and technical progress, but often at the expense of our soul or spirit. We became an unbalanced society, believing science and technology provided all the answers. We forgot these great achievements originated through the wisdom of the soul, through dreams. We believed we had made real progress, but our peasant ancestors might have been more enlightened. Their lives didn't revolve around getting rich, owning a home, or retiring with a comfortable pension fund because saving one's soul was considered more important.

Now society is beginning to realize that true progress may require a balance. In his book *Our Dreaming Mind,* Robert Van de Castle writes:

> Ancient civilizations were lit not by electricity but by the internal illumination provided by dreams. We have become an unbalanced society, in which technology is viewed as the ultimate accomplishment. Our fascination with machines—machines that can clear hundreds of acres of rainforest in a single day, machines that can unleash instant destruction on those with whom we politically disagree, and machines that, in speeding communication, also tend to homogenize our opinions into a common ideological cast—threatens our continual existence on this planet. Dreams may help us to balance our relations with nature and with each other. In dreams, the human spirit and creativity reign supreme, yet we have been taught to scorn or ridicule the messages they contain...

As we dream our way into the twenty-first century, it seems we are returning to spirit for solace, as peasants did over one thousand years ago. But science and technology have made the world a different place. Now we are realizing there are links between spirituality, science, and mathematics. We are understanding it was God who created science and math in the first place and that everything is interrelated. In Katherine Neville's novel *The Eight,* the character Shahin says, "Many people have great reverence for numbers, endowing them with divine properties. We believe the universe is comprised of number, and it is only a question of vibrating to the correct resonance of these numbers to become one with God." We are progressing beyond a world that put religion in one box and science in another, believing the two could not co-exist. Many of our great scientists have been men like Einstein who used dreams and meditation to help us take quantum leaps forward. Now we are realizing that everything spiritual is based on science, numbers are sacred, and there is a dynamic interrelationship between all living things. What better time to utilize dreams to help us further unravel these mysteries.

Chapter Seven
The Sleep Process

There is no reality except the one contained within us.
—Herman Hesse

Early Research into Dreams

Before the early 1950s, little was known about the medical and scientific process of sleep. This all changed in 1951 when Eugene Aserinsky, a graduate student at the University of Chicago, began studying sleeping infants. He noticed that at certain times during the night the baby's eyelids would flutter, darting up and down and back and forth. He reported this phenomenon to his professor William Kleitman who began studying this further with another medical student William Dement. They set up a laboratory where subjects could be monitored by EEG (electroencephalograph), which measures changes in the electrical activity of the brain. Two years later, Aserinsky and Kleitman announced that rapid eye movement (REM) sleep was characteristic in all dreamers. Their findings were published in a two-page summary in the journal *Science* on September 4, 1953.

That brief two-page article opened a floodgate of scientific research. We entered an era when doctors and scientists became intrigued with the medical and scientific nature of sleep but largely ignored the emotional or spiritual elements of dreaming. In his book *Our Dreaming Mind*, one of the most comprehensive books ever written about dreams, Robert Van de Castle discusses the document *Sleep and Dream Research: A Bibliography*, which includes over four thousand entries for sleep research between the years 1962 to 1968. The medical/scientific aspects *General Neurophysiology* and *Physiology* contained 994 and 642 references respectively. In contrast, the emotional/spiritual aspects *Special Features of Dream Recall* and *Patterns of Dream Content* had 53 and 37 references respectively.

Sleep research in the latter half of the twentieth century began taking the soul out of dreams. By today's standards, much of this early research would be considered unethical. Subjects might have been awoken countless times during REM sleep to measure its effects on their waking lives. All this sleep research occurred after Carl Jung's extensive writing in the first half of the century where he attempted to restore spirituality into medicine, psychiatry, and dreams. Jung, a medical doctor, clearly recognized that dreaming was a spiritual experience. He believed the main problem of the twentieth century was disconnection from our spirit or soul. But in 1953, the two-page publication in *Science* began a process that attempted to remove spirit from medicine and psychology.

Spirituality and Science

True science discovers God behind every waiting door.
—Pope Pius XII

Science without religion is lame; religion without science is blind.
—Albert Einstein

Early research into sleep gave us much technical and scientific information, but it's important to realize that dreaming is a spiritual experience, not an entirely scientific event that can be measured or quantified. All things spiritual are based on science and all things scientific are based on spirituality. Spirituality is us; our soul, personality, emotions, or emotional body. It's the core of who and what we are. Because most of us can't see our souls, we tend to think the soul is something separate from who we are—but it's not. Quite simply, we are a soul or spirit. When our body dies, we will still be a soul or spirit.

Science is humanity's attempt to understand the genius and workings of God or spirit. For example, thousands of doctors and scientists around the world have spent years trying to unravel the exact structure of DNA, which God invented. Science arrives at truth through experiments, mathematics, logic, and equations. Spirituality may provide similar truths through dreams, insight, intuition, reflection, and hunches. We can understand energy through the mathematical equations of God's framework. But we can also understand energy by experience, feeling, intuition, meditation, and dreams. Both are equally valuable ways of knowing or understanding. When we put the two together, we have genius. If we don't put science in one box and spirituality in another but combine the two, we achieve brilliant insights and understanding.

When Carl Jung began writing about dreams, he was trying to give us back the memories of spirit that had been buried by science. When all this early research into sleep occurred, many believed that science was somehow separate from God or spirituality. But God invented science and every enlightened scientist and doctor understands they are just unravelling the mysteries of the Creator.

How Much Do We Dream?

You have to have a dream so you can get up in the morning.
—Billy Wilder

In the 1950s, sleep researchers believed there were two distinct phases of sleep: rapid eye movement (REM) and non–rapid eye movement (NREM). During the REM cycle, most of our dreaming takes place, but we can also experience dreams during NREM sleep.

Early dream researchers believed our first dream occurred about 90 to 110 minutes after falling asleep and continued in cycles approximately every 90 minutes. They felt there might be four to seven repetitions of this cycle each evening depending on the length of time we slept. It was believed we averaged four to five dreams each night and that each dream became longer as the night progressed. There are many times when this is true. The workings of spirit in other dimensions, however, can't always be measured in precise units of time. Dreams may last from 3 minutes to 2 hours depending on what the dreamer needs to do. Although we can use past research as guidelines, it really doesn't matter how long we dream. What is most important to understand is that we all dream every night. One morning I woke up at 6 a.m., then went back to sleep until 9 a.m. When I again woke up, I had a vivid memory of three distinct dreams during that three-hour period. I was obviously dreaming a lot that night, definitely more than the four or five dreams a night we average. If I remembered three dreams in less than three hours, it's possible I could have had about eight dreams that night. Since the soul is travelling in other dimensions of time and space, it's difficult, if not impossible, to measure exactly how much we dream. However, we all dream every night. The amount of time we dream depends on how much we need to and this is different for everyone. The following have been widely regarded facts about sleep and dreaming:

• We spend 10% of our lives dreaming.

• By the end of our life, most people will have spent at least five to seven complete years dreaming.

• Premature infants spend 70 to 80% of the night in REM sleep or dreaming.

• In the two months before babies are born, they spend 80% of their time dreaming. During this time, brain growth accelerates and the grey matter in the cortex doubles in thickness.

• Newborns spend 50% of their sleeping time in REM sleep.

• Babies up to two years of age spend 9 hours dreaming.

• Toddlers from two to five years of age spend 2 1/2 hours dreaming.

• From the ages of five to fifty, we spend at least 1 1/2 hours dreaming each night. We can often dream more if we are resolving important issues, planning something major for the future, taking in new information, or if we have been sleep deprived.

Keep in mind many of these statements may be true, but they are also approximations or guidelines. You may be fifty years old, spending two hours dreaming each night because you are preparing to get married for the first time! The truth is everybody dreams differently because we all have our own issues, fears, and challenges in life. We can't put the journey of spirit into boxes. Spirit or energy can't be contained or completely understood with the conscious mind. Every soul dreams in the exact way it needs to. Trying to quantify everyone's dreams into the same pattern is much like trying to put our lives in boxes, as if we all took the exact same time to shower, eat, work, or play.

Dreaming is most heightened during the REM phase but it can actually occur at any time that we are asleep. Most of us can recall a time when we dozed off at the beginning of the night and awakened perhaps a few minutes later remembering a dream. This doesn't fit into the early theories that stated we don't have our first dream until after we've slept about 90 minutes. There is a sleeping disorder called narcolepsy where people may suddenly fall asleep during an important meeting at work or while socializing with friends. Narcoleptics immediately begin to dream as soon as they fall asleep. So it is obvious that we don't all dream in precise cycles; every dreamer is unique. There are rarely black and white rules when we talk about dreaming.

If we understand sleep as the time our body takes to rejuvenate and repair while our soul does work in other dimensions, then there is not really a dream state per se. Our soul spends the entire night exploring, testing, travelling. We can say that sleep is actually a deep meditative state where we see different things or have visions because we've crossed dimensions.

Why Do Babies Dream So Much?

When we learn of how much time babies spend in the REM state, our first question is often, why? What could a baby possibly be dreaming about? Its whole world consists of eating, sleeping, and filling its diaper. If we consider what we've already learned about the purpose of dreams, it does make a lot of sense. Dreams allow our soul to go into other dimensions while our body remains in suspended animation so that we can prepare our paths or get ready for the future. So babies need a lot of dreaming to prepare their lives because all of them come from a realm that is nothing like earth. Being born can be brutally hard. Perhaps this is part of the reason why many babies cry and scream when they come out of the womb. Their soul knows life will be tough. They've also just come from a dark, warm, sheltered environment and have been thrust into a strange new world. It's difficult to be born; there is so much to prepare. It's actually far easier for the soul to die than it is to be born. When we die, we leave the pain, suffering, and insanity of earth behind. When we're born, we spend hours in the dream state preparing to survive amidst these challenges. So babies are truly doing their inner work when they sleep. Babies may spend 80% of their time dreaming in the two months before they are born because their soul knows it's much easier to do this while they're still in the womb. They can definitely get more work done without the distractions that will inevitably occur in the hospital and their homes.

Brain Rhythms and Stages of Sleep

During the day, our brain switches from various frequencies, cycles per second (cps) or hertz (hz).

Beta 12–20 cps We are wide awake and alert.

Alpha 8–12 cps We are awake but relaxed. This is also the beginning of light sleep and dreams. Alpha is essential for mental and emotional recovery. Alpha is the frequency of genius. It is where we tap into the rhythms of our soul. Alpha is the state of dreams, meditation, lucid dreaming, visions, trance, hypnosis, channelling, clairvoyance, clairaudience, and oracles.

Theta 4–8 cps This is the cycle of deep sleep.

Delta 0.5–4 cps This is the deepest sleep, referred to as human hibernation. It is essential for body recovery and rejuvenation.

The EEG of a person fully awake shows beta rapid or high frequency brainwaves. When the eyes close and the person relaxes, somewhat slower alpha waves appear. Sleep actually begins with a quick reflexive twitch called a *myoclonic jerk*, caused by a sudden explosion of electrical brain activity. It may awaken us, but in most cases it doesn't. After a myoclonic jerk, sleep begins. When we fall asleep, the slower theta waves become mixed with the alphas. As sleep becomes progressively deeper, the slowest delta waves appear. After reaching the slowest levels of delta sleep, we move back up through theta, then alpha sleep. When the brainwaves reach alpha sleep again, we do not wake up; instead, our REM cycle or dreaming begins. Although dreaming may occur in all stages of sleep, our most vivid emotion-packed dreams occur during this cycle.

Waking and Light Sleep—Beta and Alpha Rhythms
Buzzing Beta

We operate at beta during most of our waking day. Right now as you read this, your brainwaves are operating at beta frequencies somewhere between 12 to 20 cps, depending on how interesting you consider the content. Humans are not meant to be in high levels of beta (anything above 20 cps) for most of the day. We're more relaxed, calm, better able to make wise informed decisions in the lower frequencies of beta, or high frequencies of alpha.

Astonishing Alpha (Mental Recovery)—the Realm of Dreams and Genius

Alpha one	12–14 cps	Meditation, relaxation, guided imagery
Alpha two	10–12 cps	Lucid dreams, straddling both dimensions
Alpha three	8–10 cps	Trance, hypnosis, light sleep
Alpha four	7–8 cps	Dreams

Alpha is astonishing since it is made up of several stages that range between being awake and extremely relaxed to actual light sleep. Much of our dreaming takes place in the alpha phase. This is perhaps the most fascinating cycle of human experience since it is the gateway to visions, dreams, meditation, lucid dreaming, trance, and hypnosis. Alpha one (12–14 cps) is the rhythm of genius where we may brainstorm, daydream, or tune into the collective consciousness for new ideas, solutions to problems, or even inventions.

Bulgarian scientist Dr. Georgi Lozanov began working with individuals in this relaxed alpha state in the 1960s to enhance learning. An account of this work can be found in Sheila Ostrander and Lynn Schroeder's book *Superlearning*. His technique was referred to as suggestology or superlearning. Lozanov found that learning could be accelerated when students listened to specific classical music, which lowered brainwaves to the alpha state. If they listened to music with a slow restful rhythm (such as baroque), the rhythms of the body, heartbeat, and brain synchronized to it. Dr. Lozanov was trying to get his students to rid themselves of the rumble and garbage of waking life in order to tap into the true genius of alpha, which is available to all humanity.

During alpha two (10–12 cps), we're in that delicate balance between being awake and being asleep. Since this is such a precarious position, we don't stay here long. Either we drift deeper into sleep or wake up. This can be the realm of lucid dreaming—a state of awareness that we're in a dream or altered reality. Buddhist monks spend years of training in an effort to maintain full awareness in this state. They sleep sitting up in a meditation box resembling a seat, instead of lying in a bed. By chanting prayers throughout the night, they try to awaken within a dream and realize it as a heightened reality. Buddhists believe that the lucid state is the prerequisite for enlightenment.

Alpha three (8–10 cps) is the place of deep meditation, trance, hypnosis, and light sleep. Have you ever had a dream where you experienced the sound of knocking, shouting, music playing, birds singing, or planes roaring overhead? You then awakened suddenly only to realize that you were having a dream that incorporated what were actually physical sounds. In these cases, you might have been in alpha three, a level of light dreaming where you're aware of outside sounds. But since you're close to the wakeful beta state, you've probably been jolted into consciousness by those sounds. At a slightly lower level, in alpha four (7 or 8 cps), our most vivid dreams take place. During the day, we may return to the alpha one state if we're relaxed. We may be in the shower, meditating, listening to music, rocking a baby, or taking a bath. Although still awake, we have slowed down our brain rhythms enough to journey into the land of alpha to retrieve our dreams.

Deepest Stages of Sleep—Theta and Delta
Threshold Theta

Theta is that foggy period of waking dreaminess just before we fall into deeper sleep. If it occurs during the first part of the evening, just after we close our eyes, it may last from 10 seconds to 10 minutes depending on how tired we are. It's often referred to as the Zen or *hypnagogic* state. Hypnagogia is that transitional stage between being awake and falling asleep. While we're in this state, we're really straddling two worlds. In the beginning states of theta sleep, we may experience quick visual images known as presleep hallucinations or "hypnagogic hallucinations." These images are often snapshots of the day's events. They may startle us awake or gently lure us into deeper sleep. During this stage, our skeletal muscles relax, which causes many sleepers to experience a sensation similar to falling. This feeling or fear of falling may cause us to be startled and to awaken momentarily. If we arouse someone early into the theta stage usually they will report being only half asleep.

Deep Dark Delta (Body Recovery)

Finally, when our brainwaves further decrease, we reach the delta cycle and now we're technically in a deep sleep. When we reach this state, we're totally oblivious to outside stimulation. We can't hear that phone ringing in the next room, a dog barking outside, or even someone snoring beside us. If we're awakened from delta sleep, we'll probably be confused, groggy, and disoriented. This inability to function normally until our body adjusts is called sleep inertia or sleep drunkenness. Our spirit has just travelled far into another dimension or reality and we've been jerked back prematurely which causes the disorientation. It's interesting that most sleepwalking takes place in delta sleep. This is why it's almost impossible to awaken a sleepwalker.

In his book *Power Sleep*, Dr. James Maas says the delta phase is possibly the closest to human hibernation that we come. Our muscles completely relax, blood pressure drops, pulse and respiration slow down, and blood supply to the brain is minimal. Although in delta we may seem like slumbering bears, paradoxically, it is here that our body works to rejuvenate and repair itself so that we can be restored to optimal health. If anyone told you to get lots of sleep to fight a cold, they were right—but what we specifically needed was more delta sleep. Maas explains that in this "slow-wave sleep," since our body temperature is actually turned down, we are conserving much needed energy. Metabolic activity slows enabling our body's tissue to grow and repair. Our natural immune-system modulators increase during delta sleep so that even a small loss of delta sleep may reduce the body's immune responses. Growth hormones are also secreted by the pituitary gland during this stage of sleep. This is one of the many reasons why young children and adolescents require greater amounts of sleep than adults do. These human growth hormones (HGH) synthesize protein, promote growth, and repair damaged tissue. If you've ever got up in the morning and thought that a cut or a pimple seemed to have healed significantly, it wasn't your imagination; it was actually human growth hormone which helped the tissue grow and repair during delta sleep.

Although delta sleep is most essential for body recovery and repair, we don't spend most of the night in the delta phase. This may be why many people who have difficulty sleeping wake up at regular intervals during the night. After approximately two 90 to 110 minute cycles of sleep, or roughly 3 hours, we spend virtually no time in delta sleep. As the night progresses, we spend more and more time in theta and alpha sleep where dreaming occurs. It seems we have been biologically programmed to alternate between delta sleep, which enhances body recovery, and REM sleep, which promotes mental, emotional, or spiritual recovery.

Alpha or REM Sleep

In bed my real love has always been the sleep that rescued me by allowing me to dream.
—Luigi Pirandello

A remarkable fact about dreams is that our wakeful beta state resembles our alpha/REM cycle when it is recorded on an EEG. Both are small, sharp, jerky lines in contrast to the slow longer lines of delta sleep. In the REM stage, even under closed eyelids, our eyeballs are darting rapidly back and forth as if scanning our surroundings. While we're dreaming, our body reactions are similar to those of a mild panic attack: heartbeat and breathing rate speed up, blood flow to the brain increases, more sweat and stomach acid is produced, blood pressure and cholesterol levels increase, body temperature rises, and there is an increased rate of oxygen consumption in the brain. Women experience vaginal engorgement and lubrication, while men have either full or partial erections. This occurs even in men who experience impotency during their waking hours. Male erections take place regardless of the dream content, even when there is no sexual activity in their dreams. This arousal occurs in males of every age from infants to men in their 70s and 80s.

In the REM state, although many signs of arousal are present, the body is actually in a temporary state of paralysis. While dreaming, motor neurons responsible for muscle contractions are chemically inhibited. These neuronal messages from the brain's motor cortex are blocked at the brain stem to ensure that all major parts of the body (except eyes, mouth, fingers, and toes) are in a temporary state of paralysis. This is a natural safety mechanism that prevents the dreamer from getting out of bed or acting out dreams.

Researchers have also found major body movements such as rolling over in bed or stretching increase just before and just after REM sleep. Then, as we enter into the dreaming or REM state, this stretching and rolling decreases to almost total stillness. In her book *Dream Power*, Ann Faraday compares this period of activity and stillness to the typical behaviour of someone in a theatre. We fidget, talk, and move around in our seats just before the curtain rises. As the story begins, we become still and attentive, following the action with our eyes, similar to the eyelid fluttering that occurs throughout REM sleep. If we become totally immersed in the action, our breathing may speed up, our heart may pound, we may grip the sides of our seat, or even cry. As the story unfolds, we are totally immersed, unmoving, and unspeaking. When the drama is finished, we immediately resume conversation, stretch, and shift around in our seats. Faraday says "the sleeper could indeed be watching a play during his periods of REM sleep, but a play of his own making in which he himself was the director, producer, stage manager, principal actor, and audience all at the same time."

If we think of the earlier analogy of making a movie, we can understand our entire night's sleep as part of this dramatic production. When we are in the deeper stages of sleep—theta and delta—we are often travelling to the dimension where we plan to make our movie. When we arrive, we may need to spend some time making sure the set is right and getting everything into place. Once the drama or movie begins, we are usually in the alpha or REM phase of sleep; we are excited, highly engaged in this movie, our eyes dart back and forth and our brainwaves are elevated. We keep on shooting, acting, or directing the movie as long as we are in this alert alpha phase. When the action is over, we go back into theta and delta sleep at slower brainwave frequencies while we prepare to shoot the next movie or scene. Once everything is ready to roll again, our brainwaves are elevated and we're back in alpha sleep.

In *Power Sleep*, Dr. Maas tells us that dreaming is essential for peak mental performance. He writes, "REM sleep plays a major role in facilitating memory storage and retention, organization, and reorganization, as well as new learning and performance. Without the power of REM sleep, we would literally be lost, mentally." This is especially important for teenagers, students, or adults who may be retraining or writing exams. It's possible to stay up until 2 a.m. memorizing all the formulas we need for our math exam the next day. We may do well on the exam, but if we don't get adequate REM sleep those formulas won't move from our short term to our long-term memory. Without adequate REM sleep on a regular basis, math will be really tough next semester. We may flounder and draw blanks because all that material we crammed into our brain hasn't had enough time to transfer to our long-term memory. We won't have the foundation needed to understand the next level.

What is most astonishing about the REM state is that the entire time we are dreaming, neurons are rapidly being fired upwards from our brain stem. Sleep is a highly organized, active process regulated by many neuron groups in the brain. There is, in fact, more brain activity happening when we are asleep than when we are awake. During periods of intensive learning, we engage in more REM sleep. If we've been studying for a series of exams, poring over manuals to pass a driver's test, learning a new computer program, learning a new language, or adjusting to a new relationship, there will be an increase in our REM sleep for several days afterwards. If we're deprived of REM sleep—perhaps a sick child wakes us up repeatedly during the night—it will be difficult remembering how to run that new computer program and even more difficult for our brain to transfer any new material into long-term memory. Our soul has not had the opportunities it needed in the dream state to go forward and do this preparation for us. In the dream state we would have been actually learning, rehearsing, doing test runs of this computer program. Engaging in REM sleep actually flexes our mental muscle. Dr. Maas writes, "No matter what the relevance of dreams, REM-sleep neuronal stimulation causes strengthening of memory circuits much as lifting weights causes strengthening of muscles. It is a 'use it or lose it' proposition, and REM sleep helps us use it."

Genius of the Alpha State

The dream is an involuntary kind of poetry.
—Jean Paul Richter

The alpha state is the core; it's the genius of spirit. In alpha, we're able to tap into the universal consciousness and universal records. It's that most perfect state all humanity may strive for if we were aware of its greatness. Alpha is the place of heightened brainwaves where we connect with our spirits. It's our most natural state. When we dream, meditate, or relax in the alpha state, we reconnect with our true self and remember who we truly are. We release the storms of our mind and arrive at shores of greater calm and clarity. While we're awake, our mind can be confused, unaware, disoriented, or forgetful. In the alpha state, we connect with our spirit; we have no physical boundaries; we get rid of ego and judgement, which are products of the mind, and we're ingenious.

People who are experts at navigating in the alpha state are capable of transcending the physical. The more the soul is infused in the physical mind, the more elevated the brainwaves are, and the higher a person can therefore elevate and transcend physicality. Many of the things we don't understand or consider miracles or magic are actually spirit transcending the physical body while in the alpha state. This is exactly what we do while we dream. But translating this to physical experiences is difficult to understand, especially with the limitations of the mind.

Yoga is, perhaps, the best example. It was developed by Eastern cultures more than five thousand years ago as a means of overcoming pain, transcending death, and reaching enlightenment or bliss. The first yogis achieved astounding control over their physical bodies and realized the possibility of immortality through techniques and postures that slow down the heartbeat and breathing. They perfected transcending the physical body while still consciously aware in the alpha state. We've all seen pictures of yogis lying on a bed of nails or walking on fire.

Yogis have been buried alive for several days, then returned to life. They're able to control their physical functions so completely, they actually put themselves in a temporary state of suspended animation—exactly the same state we're in when we dream. How do they do this? Elevated meditative states. Their spirit actually becomes bigger, transcends or takes over their physical body. As we enlighten, our body actually goes through profound changes for several years. Our spirit, soul, or energy enlarges or grows so that we become more *pure* energy and less dense physical mass. In other words, our spirit controls and informs our body, rather than our body controlling or pushing away our spirit. This is actually very close to dreaming, just different levels of the alpha state where our body is completely relaxed, while our brainwaves are heightened. People who do deep trance channelling actually go into a deep meditative state, the alpha state, and allow their higher selves or spirit to come through.

Edgar Cayce is perhaps the best modern example of this. Cayce was a photographer, Sunday-school teacher, husband, father, and channeller. He was a simple man, deeply religious, and not well read. He was born on a Kentucky farm and dropped out of school in grade seven to begin working. When Cayce was twenty-one years old, he took a job as a salesman for a stationery company. Around the same time his throat muscles became paralyzed reducing his voice to a whisper. Doctors were unable to cure him. As an alternative, he asked a friend to put him into a hypnotic trance. In this trance or alpha state, Cayce spoke in a clear firm voice. He diagnosed his throat problem and prescribed a cure. After this experience, he spent years going into deep trances to prescribe medical cures for thousands of patients. In this deep alpha state, he used medical terms and spoke foreign languages he didn't consciously understand. He worked directly with a group of six Kentucky physicians as a medical diagnostician in a hospital specially built for this purpose.

When he died in 1945, Cayce left over fourteen thousand telepathic-clairvoyant readings that he'd given for more than six thousand people. A record of these readings is kept at the Association of Research and Enlightenment in Virginia Beach. He's often referred to as the "sleeping prophet" because of his ability to find cures for thousands of people through deep-trance channelling while in the alpha state. When asked how he was able to access this information, Cayce explained we all have this ability to tap into what he called the cosmic mind or, in Jung's terms, the collective unconscious. He believed that working with our dreams helps bring this cosmic material into conscious awareness.

There are a few very elevated magicians in the world today like David Copperfield who can actually transport themselves or fly on stage. This is very similar to how we fly or transport ourselves in the alpha state while we dream. During his shows, Copperfield actually takes volunteers from the audience to locations miles away where they're videotaped for a waiting audience. I saw him do this during a show while he was in Toronto. He took a teenager with him to Thailand and reunited the boy with his father. We watched them in Thailand for a few moments on a huge screen from a satellite feed, then Copperfield reappeared in the middle of the audience. I sat there dumbfounded. It was so smooth, seamless—it actually seemed natural, only your brain was telling you this couldn't be possible. It was the most mind-boggling show I've ever experienced. Everything he does defies logic. One can't rationally explain it.

He has frozen himself in ice for 62 hours. He has also stood in a 2,000 °F, 140 mph tornado of fire and walked away unscathed. How does he do it? He allows his spirit to become larger than his body. Spirit controlling matter, rather than the physical body dominating spirit. Transcending physicality in the alpha state, relaxing and allowing the body to dematerialize. We perceive this as magic or simply an elaborate illusion. This is extremely difficult to understand with the mind; so difficult, in fact, that most people prefer to think it is an illusion rather than believing the possibility exists. Perhaps we can begin simply with the awareness that it's possible, and that saints, yogis, and magicians like David Copperfield have been doing this for thousands of years.

What other historical figure did this? Jesus. Like David Copperfield, Jesus could frequently materialize or appear, then dematerialize or disappear to the astonishment of His followers. The only difference was that Jesus was fully enlightened so this did not wear down or exhaust His body. It was His natural state. In the case of David Copperfield or any human being who has learned how to do this, it's physically demanding until we've reached full enlightenment. Think how exhausted we are when we travel in a plane through several time zones. The lighter or more enlightened we are, the less demanding dimensional travel is on our physical bodies.

I can never, of course, prove to you that David Copperfield actually transports his body through time dimensions, instantly arriving at the other side of the world. But I also can't prove to you that there is a God, that Jesus could disappear, that any of my theories are true, or that I haven't made up my dreams. It's possible David Copperfield isn't flying at all—perhaps he's found a sophisticated way to present an illusion. But even if this is an illusion, he is showing us the possibility of what could be. Imagine being able to fly like this. No expensive airline tickets, lineups, heavy luggage, or flight delays. If we fly in our sleep, then why not when we're awake? Less than a hundred years ago everyone believed that the Wright brothers were absolutely out of their minds for believing human flight was possible and for trying to build an airplane. Many of their first attempts failed, but they persevered. Today, most of us can't imagine a world without air travel. Perhaps a hundred years later, we're ready for the next level of flight. Maybe a hundred years from now, airplanes will be obsolete.

J. K. Rowling's *Harry Potter* series presents this possibility of flying in a humourous, entertaining fashion. The Muggles are like us—mere mortals, non-magical humans, who can't fly without an airplane. Harry and his wizard friends are all capable of transporting themselves, but this varies from wizard to witch depending on how advanced they are. Flying does not come easily; it's something all wizards must learn and there are different levels. While they're at a special school for wizards and witches, Hogwarts, Harry and his classmates receive formal instruction on how to fly broomsticks. But Harry, a messiah-like character, doesn't need to be taught. He excels at flying from his first attempt.

When they aren't using their broomsticks, the witches and wizards use chimneys and magical "Floo Powder" to transport themselves. But this too presents challenges as Harry's friends the Weasleys discover when they try to visit him and the chimney has been blocked up.

A third, more advanced method is "Apparating": disappearing from one place and reappearing almost instantly in another. Only the most advanced witches and wizards can Apparate once they have reached a certain age and have passed a test with the Department of Magical Transportation. We learn that Apparating isn't easy and it can have "nasty complications." The Department of Magical Transportation has fined people because they "splinched themselves" (left half of their body parts behind). We're told, "You don't mess around with Apparition."

We are possibly all like Harry Potter's friends. We begin by accepting the possibility that flying or transporting ourselves is part of our formal education. We also acknowledge that spiritual growth is serious—something you "don't mess around with." Then we begin the arduous lifetimes and levels of perfecting ourselves by reaching the highest level of purity or full enlightenment. Only then do we leave the broomsticks and airplanes behind.

To Dream or Not to Dream?

Early to bed and early to rise, makes a man healthy, wealthy, and wise.
—Benjamin Franklin, *Poor Richard's Almanac* (1758)

Beginning in 1959, a series of experiments by two doctors William Dement and Charles Fisher working from Mount Sinai Hospital in New York helped us to understand the importance of dreaming. Their research examined the effects of dream deprivation and showed that our need to dream is just as important, perhaps more important than our need to eat or sleep. In one famous experiment two groups were formed and both were hooked up to EEG machines that monitored REM and NREM cycles. The first group was allowed to complete their REM or dreaming cycle, then were woken up and allowed to fall asleep again. The second group was awakened as soon as the REM cycle or dreaming began, then were also allowed to return to sleep. Both groups received the same amount of sleep and were awakened the same number of times. The major difference was that the second group was not allowed to dream.

After the experiment had been running for five nights, some members of the second group tried to dream as much as *thirty* times during eight hours of sleep. It became clear that sleepers would immediately begin to dream as soon as they fell asleep trying to make up for the lost REM sleep. This is something that is rarely seen under normal circumstances, unless of course we've been dream or sleep deprived.

By the fifteenth night, Dement was forced to stop his experiment. It became virtually impossible to wake up the second group during REM sleep, and in the first two hours of sleep, twenty awakenings were needed. They resorted to hoisting dreamers' bodies upright and shouting in their ears, but they still couldn't wake them up while they were dreaming. REM sleep could only be stopped by literally dragging people out of bed, walking them around until they woke up, then forcing them to stay awake!

The next night, or recovery night, the REM-deprived sleepers were still hooked up to an EEG machine but were allowed to sleep without disturbances. When undisturbed, REM sleep began immediately and lasted longer than normal REM periods. One subject spent nearly five hours in REM sleep, four times more than the usual amount. In another of Dement's experiments, one REM-deprived sleeper had a single REM period that lasted over *three* hours on his first recovery night. Unfortunately, this person also displayed clear psychotic episodes nearing the end of the experiment.

Two clear facts emerged from this study. First, if we're deprived of sleeping and dreaming our body tries desperately to make up for lost dream time. Second, after four or five nights deprived of dreams, we begin to show signs of mental breakdown. This begins with increased irritability and ends with full-blown hallucinations. Dement concluded that continual dream deprivation would result in "catastrophic breakdown." Freud referred to dreams as the "guardians of sleep," but they are actually the keepers of sanity.

Peter Tripp

The most famous account of sleep deprivation is the story of disc jockey Peter Tripp who went 201 hours and 10 minutes (eight days) without sleep in 1959 as a fundraiser for the March of Dimes. Peter's objective was to break the world record for staying awake. For the three hours each day that his radio show was on the air, Peter sat in a glass booth in Times Square playing records and talking to his audience. During his ordeal he was supervised by doctors, nurses, and psychologists. To keep him awake, they went for walks, played games, joked, talked, asked him questions, administered mental tests, and shook Peter whenever he started falling asleep.

After two days, Peter began having minor hallucinations. He thought there were cobwebs in his shoes and that specks of dirt were bugs. On the fourth day, he became so delirious he believed a doctor's suit was a mass of furry worms and that flames were shooting out of a drawer. Simple mental tests became unbearably difficult. By the fifth day, he needed a stimulant to stay awake. On the sixth day, Peter was so disoriented and paranoid he didn't know who or where he was; he backed against a wall and refused to let anyone pass. On the eighth and final day, he thought a doctor making a routine medical check was an undertaker who'd come to bury him. During these eight days, Peter also believed he was seeing mice and kittens. He rummaged through drawers looking for money that wasn't there. He insisted a technician had dropped a hot electrode into his shoe. At the end of his ordeal Peter slept for thirteen hours and seemed back to normal, but he reported minor depression for several months. Peter's wife and closest friends said that after the eight days he was never the same again. If we go eight days without allowing our spirit to guide us during sleep we become totally disoriented in the physical dimension. While we sleep, the soul lays out our path and helps us navigate through waking life. If we don't sleep and dream, we lose sight of our path and focus. Nothing in the physical world makes sense. It's like trying to walk without our spine.

In early studies, it was believed that dream deprivation would lead to psychotic behaviour. Now we know that REM-deprived individuals are more anxious, agitated, and less controlled. They also seem to be at the mercy of their basest animal drives. REM-deprived male cats pace and eat more and will mount anything that resembles a female— even wooden blocks! All lab rats that have been chronically deprived of sleep usually die after two or three weeks. The cause of death seemed to be total collapse of their immune systems.

In humans, our need for sleep and dreaming is even more critical. A human being who does not sleep at all for ten days will die. Peter Tripp was dangerously close to his own death sentence, although he may not have consciously been aware of this. In contrast, the average human being can survive for sixty days without food. Quite simply, it's spirit, not our physical body that sustains us. Although food, shelter, and physical comforts are important, without spirit our body has nothing to animate, guide, and nourish it.

Essentially, we're all aliens; we're not originally from earth, although we get so caught up in the physical world we forget this. We're not really a physical body at all—this is just what encases or protects our core. We're really spiritual beings from different dimensions. This is why Pierre Teilhard de Chardin's words are important to remember: "We are not human beings learning to be spiritual: we are spiritual beings learning to be human." Each of us originated from different dimensions or planets in the spirit world, and we return home each night while we dream to help us navigate in this foreign land called earth.

Imagine we're sent to live in a distant galaxy called Planet XYZ. People speak strange languages. There are gadgets and machines different from anything on earth. Phones aren't needed because everyone is telepathic. Every family lives in a commune-type environment; there are few private homes. Values are different—women are equal to men, and most politicians are women. There's no upper class—everyone is the same. Their system of work is different—people have five separate jobs, but the workday is only five hours long. Some people seem to do multiple jobs, while others do the same job in five different places. People aren't paid for their work—there's no system of money. There's a confusing system of time, or no time—each day seems to just blend into the next. People don't travel by car, bus, or train—they use voice-activated flying discs. Imagine how confused we'd be. Now imagine that while we sleep, we could return to earth several times every night to do research, rehearse, plan, talk to people, and work out all the details we needed to live on Planet XYZ. This is really the function of dreams; we're all aliens in a strange but beautiful land, trying to find our way. Dreams become our lifeline home; without them, we're helplessly lost.

The Nap Debate

There has always been great controversy over napping. Should we or shouldn't we? Ten minutes, half an hour, or an hour? Early afternoon or late afternoon? Since everyone's natural rhythms and sleep requirements are different, the best advice is to listen to and respect our body's rhythms and ensure that we receive adequate sleep each night. If we're going to nap it's probably better to take a short nap or a really long one. If something wakes us up in our first delta phase, which may start about 45 to 55 minutes after we've fallen asleep, we'll be groggy and disoriented. Our second delta phase begins after approximately 2 1/2 hours of sleep.

It's also important to realize that the optimum time to dream is at night, particularly between the hours of 12 p.m. and 6 a.m. During this time, the earth is aligned in a certain way so that it's most appropriate for spirit to do its work in other dimensions. Imagine that all freeways are open to spiritual travel. There are no blocked ramps or road closures. If we nap too much during the day, it may become harder for us to take advantage of this optimum time for dreaming at night. If we need to rest or relax during the day, it may be wiser to meditate. This allows our brainwaves to go into that meditative alpha state where our soul can be activated to guide and refresh our body.

How Much Sleep Do We Need?

Sleep is better than medicine.
—English Proverb

Before Edison invented the lightbulb in 1879, most people were getting between eight and ten hours of sleep each night. In 1910, before the lightbulb was in every home, a study revealed that Americans averaged nine hours of sleep a night. But by 1997, that average had fallen to seven hours.

The individual need for sleep is a mystery that baffles scientists. Some people can get by with as little as four or five hours sleep, while others desperately need nine or ten hours. Only 5% of adults can function well on less than six hours of sleep. We also have different peak times; some people feel most alert early in the morning, while others are most productive late at night. Some are happy and alert getting up at 5 or 6 a.m., while others regard dawn with a vampiric dread. Sleep researchers refer to early risers as larks and later risers as owls.

Sleep experts generally agree that newborns need to sleep about eighteen hours. Toddlers and young children need about twelve hours. Children from the age of eight up to the late teens need eight to nine hours of sleep each night. Older teens need to fall asleep later and sleep longer in the morning. The average adult needs about eight and a quarter hours of sleep for optimum health.

In the animal kingdom, there are vast differences in sleep requirements. Giraffes need only two hours of sleep. Donkeys, horses, elephants, and deer all survive on three hours of sleep. Dogs average nine hours. Monkeys, chimpanzees, and baboons average ten hours of sleep. Cats, squirrels, chipmunks, and gerbils average fifteen hours. The top sleeper is the bat who slumbers for twenty hours each day.

Just as sleep requirements vary drastically for animals, there are huge differences in people. Thomas Edison's son Charles reported his father never slept more than four hours a night, although he did have frequent catnaps. It was not unusual for Albert Einstein to arrive at work late after sleeping for ten hours. Both men were geniuses, but Einstein needed to do a lot of work in the dream state to inform his waking hours. Much of his knowledge came from dimensional travel. Edison, on the other hand, needed to do most of his physical work in the awake state. He spent most of the day constructing, building, designing the inventions he had seen in the dream state. Some geniuses will go through different stages—lots of sleep for one year, then little sleep the next—depending on what they need to do. It's the same with most humans. When we've cleaned up all our karma and reached a state of near perfection or enlightenment, our need for sleep and dreaming decreases. It's well known that Buddhist monks who meditate for hours every day can survive on just a few hours' sleep. This elevated state, however, has been achieved by very few individuals. Before we become enlightened we all need a great amount of sleep. It's important to respect and honour these needs and to recognize we're all different.

Teenagers and Sleep

The beginning of health is sleep.
—Irish Proverb

When I began teaching high school I was constantly amazed at the number of students who were late in the morning. This varied with each class, but it was not uncommon to have thirty students in an 8 a.m. class with only fifteen showing up on time. The rest of the class would stumble in over the next hour, disoriented and half-asleep. Another common occurrence was students falling asleep during lessons. This happens to every teacher, regardless of how boring or interesting our instruction may be. Whenever a student fell asleep, I let them rest in peace. I realized if they were that tired, there was no point in trying to make them learn. Besides, they were probably doing more valuable work in the dream state. I usually asked classmates not to disturb them. This request was often met with shock and bewilderment. We live in a society where sleeping can be an embarrassment.

Since I spent nine years teaching elementary school before working in a high school, these sleepy teens were a real phenomenon. In elementary school, students were rarely late. I can't remember a student ever falling asleep, even when I taught grade one where students had just made the transition from morning and afternoon naps. In elementary school, students are perky, animated, and full of energy. In secondary school, I was trying to teach sleep-deprived zombies.

This all has to do with circadian rhythms, which we've only begun to understand in the last few decades. Circadian comes from the Latin word circa meaning "about" and dian meaning "a day." For most adults and children, this natural rhythm is close to a 24-hour cycle. But for teenagers this rhythm slows down. Typical teenagers do not want to go to bed at 11 p.m. because their internal clock is telling them it's only 8 p.m.

This is why it's often torture for a teenager to get out of bed early in the morning. If their alarm rings at 7 a.m., their body is telling them it's 4 or 5 a.m. For roughly ten years, teenagers groggily deal with an internal clock that runs much slower, on a cycle of twenty-six to thirty hours. "It's not that the younger generation is bad, lazy, or shiftless, their clocks simply are running on a slower time," write sleep researchers Shirley Linde and Peter Hauri in their book *No More Sleepless Nights*.

As adolescents mature, their internal clocks undergo a shift, pushing their pre-programmed period of wakefulness about an hour later than children and adults. This shift is due to a delay in the timing of a nightly squirt of melatonin from the pineal gland inside the brain. The pineal gland is a light-sensitive organ behind the eyes that is sometimes referred to as our third eye. In a way, the pineal gland does see since it responds to changes in light and darkness. Melatonin is only secreted at night. Melatonin, which induces sleepiness, helps set the body's circadian rhythms. This squirt of melatonin occurs at roughly 9:30 p.m. for adolescents and adults, but changes to 10:30 p.m. during our teen years. So teenagers and young adults have a physiological need for extra sleep, particularly in the morning. This may be why the absentee rate of university students for that first class in the morning has reached 40%. One Ontario study found that 60–70% of teenagers reported their sleepiest time of the day was between 8 and

10 a.m. If teenagers are allowed to sleep in as long as they want, they average about nine and a quarter hours. But the problem with most teens is that they never get enough sleep and try to operate in a constant state of sleep deprivation. Since REM sleep, where we experience our longest dreams, occurs late in the morning, many teenagers are forced to wake up in the middle of this cycle. So they're not just sleep deprived, they're REM-deprived, and at a stage in life when dreams are trying to guide them through critical life decisions. Going to bed an hour earlier doesn't help since teens can't change their circadian rhythms. If they go to bed an hour earlier, they'll be staring at the ceiling unable to sleep.

What makes this even tougher for teenagers is that most elementary schools start around 9 a.m., and most secondary schools begin an hour earlier at 8 a.m. If we lived in a culture that understood sleep, this would be reversed so that teens could sleep that extra hour—this translates to 200 extra hours of sleep per year. Mary Carskadon, from the Brown University School of Medicine is a leading researcher in the United States regarding teenagers' sleep patterns and school start times. She's been working tirelessly to convince school boards that early start times are catastrophic. Her 1999 study found that students with C, D, or F grades averaged 25 minutes less sleep every night than those with A or B grades. In Canada, Dr. Edward Gibson conducted a research study "Sleepiness and the Health of Adolescents" involving three Ontario school boards and surveying 3,400 secondary students. The findings were consistent with Dr. Carskadon's—students who felt their grades had dropped due to sleepiness, averaged 26 minutes less sleep every weeknight. Final results clearly showed that at least 24% of teenagers had lower grades due to sleepiness. One of the most telling summaries from Dr. Gibson's study is this: "No curriculum overhaul, no instructional innovation, no change in school organization, no toughening of standards, no rethinking or teacher training or compensation will succeed if students come to school sleepy."

There are many side effects for teens who don't receive adequate sleep:
- Reaction times are slower, resulting in car accidents,
- Memory loss,
- Muddled thinking,
- Mood swings,
- Behavioural and emotional problems,
- Increased irritability,

- Depression,
- Anxiety,
- Decreased sense of humour and socialization,
- Hyper-sexuality,
- Mental fatigue with reduced concentration,
- Decreased ability to handle complex tasks or to be creative,
- Increased dependency on drugs and alcohol, and
- Development of major sleep disorders.

For teens and adults in their early twenties, extra sleep is not a luxury, it's a basic need.

Can We Catch Up on Lost Dreams?

When we are tired we are attacked by ideas we conquered long ago.
—Friedrich Nietzsche

There is a formula in Dr. Katherine Albert's book *Get A Good Night's Sleep* that explains how our body can compensate for lost sleep. She tells us that all it takes to compensate for one night of lost sleep is an extra 25% of a normal night's sleep. So if we normally sleep eight hours, two extra hours is what we need to compensate for that sleepless night. If we pull an all-nighter, then sleep for about ten hours the next night, our body can catch up. In most cases, in order to replenish the body, all we need to do is make sure we go to sleep the next night and sleep soundly. Generally, if we allow this to happen, the body's natural forces will take over.

But if we've been chronically depriving ourselves of sleep—missing entire nights or continually getting an hour or less than we need, we may need weeks or months to recover. Let's say we miss one hour of sleep every night. We know that to feel rested, we need to be in bed by 11 p.m., but we never get to bed until midnight. Here's the equation:

- 0.25 x 7 hours you miss each week = 1.75 hours of missed sleep every week
- 1.75 x 4 weeks in a month = 7 hours a month you need to catch up
- 7 hours needed a month x 10 months from September to June = *70 hours* needed to catch up over the summer!

This means we would need to sleep at least one extra hour every day during July and August. Or if we wanted to catch up in one month, we would need to sleep *two* additional hours or *ten* hours each day. When I started teaching, it became obvious that most of my colleagues and I were chronically sleep deprived. We would always return in September and talk about how wonderful it was to sleep in at least an extra hour or two every morning all summer long. No surprise because we were all catching up on the sleep we lost over the entire year.

It's important to understand that although we may be able to catch up on what our body needs to replenish there is no magic formula for our soul or spirit. The effects on spirit are very difficult to correct, so we do lose time. Remember that the function of sleep is to allow our spirit to go forward and prepare our path or show us the way. If we're setting up a new business, moving, changing jobs, studying for a critical exam, or trying to figure out whether to end a relationship, our spirit will go forward in the dream state and help us prepare for these things. If we pull a couple of all-nighters before that important exam, or before our new business opens, we may feel stuck, depressed, forgetful, unaware, or panicky. This is because we haven't given our spirit the time it needed to prepare our path or guide us in working things out. We know this and so we feel scattered and unsure of ourselves.

It's not so much that our body needs extra sleep, it's that our spirit needs time to do work in other dimensions to prepare our way. We deprive our spirit when we don't allow ourselves time to sleep. When we sleep we do soul work; it's soul in the alpha state that contains true genius. So it's brutally disruptive to deprive ourselves of sleep. It's exceedingly detrimental to our true health, which is the health of spirit! Certain types of knowledge can translate into spiritual empowerment. We are empowered simply by understanding the physical as well as the emotional and spiritual benefits of sleep. If we're not getting adequate sleep, we're damaging the evolution of our soul.

Chapter Eight
Conquering Demons of Sleep

Recurring Dreams

There are three reasons for most recurring dreams:

1. We're working through a complex problem that takes time.
2. We're repeating or stuck in past patterns.
3. We're going back and reliving a trauma.

Working Through Complex or Long-Term Themes

Most of us can remember a puzzling recurring dream. We often go back to the same place many times because we want to rehearse, try new things, observe, or experiment until we've completely resolved an issue. If we're dealing with something major, like a first-time career, a career change, relationship problems, separation, divorce, illness, or a major move, it's not unusual for this type of dream to repeat for several years. In these dreams, the action will often change slightly as we make changes in the physical dimension that match our awareness. In recurring dreams, changes in landscape, people, action, or emotions can be a good sign. It may indicate we're becoming more aware and that we're making changes in life.

I spent about seven years working through dreams when I left teaching high school English. I was experiencing major health problems and needed to stop working. My spirit knew it was time to leave, but my mind or ego kept resisting. It's always easier to fall into patterns of the past. During this time, I was having dreams where I was trying to teach and every scenario was a complete disaster. Although each dream was different, every one was telling me that this didn't feel good, I wasn't helping anyone, and I wasn't helping myself. Sometimes I was trying to teach wild unruly classes. In other dreams, I'd show up and realize another teacher had replaced me. I'd go to the school and feel terribly out of place, knowing I didn't belong. In other dreams, the staff ignored me; it felt like I was invisible. All these dreams were trying to tell me I needed to change what I was doing. I finally did leave, but each time I contemplated going back to start a new semester, these same awful dreams would resurface. Each dream was a mirror showing me all the horrible emotions I would feel if I went back.

When I started to feel healthy again, my dreams started changing. Now I was going into classrooms, but it felt completely different. Teaching was enjoyable again. My students were cooperative and a pleasure to be with. I wasn't having discipline problems. In one dream, I was given an idyllic country cottage to teach in, and there were only eight students. My principal said things had been very difficult for me in the past, so now they were going to make it easier for me. When I had this dream—after many agonizing years—I knew I was finally making the transition.

One of my neighbours told me about dreams that took him ten years to resolve. In his early twenties, he spent five years working as an ambulance driver. It was an emotionally stressful job. He'd receive calls to remove the noose from around the necks of people who had just hung themselves. He'd be called to homes where people had experienced heart attacks, stabbings, and where women had been beaten by husbands or lovers. At night, he would dream about these horrible experiences, probably his spirit's attempt to work through and release the horrors of that day. But he didn't want to remember these dreams so he started drinking heavily before going to bed, falling into a stupor and not remembering anything in the morning. But consuming alcohol late at night disturbs our normal sleep patterns. Sleep becomes fragmented and we may actually wake up several times during the night, so we actually sleep less. People with chronic drinking problems often have less REM sleep or dream time, which prevents them from working through problems. In my neighbour's case, he didn't remember his dreams in the morning due to the alcohol impairing his sleep, but he said it was ten years before these "nightmares" stopped completely. It's impossible to know how long these dreams would have lasted without the alcohol, but it's a fascinating story showing that difficult or complex issues do take a long time to work through.

Repeating the Same Patterns

If we're repeating the same patterns in life, similar themes will keep recurring. This is usually because we're stuck and can't figure out how to make changes that are in our best interests. One of my recurring dream themes is losing my car. I may be at a huge shopping mall and when I go outside I search endlessly but can't find it anywhere. In other dreams, I panic because I'm sure my car has been stolen. I also repeatedly dream of losing my credit cards, wallet, or purse. Every time I have one of these recurring dreams, I know I'm feeling insecure, afraid, or worthless. When I left teaching, I had these dreams more frequently. All of these symbols: the car, purse, and credit cards represented me. Purses, wallets, and credit cards represent money, self-worth, and buying power. Unfortunately, we often define ourselves by how much we earn. So these things are my identity and a form of personal power. When I left teaching, I felt I had lost my identity and self-esteem, so in my dreams I kept on losing things that represented myself. In physical life, I felt as if my identity had been taken from me, in the same way that my car, purse, wallet, and credit card were being lost and stolen in dreams.

If the exact same dream repeats over and over, they may be telling us we're not evolving. It may be our spirit showing us we're stuck and unable to move forward. A woman told me about a recurring dream in which she kept going back to a house she had owned. She kept revisiting this place because part of her longed to live there again. In the dream, new people had purchased the home, so she had to sneak out before they discovered her. This dream repeated for over *ten* years because she never really wanted to sell this home. She referred to it as her "tiny perfect dream home." She adored this house and sold it when she moved to another city to look after a sick relative. Although her present home was much larger, she held a nostalgic longing for this "tiny perfect home." (This can be similar to feelings we have for a childhood home years after we've moved on.)

If we're not willing to give something up in our physical life, often we go back in dreams and keep on trying. But in the dream, it never feels comfortable—there's always something out of place, or it's awkward and embarrassing. Let's say our first marriage didn't work out. In dreams, we may go back and try to remarry and remarry until we realize it's never going to work. If we are dismissed from what we believed was the perfect job, we may go back to that job over and over in dreams trying to make it work, trying to fit in, until we realize it was never an ideal situation, or we may find another job to replace it.

Recurring Dream Traumas

Perhaps the most unnecessary dreams are those where the dreamer goes back and relives a traumatic experience. We've all heard stories of people who had recurring dreams after being raped, attacked, or involved in an accident or war. These dreamers are crossing the time barrier, going back in time and reliving the experience with all its horrors. It's important to understand that *this is completely unnecessary*. It doesn't serve our soul in any way to repeat a karmic or traumatic experience. Reliving it over and over again in dreams is simply not empowering. Why would anyone want to remain a victim? It's better to move forward and determine future possibilities. Instead of being a victim forever, it's far healthier to understand why the soul needed this experience. What kind of karma could be released or corrected? Why would this be necessary for the soul's growth?

Imagine we were robbed or attacked while returning home at night. We may reflect or meditate by asking, why would my soul choose to be robbed? What was I trying to figure out? Was I trying to stand up against some form of darkness? Was I trying to empower myself? What was I trying to face? Am I trying to break out of a pattern where I have been a victim? When something like this happens, it's not always that the soul did something wrong or needed to be punished. It's often that the soul is trying to stand against some form of darkness and reclaim its power. Perhaps someone has robbed us lifetime after lifetime and we need to break this pattern or correct the karma. It's karmic for anyone to allow himself or herself to repeatedly be a victim.

After this pattern is recognized, we may become a speaker who teaches others how to protect themselves from danger. We may begin teaching people how to stay empowered so they aren't susceptible to attack. As a public speaker, we are standing against darkness and reclaiming our power. Or perhaps we've never learned how to emotionally crawl out of this experience. Maybe we've always sunk into a deep depression and this provides an opportunity to reverse those negative thought patterns and replace them with self-acceptance, faith, and much needed peace.

Demons That Keep Us Awake

We've talked about how negative entities can produce night terrors by seducing us into their dimension when we're in the delta phase of sleep. In rare cases, the same entities or demons can also seduce us into staying awake! This is why we have the concept of "personal demons." Our personal demons may be chronic insomnia, staying awake until 3 a.m. eating pizza and watching movies, working so many hours that our mind cannot relax, or working incessantly and believing no one else can perform our job. This type of activity prevents our spirit from moving forward. So although there are demons that seduce us during sleep, there are also demons of the mind capable of seducing us while we're awake. Some people battle demons their entire lives without awareness of what is happening. Becoming conscious that demons do exist is the first important step in eliminating them.

As we're lying in bed trying to fall asleep after a busy day, our mind may try to keep us awake. It fills our head with all kinds of trials and tribulations, anxieties, problems, insecurities, or obligations in order to prevent us from going to our natural state and doing our real work. Our true work—our spiritual work—occurs in the alpha or dream state. This spiritual work informs us so we can successfully navigate in the physical dimension. So yes, there are demons that can fill our head with all kinds of physical problems to prevent us from gaining the wisdom we need while dreaming. Dreams enable us to go ahead, clear our path, prepare, and allow our body to replenish. Negative entities, however, can invade when we're attempting to fall asleep because they know if we're not allowed to go ahead and prepare our path, we're powerless.

Demons or other forms of negativity work through the lower vibrations of the mind. The mind can be compared to a sophisticated computer. On its own it has no inherent wisdom, no memories or insights. It needs power or electricity to be activated and then software that makes it seem brilliant. To our mind, this power or electricity comes from God or spirit, and the software is our dreams. Spirit or soul always works through your intuition, dreams or gut feelings. Our mind can keep us awake forever—wrestling, worrying, stewing over things that we could actually work out in the dream state.

Even Mother Teresa wrestled with personal demons. After she passed away, the archbishop of Calcutta, Henry D'Sousa, reported that while she was hospitalized, Mother Teresa had difficulty sleeping. With Mother Teresa's consent, Archbishop D'Sousa brought in priest Rosario Stroccio to perform an exorcism. After the ceremony, she was able to sleep peacefully and the Archbishop stated, "Mother Teresa was not at all possessed by devils." An exorcism is an extreme route that most of us will never need to follow. If we're aware of the importance of shutting down the endless chatter of the mind to allow sleep to take place, we can all be our own exorcists! All we have to do is call on God, spirit, the universe, whatever we believe in and ask to be watched over and protected while we sleep. Armed with this knowledge we can all sleep peacefully and fulfill our destinies.

Craziness Is the Inability to Dream

Jung believed that mental illness was actually disconnection from spirit. He was absolutely right. If we haven't slept for a long period of time, we become neurotic. If this goes on even longer, psychosis occurs. In some cases psychotic people need to sleep so badly that their dreams break through into physical reality—they start hallucinating and seeing things like dream images while they're awake. These visions and hallucinations do exist—others just can't see them. We can't see someone else's dreams even if we're sleeping in the same bed with them, but this doesn't mean these nocturnal experiences aren't real.

Psychosis is a complete disconnection from physical reality. We interpret reality as being the physical world. However, a truer reality is the world of spirit. If we've become neurotic or psychotic, somehow we've lost or become disconnected from our spirit, which is our true navigating wisdom. Psychosis, therefore, is when the physical mind becomes disconnected from spirit. If we're emotionally or spiritually healthy there is harmony, balance, and connection between our mind and spirit. Spirit informs the mind each night as we dream and enables it to make wise decisions. Mind and spirit work together as partners for our well-being.

When the body or mind fragments from spirit, it's like trying to run a computer without any software or programming. For human beings, it's like trying to walk around without our spine. Without the wisdom of the soul or spirit, we have absolutely nothing to support us. Without the wisdom of spirit, the mind becomes an empty vessel. When the mind is empty, it's inundated by everything in the physical and non-physical world without being able to make sense of it. The only way we can make sense and translate experience is to be connected, plugged in, or melded to our spirit. Spirit is our core, fuel, focus.

People are driven into neurosis or psychosis because their spirit hasn't been allowed to go ahead and prepare their path. It's like going to a foreign country without any translators, guides, or people to assist us. Imagine how difficult this would be. We're in a strange place, we don't know the language and customs, and no one understand what we need. This is similar to how psychosis feels. Eventually, psychotics reach a heightened state of anxiety because they're too long in a strictly conscious state. They're inundated and overwhelmed without the benefit of having spirit explain things to them.

Anyone who goes into a coma has made a decision at a soul level that they need a prolonged period of time to work through issues in the spirit world. This is why people go into comas after they've been in a car accident, while they're experiencing a serious illness, or before they die. After they've gained the insight they need, they may come out of the coma. This is also why people who are severely depressed will sleep for hours and hours. If they're able to sleep and not be judged by others for this, they can and do heal themselves. Depressed people know intuitively that they can't heal themselves as effectively in the waking state. So they go into their real state, or dream state, in order to heal.

So if we've been chronically sleep deprived this is a danger zone, red flag, put it up, recognize we're running down the road to serious trouble. It's not cool or trendy to survive without adequate sleep—it's the path to insanity. The dream that follows was written by a grade eleven student in one of my English classes. It's an excellent example of how dreams will let us know if we're not getting enough sleep.

Sample Dream Journal Entry

Choices — *Eleventh-grade male student*

This dream has recurred approximately five times. It is the fifth dream which was special. The first four dreams begin with me running and running from some unknown entity. I am too afraid to look over my shoulder. My body starts to shake I can hardly run. I start to panic. All of a sudden I reach two doors. In panic I choose the left door. Behind this door is nothing but a black emptiness. I begin to fall. That is when I awake. In this dream I am frightened and erratic. I want nothing more but to escape what is chasing me.

In the fifth dream I am running and running trying so vehemently to escape my predator. I reach two doors. I am picking the left when all of a sudden I remember what happened the last time I picked the left door. I make up my mind and choose the right door. I open the door and it is my room. I close the door. Slowly I get into bed and close my eyes. That is when I woke up. Contradicting my first dream, in this I was feeling relieved. I also had a sense of peace.

The dream *Choices* did not take long to figure out. My unconsciousness intertwines with my consciousness to produce some surprising results. The symbols in these recurring dreams are my bed, the left door, the right door, the entity, and my room.

The entity which is chasing me in my dreams is the pressure and stress from school. It is also the pressure from work. Similar to the entity, it has forced me to make a decision too quickly. The left door represents the rushed choice. Which is often the wrong choice. In life I am choosing work, school and friends over sleep. I did not think that sleep was important.

My unconscious mind thought differently. The right door was its way of telling me to relax and think before I make a decision. My room symbolizes the path to good health. It literally states that if I do not choose sleep then the side effects would eventually catch up to me. The bed represented the needed sleep that my body wants to maintain its life processes. Before I interpreted this dream I was averaging four hours of sleep a night. Now I am currently averaging six to seven hours of sleep a night. A little improvement, however, it makes me feel better.

In summary, my dream through a recurring sequence teaches me a great lesson in how to maintain my physical needs of sleep and relaxation. This important lesson is one that I must not ignore or take too lightly. The consequences may be more serious though.

Night Terrors

Many parents can relate incidents of a child or teenager gripped by night terrors. They affect up to 5% of children aged three to six years old but are also experienced by teenagers and some adults. They occur during delta or slow-wave sleep when the brain is virtually half-asleep and half-awake. Children can be more susceptible to night terrors because they sleep longer and spend more time in this phase of sleep. Since slow-wave delta sleep occurs at the beginning of the night, children will often awake with night terrors during the first two or three hours of sleep.

Night terrors can be just as traumatic for a parent witnessing them since they seem powerless to help. They usually begin with a blood-chilling scream, the eyes are wide open, and the child is sweating and trembling. They may jump out of bed, knock things over, become uncharacteristically aggressive, and even break a window or lamp. They're noticeably panic-stricken but can't tell you what's wrong, and their behaviour can last from ten minutes to one hour. Although it appears they're awake, they're actually in a deep phase of delta sleep or "human hibernation" with brainwaves between 0.5 and 4 cps. In the morning, they usually have no memory of what took place.

During a night terror, a child or teenager risks physical injury, but anyone trying to restrain them puts themselves at risk. In the short term, the best advice is to block access to any stairways, doors, or windows where they may hurt themselves. Make their environment safe by turning on lights, pushing away clutter on the floor, and simply being there to calm them.

Parasomnia and Sexsomnia

We've all heard stories or read about parasomnia—a group of sleep disorders that includes sleep walking, waking up in a cold sweat, being paralyzed by fear, and leaving the house while still asleep. In one dream class I taught, a woman said one of her relatives would often get up in the middle of the night to cook bacon and eggs with no conscious memory of doing this in the morning.

Dr. Harvey Moldofsky, director of the sleep disorder clinic at Toronto's Centre for Sleep and Chronobiology, has dealt extensively with many parasomnic patients. In a *Toronto Star* article entitled "While you were sleeping..." by Christian Cotroneo, Moldofsky is quoted as saying, "There are people who can do very complicated things and look as though they're awake. But they are not with it. They are behaving as an automaton—a robot. There are people who are violent during their sleep and within that group, there's a very small group that murders people." He has worked with and studied sleepers who have "beaten up their partners, torn apart things, gone out windows and lacerated their arteries and almost died. There are those people who grab their spouse and strangle them or beat them. Then there are people who destroy things, tear things apart in the rush of their terrifying experience in the context of sleep."

Some of Dr. Moldofsky's patients experience as many as four night terrors a week. Their sleep becomes a living nightmare. "They see snakes, rats, spiders, ominous shadows. But they're not actually dreaming. These are illusions or confusional states. They might actually be staring at a telephone cord by the bed and believe it's a snake. Or they look at their closet and see people standing there."

A famous case of a parasomnic was Kenneth Parks who left his Pickering, Ontario home in 1987 while asleep, drove twenty-three kilometres to his mother-in-law's home and stabbed her to death. He made medical history when he was acquitted for claiming he was sleepwalking. At the trial, a team of sleep researchers, psychiatrists, respirologists, and scientists concluded that Kenneth Parks suffered from parasomnia.

Recently, a new sleep disorder has been documented called sexsomnia. In this type of parasomnia, men can be fast asleep but initiating aggressive sex with their wives. But they're in such a deep sleep that in the morning they have no memory of the experience. In June 2003, Canadian doctors Colin Shapiro, Nikola Trajanovic, and Paul Fedoroff reported this new parasomnia in the *Canadian Journal of Psychiatry*. Their research report entitled "Sexsomnia–A New Parasomnia?" states that "a person with parasomnia can walk, operate a motor vehicle, eat, perform a sexual act, or even kill without the ability to, if we simplify, (fully) control his action." They say although the reasons behind these actions are not fully understood by the medical community, it's apparent "the most common precipitants of parasomnic behaviour in adults are stress, sleep deprivation, and alcohol or drug consumption." They noted that 2% of the sexual assault cases brought before the courts involved people who were sleeping!

One of the case histories in this article told the story of a twenty-seven-year-old nightclub bouncer referred to Dr. Fedoroff by his wife's psychiatrist:

> She had complained that her husband frequently sexually assaulted her while she was sleeping. Criminal charges had been laid, and she was considering leaving the marriage... He had a history of multiple-substance abuse... His sleep history was significant for snoring and a personal (as well as family) history of sleepwalking. His wife also described instances in which he screamed and talked in his sleep. He had daytime sleepiness which he self-treated by consuming up to thirty cups of coffee a day and by taking "power naps."

Another case involved a thirty-seven-year-old married police officer with a history of "severe parasomnia especially sleepwalking with driving in sleep, particularly when under stress and amplified by alcohol consumption." His wife reported that his episodes of sexsomnia occurred about once a month:

> His wife describes him as more aggressive and more amorous at these times than when he is awake. He indulges in behaviours while asleep that he does not undertake when awake. She says that, in some of these episodes "there is no stopping him"; however, on one occasion when he grabbed her around

the neck, she slapped him hard, and he immediately awoke and stopped the behaviour.

What is most fascinating about parasomnia is that it usually doesn't occur while people are dreaming or in the alpha state, when our soul is doing its work to help us through life. Most parasomnic episodes occur in the delta or slowest brainwave phase of sleep, but, like dreams, they may occur in any phase of sleep. Drinking alcohol can increase the time someone spends in delta or slow-wave restorative sleep, so sleep doctors will often explain this to patients first. If parasomnia becomes chronic, antidepressants such as clonazepam or lorazepam are prescribed, which also decrease the amount of time people spend in delta sleep. But as we've learned, delta sleep is essential for our body to rest, heal, and rejuvenate.

What do you think is really behind parasomnia, sexsomnia, or night terrors? What could make a sane person lacerate their arteries, attack, rape, or kill someone while they were in delta sleep? Perhaps, like St. Jerome, they're being controlled by a dark being. For most people, it's a scary proposition to admit that demons, entities, or dark forces could actually take over our bodies while we're in the deepest phases of sleep. If we think about it, each episode of parasomnia puts the dreamer or someone they know in danger. This is the way darkness operates, not beings of light. Even seemingly harmless episodes like cooking bacon and eggs at 3 a.m. don't really help. There's the possibility we could hurt ourselves since we're virtually automatons being controlled by entities wanting to vicariously enjoy this food by our bodies as hosts. It's also extremely unhealthy to eat then go to sleep because food is difficult to digest. Trying to sleep with an undigested meal can actually induce more unsettling dreams. Spirit at work never scares, terrifies, or hurts anyone. Darkness is not the natural enlightened state of spirit. It's only darkness that can scare, hurt, maim, and turn people into virtual robots while they sleep. Armed with this awareness, we'll see there are always easy drug-free ways to outwit any demon.

Nightmares

Nightmares are quite different from bad or unpleasant dreams; bad dreams usually don't wake us up although we may remember them in the morning. Bad dreams may make us feel uneasy or uncomfortable, whereas nightmares terrify us. Bad dreams can make us painfully aware of things we don't want to face; nightmares invoke guilt, shame, fear, horror, and despair. The difference in intensity is like seeing a friend fall off their bicycle and receive minor scrapes and bruises. We may characterize this as a bad experience, but we can still resume our day-to-day life. A nightmare is seeing your best friend riding their bicycle, then they're hit broadside by a car, killed, or horribly disfigured. After the nightmare, you're shaken for a long time. It's impossible to go through your day without its repercussions affecting you.

Nightmares are also quite different from night terrors or parasomnic episodes. First of all, we can't wake someone from a night terror or from parasomnia because they're in delta or slow-wave sleep. During a nightmare, we wake up on our own because of its blood-curdling intensity. Nightmares occur mostly during alpha or REM sleep when the brain is more active and alert. Because of this, we always remember a nightmare with all its horror. A former high-school student wrote about a nightmare that was definitely not helping him:

> I woke up out of bed hearing my family singing gospel songs and getting ready for church. I thought they were trying to make me feel left out because I refused to go to church with them on Sundays. In a way I did feel left out, on the other hand it did not bother me at all because I played my favourite music, watched my favourite television programs and had the house all to myself every Sunday morning. This was going on for a long time now.
>
> After a while, I started having nightmares of the devil chasing me and God disowning me. It seemed like I was separated from the rest of the world, I got very scared. One Sunday morning, I got out of bed and ironed a suit for church. I opened my bedroom door and went downstairs. No one was home. I thought they went to church extra early that day to leave me behind purposely. I went outside and saw the most incredible thing. Everyone was being taken up into heaven by God and his angels. I was the only one being left on earth. I was shouting and screaming for them to hear me, while they all went up but no one listened. As soon as no one was in sight, God came back down and threw a big ball of fire towards the earth, which went up into flames, along with myself.

Again it's important to understand that something like having huge balls of fire thrown on us in a dream just doesn't happen if our soul is trying to gently prod us forward and help us become aware.

This was all part of the drama used by negative forces to make him feel guilty, insecure, and worthless. It's very similar to St. Jerome's dream, where he was led to believe that God was an angry vengeful being. In both dreams, a demon or trickster impersonates God.

Understanding How Demons Work

In all of us, even in good men, there is a lawless wild-beast nature, which peers out in sleep.
—Plato

What is not widely understood or known regarding sleep terrors and nightmares is that these experiences are actually occurring in other dimensions while our body is in suspended animation. So while our soul is free to explore other dimensions, we can be seduced by negative entities. We may be on our way to the dimension that is most appropriate to enact our dream. As our soul is travelling, we're tricked or coerced into a realm we don't need to explore. Children experience night terrors most frequently because they're so vulnerable. In a night terror our soul or spirit is tricked, seduced, coerced into entering terrifying dimensions inhabited by entities who are far from kind. It's like an innocent child at a carnival being seduced into the haunted house or chamber of horrors when they really wanted to see animals at the petting zoo. Once our soul is in their realm, we're subject to their tricks and illusions and they attempt to gain power over us. They're masters of illusions because they've had lots of experience. However, our spirits are far wiser. It's important to realize their tactics are only illusions. They're elaborate illusions just like those monsters in the chamber of horrors that can be unplugged, disassembled, and taken away. But to a naive inexperienced dreamer, they're terrifying blood-curdling events. Why do dark beings do this? The same reason dark manipulative beings seduce us on earth—for power and control. It's the classic battle of good versus evil played out over and over again to prevent us from achieving full enlightenment.

Our souls don't travel in other dimensions just to have a good time or go on a holiday. We sleep to clear up karma and to have experiences that pave the way for growth, dharma, or enlightenment. If we are seduced into entering a negative realm it prevents us from doing our real work in the dream state, which is empowering. This prevents us from clearing our path and moving forward. These demons terrify us so that we immediately go into a state of fear. As soon as we become afraid, we lose our power. As long as we're terrified and rendered powerless, we're temporarily trapped in their dimensions.

When these dream experiences terrify us, there's usually a spillover to waking life. If we go through life feeling insecure, afraid, and powerless there's a ripple effect on everyone we meet. Instead of everyone feeling peaceful, loving, and exuberant about life, people simply go through the motions, crippled by low self-esteem and fear. This is exactly what these demons want to instill—fear and lack of control. If we're rendered powerless, we may never achieve our destiny and give back to the world. We'll never discover our core or essence. We'll never reach our greatness—that place of harmony and peace. Imagine how different our world would be if Mozart believed he was too worthless to write music, Christopher Columbus never had the confidence to sail around the world, Edison was afraid to go public with his light bulb invention, or Gandhi didn't believe in his visions and dreams for a more peaceful world.

Between 5% and 8% of adults have ongoing problems with nightmares, but all of us experience nightmares at some point in our lives. It's like someone getting a virus on a computer because of something they downloaded or maybe they didn't install anti-virus protection. To outwit these demons it's important to understand that on some level we have invited them in or left a door open. They may see us as easy prey because we go through life feeling or acting like a victim or because we become susceptible to fear, self-doubt, or low self-esteem. For others, the door may be a huge ego, judgement of others, or a desire for more power, money, prestige, or control. In short, anything that is not a true attribute of spirit allows these demons easier access. The number of people having nightmares rises to 25% for psychiatric patients, alcoholics, and drug addicts. In the cases of sexsomnia, there was a pattern of stress, sleep deprivation, and/or alcohol and substance abuse. But if we open a door, it certainly doesn't mean we're dark or bad people. On the contrary—it is often the energy of our light that they're after! Because we're human, we've all opened physical doors to negative people in our waking life and energetic doors to negative entities in our dream life. Armed with this awareness, it's entirely possible to outwit these demons.

Awareness begins the process of eliminating any form of darkness. If we fall into fear, we have fallen into the illusion that darkness is stronger than light. Demons, illusions, and psychic invasions are the reality we buy into. We have replaced faith with fear. We constantly need to remind ourselves that light and love are ultimately stronger than darkness. For an eternity, the forces of light have always defeated darkness. Light is the original source that darkness tries to feed from. Darkness has nothing to sustain itself without light. It's really hollow; it has no core or essence. Armed with this wisdom, it's not difficult to permanently rid ourselves of any witch, goblin, or ghoul.

In the television series *Buffy the Vampire Slayer*, Buffy Summers is always defeating the most horrendous demons. When she drives a stake through their hearts, their energy crumbles into nothingness. As we see their energy dissolving, we realize they held no true power, only the illusion of power. It's like the Wicked Witch of the West in the movie *The Wizard of Oz*. Dorothy destroys the witch simply by spilling water on her. When the witch dissolves into a heap of black clothes, we realize how easy it was all along to outwit her. At the end of the movie *The Matrix,* Neo is being chased by dark characters. They fire several bullets at him, but Neo is able to stop those bullets in mid-air. They had no power to kill him because Neo understands they aren't real. They're part of the matrix or web or illusion that is controlling most beings on earth.

Like Neo, once we understand that every form of darkness is just a sophisticated illusion, everything changes. Nothing can harm us. We take back our power and step into the true world of light where fear and disempowerment do not exist. It's not that easy to extinguish the light of a soul. Our essence or core can never be reduced to crumbling ashes or a pile of black clothes in a second. Our essence, spirit, or core is eternal and indestructible.

Protection While We Sleep—How to Cast Out Demons

The simple awareness of what is happening begins to give power back to us. All of these negative entities use illusion to lock fear into us. Realizing the monster or the witch isn't real can empower us in the dream state. Whether we're children or adults, as long as we're gripped by fear, we're powerless. As long as we're powerless, our souls cannot grow and evolve; we never step into our essence or greatness. It's not just temporary power we're after—it's the eternal empowerment of enlightenment. Power can corrupt, but true empowerment soothes and heals.

There is a children's book called *How To Get Rid of Bad Dreams* by

Nancy Hazbry and Roy Condy that gives children creative techniques to outwit these demons. It may be worth reading for adults who are terrorized by nightmares too. In the book, children are given a variety of methods, such as holding a mirror in front of the monsters to scare them, beginning to laugh at them, or shrinking them down to the size of a kitten.

There are several practical techniques that will dispel demons while we sleep. Before we go to bed, it may help to say the prayer at the back of this manual. We can ask God, angels, or archangels to protect and guide us while we sleep. We can call on any angel, saint, Mary, or holy person we are familiar with and ask them to shelter or protect us. Although archangels, angels, and enlightened beings are assisting us all the time, there are times when they cannot interfere or control our lives without our permission. This may seem strange because we assume they're always at our beck and call. But even enlightened beings must abide and respect the laws of free will. At times, they can't assist because without consciously being aware, we've made it imminently clear that our allegiance clearly lies with things like drugs, alcohol, ego, judgement, guilt, greed, money, fear, or self-loathing. It's a bit like this: Imagine that against your family's wishes, you've become involved with someone who frequents a trendy nightclub, hosting all kinds of dark characters behind its glitz and glamour. Then one night, while you're at the club, shooting and fighting break out. When your friend takes off with no regard for your safety, you frantically make a cellphone call home asking for help. Now with your permission, family members rush to assist you. Prayers to enlightened beings are sometimes like that phone call home.

We can also perform a visualization technique in which we surround ourselves with pure golden light. Gold vibrates at the high frequency of enlightenment—demons cannot come near it. It's similar to a vampire being terrified by the light of day. We can visualize a ball of light, egg shape, or pyramid surrounding and protecting us. The more we do this visualization or protection exercise, the stronger we make the energetic force field around ourselves. In time, nothing can penetrate it. It's like building a huge gold brick fortress. If demons have invaded our sleep for a long time, it's important to use these techniques every night. It takes only a minute or two to ensure our safety.

If we're aware in the dream state, we can cast out demons by saying, "In the name of the One True God of light I cast you out," or "In the name of God be gone—you have no power over me." If we find ourselves falling into fear or self-doubt, we can say any prayer that raises our vibration and brings us back to the light. We may say a few words such as, "I align myself with the light," "I stand in my power as a child of the light," or "I honour and believe only in the light." These techniques work well and they're easy to do.

Monsters, Inc.

After learning about nightmares and sleep demons, it's nice to end on a humorous note. The Disney movie *Monsters Inc.* cleverly illustrates that monsters do try to steal our energy while we sleep. The story takes place in another dimension inhabited by monsters of all shapes, sizes, and colours. The two protagonists are James P. Sullivan (Sulley), a big, furry, blue monster, and his best friend, Mike Wazowski, a green one-eyed monster.

Sulley and Mike desperately need children because their entire dimension is run by the energy of children's screams. Mike and Sulley work at a huge factory called Monsters, Inc. that captures the screams of children. The company's motto is "we scare because we care." The factory has an elaborate system of doors leading to children's bedrooms. Every night, monsters (known as "scarers") walk through these doors, cross to the dimension of earth, scare children, and trap the energy of screams in special cylinders. The more energy they trap, the more valuable they become to their employer. Sulley is a hero because he has the distinction of being the top scarer at Monsters, Inc.

When the story opens, however, there is a severe energy shortage. Kids just can't be scared anymore; they've been desensitized by all the violence on earth. The energy shortage is so severe that Mike and Sulley walk to work instead of using their cars. In fact, very few monsters are using their cars any more.

Surprisingly, monsters are terrified of children. They believe if they touch a child or the child's clothing or toys, they will be seriously contaminated. So each monster quickly crosses the dimensional door to the child's room, collects as much scream energy as possible, and makes a quick exit. One night, Sulley is investigating a door to the earth dimension that's been left open. A little girl named Boo follows Sulley. She thinks big furry Sulley is cute and calls him Kitty. But, unfortunately, once she's in the monster's world, the door to her bedroom disappears. This begins a frantic attempt by Sulley and Mike to hide the little girl until they can return her to earth. While they're hiding Boo in their apartment, there is a power blackout because of the energy shortage. When Boo laughs, all the lights go on. Sulley and Mike discover that a child's laughter actually contains *ten times* more energy than screams. This revelation changes everything.

By the end of the movie, all the monsters have taken different training to become clowns or comedians. Instead of learning how to scare children, they're trained to make them laugh. Their main work is still crossing dimensions each night to interact with children, but their new goal is to entertain them so they can trap their laughter.

The energetic theories in *Monsters, Inc.* are quite true. There are monsters, tricksters, and other forces that may try to steal our energy, soul, or spirit each night while we sleep. This energy is largely what keeps them going since they're not connected to the major source of energy, which is God or spirit. As humans, we have a constant supply of energy, unless we've totally turned to the dark side. As long as we stay connected to the light, we're walking light bulbs or energy sources. The more joyful, enlightened, peaceful we are, the more available energy we have. There is indeed more energy in a laugh. Our energy is depleted when we're sad, depressed, or fearful. When we raise our vibration by laughing, smiling, loving, and doing things that give us purpose or joy, we really do outmanoeuvre those demons.

Chapter Nine
Understanding Our Soul's Journey into Other Dimensions: Twenty Keys

He who knows others is wise, he who knows himself is enlightened.
—Lao Tzu

Hard and Fast Rules Do Not Apply to Understanding Dreams

Even though we're going to break down the process of understanding dreams, it's important to realize there is no *one* correct way to do this. This may seem like a contradiction, but there is no magic formula for understanding dreams. It is a completely individual intuitive process. It has nothing to do with intelligence or academic experience. It's often a humbling process achieved by anyone who is sincerely open to growth and change.

When we dream, we're visiting other dimensions, and everyone does this differently. It's like travelling to different cities or countries on earth; every traveller follows the nudges of their spirit and we end up in different places. Dreams are unique to every dreamer because no two souls are the same. We all have different spiritual merit, abilities, tastes, and preferences when we dream. You may routinely choose a dimension that I will never visit, and when you describe this dream, I learn by listening to your experiences. Just as in life, you may routinely visit France because you have friends there, but I may never set foot on French soil.

After we've read and understood all the keys presented here, our mind will file away whatever is important to us. This gives spirit and mind an opportunity to work together. Once this information is filed away, the meaning of a dream will come intuitively in a flash of insight. We won't need to review all kinds of theories or steps to understand what spirit is showing us.

Carl Jung was instrumental in bringing dreams into the twentieth century. Near the end of his life, Jung estimated that he had studied at least eighty thousand dreams. Despite this, in his book *Man and His Symbols* he explained that there is no straightforward way to understand a dream. Each individual varies so much in the way their unconscious or spirit works with the conscious mind that it is "impossible to be sure how far dreams and their symbols can be classified at all." Jung told his pupils to learn as much as they could about symbols and dreams, then to forget it all when they're deciphering their dreams. He said, "This advice is of such practical importance that I have made it a rule to remind myself that I can never understand somebody else's dream well enough to interpret it correctly." Once Jung had two patients, a young man and an old man, who brought him the same dream:

> ...a dream in which a group of young men are riding on horseback across a wide field. The dreamer is in the lead and he jumps a ditch full of water, just clearing this hazard. The rest of the party fall into the ditch. Now the young man who told me this dream was a cautious, introverted type. But I also heard the same dream from an old man of daring character, who had lived an active and enterprising life. At the time he had this dream, he was an invalid who gave his doctor and nurse a great deal of trouble; he had actually injured himself by his disobedience of medical instructions.
>
> It was clear to me that this dream was telling the young man what he *ought* to do. But it was telling the old man what he actually was still *doing*.

With this in mind, let's begin the process of filing away information that will give us insight into our dreams.

The Twenty Keys

1. Recognize that dreams are just as real as our physical life. We're travelling and learning in other dimensions.

2. There will be people, characters, and animals in our dreams from all dimensions and from the past, present, and future since we enter a world without linear time.

3. Dreams are about *us*. They always deal with our karma or dharma.

4. Consider the main emotion felt in the dream. This is key

to true understanding. Look for a key phrase or sentence that sums up the emotional meaning of the dream.

5.   The meaning of dreams is rarely to inflate our ego or to congratulate us. Dreams are pushing to help us understand tough issues we're not consciously aware of.

6.   Dreams are helping us work towards enlightenment: a place of ethics, insight, wisdom, peace, and compassion. This means dreams will never instruct us to do anything that is unethical or uncompassionate towards ourselves or others.

7.   Every symbol in our dreams can have thousands of meanings. There is never just one fixed meaning. The symbols often come from our personal life experiences.

8.   For every symbol there is always duality and directly opposite meanings.

9.   The more we talk about our dreams with family members and friends, the better our chances are of understanding them.

10. If someone or something we're familiar with appears in a dream, ask yourself, what does this represent to me?

11. Look at the overall picture, truth, or metaphor contained in the dream. Try to find one central question that brings it all together.

12. Look for patterns and themes over time.

13. The content of movies and television shows we watch will be transferred to our dreams. This content is often of minor importance.

14. Dream or symbolic dictionaries may be helpful when we begin working with dreams. Over time, we may find we rely less on dictionaries and more on our intuition and knowledge of how symbols work.

15. Some dreams are of major significance, while others have minor importance.

16. Each dream may have several layers of meaning. Over time, these multiple levels or overlays will become more apparent.

17. Allow a period of incubation when we simply leave the dream. Remember, all dreams cannot be understood right away, especially if they are predictive or dreams that prepare us for the future.

18. Try to keep an open mind to new ideas and challenges. Dreams are working to inform our mind. The mind is always resistant to change, even if that change is in our best interests.

19. Trust internal wisdom. Be grateful for this wisdom.

20. Don't feel we have to understand every dream. Just be in awe!

1. Recognize that dreams are just as real as our physical life. We're travelling and learning in other dimensions.

Most of us experience three types of dimensions in dreams.

A. Dreams that are the same as earth, where we stay in the present or go forward in time.
B. Dreams where we perform astral travel or go to a dimension that is slightly different or more evolved.
C. Dreams where we earn the right to travel to more enlightened dimensions where nothing is familiar.

Most of the time we will visit places that are actually on earth but we go forward a week, month, or a few years. In these dreams, everything will be familiar and it will seem incredibly real because it is! Often, we hear people relating a dream followed by the words, "It was so real." The implication in their voices is that this was just a dream, so how could it possibly appear so realistic. If we all understood that dreams are real, a separate reality where our soul is free, we would take a quantum leap forward in our own awareness.

Another scenario is visiting places that seem just like earth, but with slight differences. We may be in high school, an office building, a park, a house, a neigbourhood that *seems* familiar, but we may get lost because it's not exactly the same as that place on earth we know so well. Or it may seem very similar to earth, but then we see something like a computer that we've never seen on earth. In these dreams, we're in parallel dimensions that only seem similar to the earth we know.

A friend described a dream to me once where she had visited a beautiful white temple. Because the architecture was like nothing she had seen on earth, she thought this might be a fantasy or something that wasn't real. If something is extremely beautiful, but not familiar, we may have visited more evolved planets or dimensions. Sometimes we visit more advanced dimensions and we have nothing here that can translate into what we see. Imagine trying to explain a television or CD player to someone living in 1800, before electricity was invented. When we are in more evolved dimensions the colours will often be more brilliant and vibrant. We may see energy vibrating and pulsing. We will witness architecture, nature, paintings, and people of enormous beauty. We may see the energy forms of other beings merging and melding. It is like nothing on earth!

Travelling to other dimensions while we dream is very much like travelling to other countries. Let's say we go to Florida for the first time. We've never seen a book, picture, television commercial, or movie that gave us any information about Florida, so we have no idea what it's like. Imagine the differences when we step off the plane. The temperature feels hotter. People will not look familiar. They may speak with a different accent and use phrases we're not accustomed to like, "Y'all come back now, y'hear." They dress in brighter colours and different styles. There will be palm trees, flowers, and vegetation we've never seen before. Everything will be lusher and greener. We pick fruit from orange and lemon trees in our backyard. As we pick this fruit, two lizards scurry by. The streets are arranged differently—they may even be made with cobblestones. There is a different type of money. Alternatively, we visit a place filled with real mermaids. We may also go to another place inhabited by cartoon characters and a huge mouse wearing red pants. There's a beautiful white castle in the middle of this enchanted land. We can use this analogy of Florida with its different signs, customs, and symbols; it's like going to another dimension while we sleep. Some things may be familiar, but you will encounter symbols, people, and animals that are very different from the physical dimension.

2.   There will be people, characters, and animals in our dreams from all dimensions and from the past, present, and future since we enter a world without linear time.

We will sometimes travel with friends, family members, or people we know. Their soul has agreed to accompany us so that we can enact situations together to help us grow. There will be people in our dreams we don't know but will meet in the future. That is often why there is a spark of recognition or a familiar feeling when we meet someone. One of my friends had dreams when she was pregnant where she was holding a baby up to the sky, laughing, and marvelling at the beauty of his face. Several months after her son was born, she realized he was definitely that baby from her dreams.

Since we're travelling in dimensions without linear time, deceased loved ones can frequently visit our dreams. After my mother died, for a while I actually saw her more then I had in physical life! We may enact situations with people we knew in other physical lifetimes or in other dimensions. Most frequently, we go forward in time in the dream state to observe, experience, rehearse, or test out anything our soul realizes is necessary to help us prepare. Our soul knows exactly who to take along.

3.   Dreams are about *us*. They always deal with our karma or dharma.

The purpose of dreams is to help us evolve and move forward. Every dream is either helping us work through our issues or karma, or they are helping us carry out our destiny or dharma. Dreams rarely give us information about what other people need to do because they focus on how we can personally become aware and move forward.

Dreamwork, however, is never black and white; there are always exceptions. Let's say we run a restaurant and have a business partner Nick, who we trust implicitly. Unfortunately, Nick is doing a few underhanded things. We may have a dream of being in the restaurant making coffee and we notice that Nick should have given a half-blind little old lady $20 in change but he only gives her $5. Then we watch as Nick tells a teenager we're all out of pizza, then goes into the kitchen where he begins devouring the last two large pizzas. This dream may be making us aware that we can't always trust Nick the way we thought.

We're not likely to have a dream telling us that our next-door neighbour "Fanny" needs to lose seventy pounds. However, if at 2 a.m.

Fanny is taking our car without telling us and driving to Tim Horton's to sneak home a dozen donuts, we may become aware of this in a dream. We're not given information about other people in dreams unless that person has a direct effect on our lives. Most dreams are about us and the people and places that impact our lives.

Since dreams are personal, it often helps to consider what the most important issues are in our lives. Are we dealing with changes in our career, relationships, friendships, or place of residence? Are we embarking on a new venture? What fears, anxieties, or challenges are we dealing with? Are there things we're afraid to change? What have we been putting off doing? Is there anything stressful or unpleasant that seems to repeat over and over? If we're honest, what would our weak areas or issues really be? If someone were to ask what the most important issue in our life is right now, how would we respond? In many cases, this will be what our dream is about (or it will be about anything that is difficult or painful for us to face). If we're totally naive about Fanny's propensity to "borrow" our car because we believe she's the best neighbour in the world, then our dreams may enlighten us.

Since our lives are incredibly complex, it's possible to be working through several issues simultaneously while we dream. If we were able to remember four dreams in one night, the first dream may deal with our naiveté surrounding Fanny's borrowing the car. In the second dream, we may be exploring other job possibilities. The third dream may be helping us release feelings we still carry for an old relationship. And dream number four may be helping us decide whether to buy a new car.

4. Consider the main emotion felt in the dream. This is key to true understanding. Look for a key phrase or sentence that sums up the emotional meaning of the dream.

Our emotions do not lie to us in dreams. Our emotional body is really our soul. Words may lie, but emotions don't, so they bring out personal truth while we sleep. While it's possible to twist, distort, misunderstand, or misinterpret words, emotions are conveyed with honesty in dreams. This is probably the single most important key to remember when working with dreams.

It's through emotions that our soul communicates with us. The emotions that emerge in dreams provide a barometer to gauge exactly how we're feeling in our outer lives. They provide a mirror image, outwardly reflecting our fears, joys, and frustrations so that these feelings may illuminate us with greater clarity.

For example, we can take the exact same dream: someone trying to swim across a lake. In the first dream, as we're swimming across the lake, we easily reach the opposite shore feeling energized and invigorated the entire time. Our spirit is showing us that whatever challenge we've dived into will be positive and energizing. In the second dream, we feel exhausted and defeated while we're swimming, and we never reach the opposite shore. Our spirit may be telling us if we pursue this challenge it may leave us drained and exhausted so perhaps this isn't the best time to dive into this venture.

Often, when we write or talk about a dream, there is one key sentence that summarizes everything. I've listened to countless people retelling a dream for their first time. They end with one or two sentences, often emotional in nature, which brilliantly summarize the entire dream. This may be followed by a blank or puzzled facial expression when their mind clicks in, and they think they have no clear understanding of the dream. Their soul, however, has already provided great insight:

- "I felt scared to death,"
- "I knew I had to change something,"
- "I felt everyone was always after me,"
- "The car was moving too fast, I felt completely out of control,"
- "I knew I had to keep driving through this storm, although it would be difficult,"
- "I knew inside that everything would be okay,"
- "I felt completely trapped and closed in,"
- "I knew I just had to take one more step to get there, but I was afraid to,"
- "I was carrying around so much heavy baggage it was impossible to do anything,"
- "I was so excited because I knew this wasn't as difficult as I thought,"
- "I was so happy because this felt exactly right," or
- "I realized with dread I'd done this over and over before and it was a huge mistake"

These examples from dreamers convey exactly what emotions we're experiencing in our physical lives.

5. The meaning of dreams is rarely to inflate our ego or to congratulate us. Dreams are pushing to help us understand tough issues we're not consciously aware of.

Dreams will direct us towards our dharma or destiny, but they usually don't tell us what we already know. This would be a waste of our soul's valuable time. If we're successful athletes, we're not going to have a dream telling us how great we are. Dreams rarely complement or boost our ego since the purpose of dreams is to help us evolve. Overinflating our ego only keeps us trapped in karma and illusion. As we enlighten, we're working to substantially dissolve our ego until we reach a place of greater humility. It's important to keep this in mind. If we choose a meaning that's self-congratulatory, or anything that says we're wonderful—smarter than our best friend, or better looking than our sister—we may be inflating our ego and staying trapped in illusion rather than gaining new insights and awareness. Dreams usually push us gently in directions our mind has great difficulty accepting.

6. Dreams are helping us work towards enlightenment: a place of ethics, insight, wisdom, peace, and compassion. This means dreams will never instruct us to do anything that is unethical or uncompassionate towards ourselves or others.

Generally, dreams don't tell us what to do; they simply give us heightened awareness and it's usually up to us how to act on these insights. It's pretty safe to say we'll never have a dream that instructs us to start a war, blow up a building, scream at our best friend, or demonstrate any type of hostility, anger, or aggression. Spirit always operates in a moral, compassionate, sometimes humorous way. Dreams may help us break through powerful illusions and gain important insights. It's important to act on these insights within a moral framework. If a series of dreams helps us become aware that someone has never loved or respected us, our mind may be tempted to yell and scream at this person, or to break off the relationship in bitterness and anger. The trap here is that this only creates more karma. A dharmic course of action may be to sit down with this person, have a heart-to-heart talk, end the relationship on good terms, and then look forward to continued guidance in dreams.

7. Every symbol in our dreams can have thousands of meanings. There is never just one fixed meaning. The symbols often come from our personal life experiences.

Our soul is highly creative, so it will adapt symbolic meanings from our life experiences. These are called personal symbols. For example, if our favourite grandmother always wore the colour red and had a vase of red roses in the living room, red would represent her warmth and love for us. Or maybe we had a cruel sadistic grandmother who always wore red. Or if we had a severe nosebleed as a child and bled all over our favourite red outfit, we may remember this day as extremely traumatic. If our nosebleeds continued for several years, the colour red could symbolize loss of control, anxiety, and fear.

In many dreams we're doing things that are familiar to us. If riding a bike is a great source of freedom and fun for us, bicycles could frequently appear in our dreams in a positive way and could show our life was balanced. Or we may ride our bike in dreams to explore. But if we experienced a terrible accident—perhaps we were hit by a car while riding a bike and this memory was painful—we may seldom, if ever, ride a bike in our dreams. If we did, they would represent trauma or loss of control.

If we always grew up with a dog and we had a close relationship with dogs as a child, dogs in our dreams could represent companionship, comfort, or guidance. Dogs may often appear in dreams since they're part of the landscape of our life. But if we never had a dog and we were bitten by the neighbour's dog when we were six years old, then dogs in dreams may represent danger or terror.

Some of my students who were hockey players always visited hockey arenas in their dreams. Other students who were promising singers or performers were frequently rehearsing or singing on stage. When I was a photographer, for many years I was often in darkrooms in my dreams trying to see what develops. Now that I am also a teacher, I frequently have dreams in classroom settings.

Archetypal symbols are often different from personal symbols. They represent first forms or blueprints. They are charged with energy and deeper emotions that can be the same for many people since archetypes come from the collective unconscious, rather than from personal experience. For example, the devil is usually associated with evil; magicians are associated with magic and mysticism; and rings or circles symbolize union or wholeness. White is most often associated with purity or heaven, and angels always represent good. But the archetypal mother can bring up different meanings depending on the experiences you've had. Mother can evoke images of a loving caregiver or a rough taskmaster. To determine the meaning of any symbol, we need to ask what experiences we've had with this symbol.

8. For every symbol there is always duality and directly opposite meanings.

Almost every symbol can have directly opposite meanings. Colours are good examples of this duality. Green is the colour of grass and living things and often denotes growth. It's the colour of the fourth chakra or heart centre denoting love, warmth, and compassion. It is also the colour associated with money or abundance. But we've all heard the phrase "green with envy." In Shakespeare's *Othello*, the villain Iago's famous words are "O beware, my lord, of jealousy! It is the green-eyed monster..." So green can denote growth, nature, love, compassion, abundance, affluence, or negative qualities such as envy or jealousy.

Blue is a colour often associated with wisdom or spirituality. Mary, the mother of Jesus, always wears blue. When we're depressed, we feel blue, so the same colour also represents sadness or depression. In the West, black often symbolizes evil, darkness, depression. But to the Egyptians, black was the colour of rebirth and resurrection. It can symbolize new life and regeneration since babies are born from the darkness of a mother's womb. The colour white in the West is associated with purity, virginity, peace, innocence, and cleanliness. But Chinese and Indian traditions link white with mourning, funerals, death, and ghosts. Snakes in the West usually symbolize Satan or evil. But in ancient times, they symbolized wisdom, regeneration, and healing since a snake has the capacity to continually shed and regrow its skin. Fire can represent death, devastation, and destruction, but it can also represent purification or rebirth. Again we can always look at our experiences and emotions around any symbol to discover its meaning for us.

It's also important to understand that many sacred symbols have developed opposite meanings after they were manipulated by dark forces. The *swastika* is an example most people are familiar with. In ancient cultures, it was a symbol of peace, joy, life, and luck. It was found in India, China, Japan, and was well known to the Vikings, Celts, Greeks, Christians, Mayans, and several North and Central American aboriginal groups. The word *swastika* came from Sanskrit *su* meaning "well" and *asti* meaning "is" or "to be," and translated as "well-being." In its original form, it was a wheel representing perpetual regeneration, the motion of the sun, transcendence, and was associated with saviours such as Christ and Buddha. After the Nazi party in Germany adopted this symbol, Hitler had the swastika rotated to a 45° angle to symbolize revolution. For many, it became a symbol of terror, hatred, and fear.

In ancient times, the number *thirteen* represented God. This is why in Christianity there were twelve apostles and Christ—thirteen—representing God. Since this number held great power, it was utilized by dark forces until we came to believe it was an unlucky number. We think we'll have bad luck on "Friday the thirteenth" when this was originally a powerful sacred day. Today, when we go into high-rise buildings, the number thirteen is rarely listed on elevators because it's considered unlucky.

The *pentagram* or five-pointed star, was a symbol of the goddess Athena. It stood for light, perfection, and wholeness. When it was later used for magic, both its name and position changed. As a dark symbol, it's called a pentacle. In its pure spiritual form there is one point upward and two points downward. As a dark magical symbol, there are two points upward and one point downward representing a goat's foot or the horns of the devil.

Whatever we believe about a symbol is usually the way it's used in dreams and our waking life. If we believe thirteen is an unlucky number, that's how it will be represented in dreams. If we believe all dogs are vicious, that's how they'll appear when we sleep. If the colour red causes us great anxiety, that's the way it will manifest in dreams, but for someone else, red could symbolize warmth and love.

9. The more we talk about dreams with family members and friends, the better our chances are of understanding them.

It's tough to be honest and objective when trying to understand our own dreams. Since dreams often reveal what we don't want to see or admit, it may be easy for others to instantly see the meaning of our dreams even if they've had no experience with dreamwork. It can be easy to see the messages in our best friend's dream but difficult to understand our own. Family members and friends often intuitively know. Since they're familiar with our life they can usually provide great insight. Often, just by telling someone a dream, we start to recognize its meaning. Sometimes just one word or phrase in our description makes things clear. It's important to only share dreams with people we trust—those who have our best interests at heart or someone who respects and honours dreams. If we begin revealing intimate details of our life or dreams to someone who may belittle or devalue us, we're not acting in our best interests.

10. If someone or something we're familiar with appears in a dream, ask yourself, what does this represent to me?

This question is often the key to understanding many dreams. Everything can have completely different meanings depending on what our life experiences have been with that person or thing that shows up in a dream. One of my friends had a detailed dream involving an aquarium; below is a small part of it. I love aquariums and can watch them for hours. It's a very meditative, soothing activity for me. But, as my friend explains, she certainly didn't have warm fuzzy emotions around aquariums. Without her providing background information, I could have never guessed what this dream was about:

> My dream was that I was watching fish in an aquarium (home-size variety). When my ex-husband lived here, he dealt with aquariums—it's the first time that I was up close to these things, and even though fish are supposed to be calming I saw some pretty ugly battles where fish would fight to the death and I couldn't stand watching the male fish not leave some of the females alone. One time it practically looked like the female fish would die the way the male was pushing and slamming her around and then finally penetrated her. I never had "nice" feelings about aquariums as other people do. Plus, it was my former husband's hobby, which also had negative feelings for me. The other part I detested about home aquariums was watching the female fish hatch babies, and then the babies would all be eaten—ALL of them. There was no respect for new life or life in that old fish bowl.

Now let's examine people and their unique significance or meaning in a dream. Imagine you're a tall skinny kid growing up in Saskatoon. You always feel out of place because your father is Black and your mother is White. You're shy, a loner; everyone teases and ridicules you, including your parents. Your parents tell you you'll never amount to anything. Eventually, you leave and become a successful model in New York, achieving international status because of your unique look. You begin acting in movies and enjoy further success. Then you're temporarily out of work and all those emotions of insecurity and self-doubt from childhood resurface. You begin having recurring dreams in which you're wandering around the streets of Saskatoon desperately trying to find modelling jobs. People from your past are making fun of you and you wander aimlessly up and down streets never finding work. In your physical life, you may be thinking, "I'm a total loser, I can't get work, I should move home with my parents." If this dream repeats, you could ask, "What does Saskatoon represent to me?" The answer is that Saskatoon was a place where you felt uncomfortable, judged, and dishonoured. Your dream is telling you that you're trying to go back to a place that doesn't respect you or recognize your gifts. You'll just keep wandering around aimlessly as you did in the dream.

In another dream, you may be successfully flying a plane that is carrying many passengers. Then a relative, Uncle Jimmy from Saskatoon, gets beside you in the cockpit and announces he'll give you flying lessons. As soon as Jimmy takes the controls, the plane crashes into a lake. No one is killed, but the dream ends as everyone is floundering about the water in complete chaos. Suitcases and parts of the plane are everywhere. You could ask, "What does Jimmy represent to me?" The answer would be your old way of doing things, the way you've navigated through life before you became independent and successful. Maybe Jimmy's entire family believed modelling or acting weren't real jobs. So here, the dream is indicating that if you fall back on your old belief systems, it will be disastrous; you may crash in life. You won't die, but it certainly won't feel good.

Conversely, people and places may appear in dreams that represent positive experiences, directions, and possibilities. Maybe your destiny is in London, England, and Uncle Nick who lives there is the kindest, wisest, most compassionate person you know. You're living in Texas, but things just didn't work out; you're broke and going from job to job. Meanwhile, you keep dreaming about Uncle Nick's busy upscale restaurant in London. In these dreams, you're preparing fine cuisine and loving it. In one dream, you actually win a prestigious cooking award. Again, you could ask, "What does Uncle Nick or cooking mean to me?" The answer may be a job opportunity as a chef-in-training you were offered but declined. Maybe Uncle Nick represented a warm family member who respected and nurtured you.

11. Look at the overall picture, truth, or metaphor contained in the dream. Try to find one central question that brings it all together.

Try to see the big picture, rather than getting lost in all kinds of details. Dreams often provide brilliant metaphors or comparisons to our life. We can look at the main character and ask ourselves, "How am I like this person?" or "What themes are similar in my life?" For example, a married man with two children dreams he's stranded on an island. He suddenly realizes that his body parts, including his arms and legs, are floating away. He had this dream just after making the decision to separate from his wife. Rather than trying to understand each symbol separately—island, water, stranded, arms, legs, body parts—it's easier to see the story as a whole. His central question could be, "What am I losing?" "What parts of me are drifting away?" "What's really happening to me in this dream?" or "Is this like my life in any way?" The answer is obvious: he's losing parts of himself, his wife, and his children.

Another man had a dream in which he watched in horror as his house burned down. His wife was upstairs frying eggs, and she died in the fire. This doesn't mean his wife is really going to die. During this time, he was seeing his wife less because she had started a new business. The eggs represented the new life she was cooking up. Rather than getting caught up in all the details—the burning house, second floor, frying pan, eggs, flames, wife, death—and trying to understand each symbol separately, he could ask, "What is happening to my wife in the dream and in physical life?" The answer: her time as a stay-at-home wife is dead or over. She's cooking up new things.

Let's imagine in dreams we have antiques and useless junk, and we're always carrying it with us to work, restaurants, and social situations. We may be carrying around old clothes, books, kitchen utensils, lamps, rope, small kitchen appliances, rugs, and ornaments. Rather than looking all these items up in a dream dictionary, we may ask:

- "What am I doing in this dream that is the same as my physical life?"
- "What do I need to unload from my life right now?"
- "Have I surrounded myself with too much dead energy?"
- "Am I carrying around too much from the past?"
- "Do I have too much junk in my life?"

- "Am I carrying around a lot of garbage in life?" or
- "Do I carry around a lot of ideas that are just garbage?"

12. Look for patterns and themes over time.

Once we start keeping a dream journal, we'll realize that themes run from dream to dream. A theme may continue for months or even years until we've worked it out. For example, over a three-month period we may realize we had five driving dreams in which we took a left turn. This may symbolize an unwise decision since we did not make the *right* turn (or it could be the other way around, left may always work out for us).

We may remember having several dreams in which we crossed different bridges. This could indicate we're making a transition, reaching a destination, crossing over to new territory in life, or exploring a new idea. We may have dreams in which we're wandering around in basements, which may represent our desire to uncover issues from our past. Or it may represent that we've delved into the dark recesses of our unconscious through dreamwork for the first time. If we start to journal our dreams, we'll be able to pick up personal symbols used repeatedly. Usually, the symbol is something we're familiar with. We may start seeing bedrooms in our dreams every time we're not getting enough sleep. We may be driving a car and making a left turn rather than the *right* turn every time we've made a decision that isn't working.

13. The content of movies and television shows we watch will be transferred to our dreams. This content is often of minor importance.

If we frequently watch *Star Wars*, the characters and props from this show will frequently become part of our dream landscape. We may be a Jedi warrior fighting Darth Vader in our dreams. Someone who takes a bus to work every day may take buses in their dreams. If we watch a lot of horror movies, the sets of our dreams may be horrific and scary. If we like westerns, there may be cowboys and horses in our dreams. In most cases, these are merely the props or movie sets of our dream landscape. It's more important to examine what we're doing and the emotions we're feeling in the dream and in waking life.

Sometimes there are exceptions. If we watch a movie or television show and the theme is similar to our life, our spirit may cleverly incorporate this into a dream. But my hunch is that this phenomena isn't that common. It's only happened to me once when I watched a

SpongeBob SquarePants cartoon. In the episode, SpongeBob's boss Mr. Krab decides he's going to make some fast money by taking things from his neighbour's garbage cans and selling them in a garage sale. During this time in my life, I had accumulated an incredible amount of junk since I had lived in the same house for twenty years. I hated to throw things away, so I'd become a real pack rat. That night in my dream, I realized I had an incredible amount of junk around me, useless things I didn't need, like old pieces of lumber. I was at a workplace so I took this junk to the designated spot for garbage. I returned a few minutes later with another load only to find an employee had taken her garbage to the same spot, but, like Mr. Krab, she'd put a price tag on it hoping someone would buy it. In the dream I was really upset and realized even more the stupidity of keeping old things that often just weigh us down physically and emotionally. Unfortunately, I didn't have *SpongeBob SquarePants* cartoon characters in my dream, but watching that show definitely piqued my awareness.

14. Dream or symbolic dictionaries may be helpful when we begin working with dreams. Over time, we may find we rely less on dictionaries and more on our intuition and knowledge of how symbols work.

A good symbolic dictionary may be an extremely useful tool. Always pick a dictionary that gives *several* meanings for one symbol. There are many excellent dictionaries, but some are absolute garbage. To begin, it's often helpful to have two or three different dictionaries to consult. Often, one will not contain the word we're after. Sometimes the wording or information will be different in one dictionary and it will immediately fit or feel right for us. Remember, intuition is our most useful tool in understanding dreams. Some dreamers don't need dictionaries at all; others use them all the time. If symbolism really interests someone, they may accumulate a small library of dream and symbolic dictionaries. There's no right or wrong; it's a matter of individual choice.

15. Some dreams are of major significance, while others have minor importance.

Our lives are filled with routine days and days that may be significant or life altering. Dreams work the same way; some can be life changing. Carl Jung referred to these as "big dreams." These dreams are so vivid and essential to our growth that they're unforgettable. Their memory and the accompanying emotions remain etched into our psyche. We may have an extremely significant dream that deals with changing careers, moving to a new country, starting a new relationship, or overcoming something we've always feared. I've had only two or three of these "big dreams" in my life. Other dreams simply run through our day and provide a mirror of daily events. They may indicate we went to work, did our job, and at the end of the day felt exhausted because we didn't get enough sleep. Every dream will not be earth shattering, but each of them are important steps in our journey, and each step is required to arrive at our destination of enlightenment.

16. Each dream may have several layers of meaning. Over time, these multiple levels or overlays will become more apparent.

Any dream is like an intricate symbolic novel. With each reading, we gain new insights and awareness. We see and understand things we didn't see before. This doesn't mean that our first understanding was incorrect, only that we've added new layers to our understanding. It can be like peeling away layers of an onion to get to the core. As we grow in awareness, our appreciation of the dream becomes deeper and more multifaceted. This is why it's always a great exercise to go back and reread our dream journals. It can be great verification of just how far we've come.

17. Allow a period of incubation when we simply leave the dream. Remember, all dreams cannot be understood right away, especially if they are predictive or dreams that prepare us for the future.

If we've written down our dream, looked up the symbols, talked about it, and the meaning still isn't clear, it may be a good idea to just let life unfold. This is most important with dreams that are helping us prepare for the future. We may go back to the dream in two weeks or two months with completely different insights. Sometimes we can go back to a dream a week later and the meaning is immediately clear. There will be other times when the wisdom of the dream isn't evident until a year or two later. Usually, something needs to occur in our waking life before the dream will make sense.

18. Try to keep an open mind to new ideas and challenges. Dreams are working to inform our mind. The mind is always resistant to change, even if that change is in our best interests.

Dreams take place in the spirit world and are brought into memory by our conscious mind. Our minds are often resistant to change. They're like computers designed to continually run the same programs. Our mind always chooses what is familiar. It also likes to be the boss and have all the control and not let spirit in. So when we start journalling dreams, spirit is informing the mind and working like a partner. This becomes like a dance between mind and spirit. It may begin with mechanical steps but has the potential for a rhythmic flow. The goal of this dance is actually marriage or melding of the mind and spirit. We can't understand dreams solely with the mind—it's too mechanical and relies only on what has happened in the past. Intuitive nudges, all genius and insight, come from the soul. If we sincerely want to understand what the dream is showing us, it will eventually come. If our intent is pure, it will happen. If we pay attention to spirit, it pays attention to us.

As we work with dreams, we invite spirit into our mind or intellect. Eventually, our mind becomes whole or holy. We will have more flashes of insight and awareness. We will begin to see things with greater clarity and wisdom. Instead of slow mechanical steps, there is a harmonious flow of information.

19. Trust internal wisdom. Be grateful for this wisdom.

We're the experts on our life and emotions so we're best equipped to make sense of our dreams. Trust in soul's desire to move us towards wholeness and wisdom. Having faith in this wisdom can be one of our greatest assets. Spirit, not the mind, knows why we are here, what karma needs to be cleaned up, and how we can fulfill our destiny so that we live with purpose, passion, and peace. We're all inherently wise if we listen to the rumblings of our spirit.

20. Don't feel we have to understand every dream. Just be in awe!

Over time, we can begin to see our dreams as nightly soul travel. If we don't understand a dream with our mind right away, that's fine. Our mind may have no idea what a dream is all about, but our spirit knows. We can still be in awe! We can still be grateful. It's not necessary to make sense of every dream. Some may be preparing us for events that may happen five or ten years away. If we have the right intent—spiritual growth—we eventually get what we need. Dreamwork can become a frustrating mental process, rather than an exciting spiritual journey if we try too hard or feel we should understand every dream. There are no "shoulds" with dreams, only continual challenges, insights, and new levels of awareness.

Chapter Ten
Common Dream Symbols

In symbols there is meaning that words cannot define.
—Ibn al-Farid, Arab poet

We learned in the previous chapter that everyone dreams differently. Although the twenty keys may be important in the beginning, most dreamers will gradually file away the information. They'll understand their dreams without having to read, analyze, or mentally go through a lot of steps. It's the same with symbols. Most of us need to understand how symbols work in the beginning before making sense of our dreams. But this can be different for everyone. When I was doing dreamwork with high-school students, I always had five or six dream dictionaries in the room. Since I needed several dictionaries when I got started, I assumed everyone else would too. But over the years, I observed that some students loved symbolism and couldn't get enough of it, others looked up symbols occasionally, and some didn't need dream dictionaries at all. Intuitively, they were able to make perfect sense of their dreams.

If we study Jungian psychology, it may seem that everything revolves around symbols and the deep understanding of these symbols. Dreamwork can almost become an academic or mental study of symbolism. But what's most important is understanding the emotions that lie beneath these symbols.

For the novice, understanding symbols will provide real guidance—a starting point or foundation. Working with symbols is like learning how to print for the first time. We learn the mechanics of printing to prepare us for the more flowing process of writing. Or it's like learning to play a song using musical notation as a guide. In time, musicians don't need to look at these musical symbols to play everything. Their music ceases to be mechanical and comes from inside. The best musicians close their eyes and play from the heart. It's the same with dreams and symbols. Once we have a foundation in symbolism, understanding dreams isn't mechanical any longer—like writing and music, it begins to flow from inside us.

As we read these common symbols, we'll notice there is a relationship or logic between each symbol and our lives. For example, if we're dreaming about a caterpillar becoming a butterfly, this probably corresponds to a major breakthrough or transformation in our life. Perhaps life lacked scope somehow; maybe it was routine, physical, earthbound, based on illusions, and something has happened that gives us greater freedom or allows our spirit to soar. This type of dream could occur when we get married for the first time, have our first baby, land a job we've been working towards for years, leave an abusive relationship, or see through faulty belief systems that have trapped us for years. Symbols will rarely mean something that is totally unrelated. In working with dreams, we use the logic of these symbols along with intuition to arrive at a meaning that makes sense— mind and spirit working in harmony. Once we have this foundation, symbols no longer become a mystery. Instead, like music and writing, they become instruments that can illuminate and inform our lives.

Animals

The word *animal* comes from the Latin word *anima*, meaning "soul or breath of life." The energies of animals can offer tremendous healing qualities and insights. We often need to consider the unique qualities of this animal. Our dreams may be mirrors showing us that we've been acting or feeling like this animal. If we've been dreaming of turtles, perhaps we've become too timid or developed a hard outer shell. Or perhaps we need to acquire the slow and steady patience of a turtle to win the race of life. In the dream *The Frustrated Frog*, the dreamer felt like a rubbery frog stretched to the limit because of school, exams, essays, and social activities. But a frog is also a symbol of transformation since it changes from a tadpole to a quite different creature. So frogs can remind us that anything in life can change or transform drastically.

Animal dreams may also be showing us qualities we need to merge or integrate. A tiger in a dream may be telling us we've been acting like a tiger, stalking and growling at people, or we may be too submissive and our dream is encouraging us to integrate or develop the strength and confidence of a tiger. Examining our personality and what is going on in our lives always gives us clues to understand these dreams. (The dream *Devil Bear* in the next chapter is an excellent example.) If the energies of an animal hold important insights for us, we may begin seeing this animal in our waking life too. My favourite resource on animals is Ted Andrews' book *Animal-Speak*.

Birth

People often dream of having a baby or giving birth when something new begins in their life. So dreams of giving birth can be common since there are so many potential new things that can happen. Both men and women can dream of having a baby when they're in the process of initiating something new or promising. We could have this type of dream if we start a new job, relationship, marriage, move to a new home, start attending a new school, find a new friend, start a new sport or hobby, or give birth to a new level of ideas, insights, or understandings. We can also have birth dreams symbolizing a new beginning when we retire from a job, leave a relationship, or let go of people, places, or activities that were holding us back.

Bugs

This usually indicates something that is *bugging* or annoying us or is a real *pest* in our life. The location of the bugs often tells us where the problem is. Are they in our home, place of work, or on our body? If the bugs are biting, this may indicate the problem is literally getting under our skin. Bugs on our body could also mean we have caught some "bug" or may be getting a cold or the flu. If the bugs are slowly creeping or crawling toward us, this may indicate an approaching problem. Sometimes bugs can be positive creatures. It may be important to distinguish the type of bug. For example, dreaming of a ladybug may symbolize good luck. The ladybug was named after Our Lady the Virgin Mary because of its hard work in getting rid of pests on plants. Other bugs may help us sift or sort through problems. In many myths, fables, and fairy tales, bugs often appear in a crisis to help the heroine.

In the myth *Cupid and Psyche*, Psyche is given the impossible task of sorting piles of the smallest seeds: wheat, barley, millet, and poppy. Her jealous mother-in-law Aphrodite gives her this job believing Psyche will never succeed. Psyche cries in despair, but is comforted by armies of ants who arrive and work through the night skilfully separating and dividing the seeds. By morning, the seeds are arranged into perfect order.

Buildings

Buildings in our dreams are the sets or backgrounds in our dream movies. They reflect the mood, tone, and atmosphere of our life. So buildings symbolize what we've constructed in life along with the perceptions and emotions we have toward these places. Leaving a building could mean we're leaving behind ideas or moving from one state of awareness to another. Exploring buildings may symbolize exploring or investigating ideas or options in life. Decrepit, decaying, or old-fashioned buildings can represent old ideas or places that no longer serve us. New buildings or places under construction may symbolize a new venture in our life, rebuilding, or developing new attitudes.

Cars

Cars are one of the most fascinating symbols. They represent our body, ego, or the state of affairs in our life. They symbolize our internal drive or the way we're moving through life. Where we are in the car is often important. If we're in the driver's seat, this may symbolize that we're in control. If we're in the back seat being driven by someone else, we're often under the control or authority of others. Teenagers frequently dream of being driven by their parents. If we're in a car that's running out of control, this may represent that our life is literally out of control. If the car is running too fast, not stopping at traffic lights, or if we can't apply the brakes, this may symbolize that our life has become fast paced or hectic. If we're driving too slowly and others are passing us, we may need to speed up something in life; maybe we're being left behind. If our car is on fire or overheated, we've probably been hot-headed, angry, or involved in an explosive situation. If we have a flat tire, this could be showing us we've been totally deflated by someone, or we've somehow lost our drive or energy. If we're driving a miniature or children's car, the dream may be encouraging us to grow up. If our car is full of garbage, we may need to clean up some aspect of our life. If the car's windows are covered so that visibility is poor, this could suggest we're going through life with blind spots. There may be important things on the road of life we're not seeing or don't want to face.

Imagine a dream where you've been driving a beat-up rusted Volkswagen. You're almost out of gas. Then your boss gives you the keys to a new Mercedes Benz and says it's yours to drive for the next year. What could this indicate? What if the dream was the other way around?

Child

We've all heard the expression "out of the mouths of babes." A young child may utter unbelievable wisdom, possibly something we've been trying our entire lives to understand. They represent purity, innocence, simplicity, and clear meaning. In dreams, children may impart great insight; this may be the wisdom of our soul or unblemished "inner child" speaking to us. These children may help us see that we're not meeting our full potential, that we've been acting immature, impulsive, self-centred, or childish; or that we've cut ourselves off from expressing true joy and emotion, or they may help us regain a sense of childlike innocence, trust, awe, and wonder.

In dreams, children may also act as mirrors showing us both positive and negative characteristics. A neglected, battered, or abused child may be showing us that we've neglected or have not nurtured ourselves. If we watch a child bullying or hurting someone else, this may be mirroring our own behaviour. Perhaps we've been a bully with friends, co-workers, siblings, or our children. Looking to patterns of our lives always provides answers. If we dream of a stubborn, insolent child who has been screaming and yelling just after we've had a huge shouting match with our best friend, then the dream's meaning becomes obvious.

If we learn the age of the child, perhaps we're a five-year-old, we may consider what important event happened to us at age five, or we may ask what happened five years ago. If we're going back to our childhood home in dreams, this usually indicates there are childhood issues we have yet to resolve. It's not uncommon to spend months or years revisiting the haunts of our childhood to understand what happened and heal our wounds. Without this important function of dreams, we would remain wounded children forever rather than fully conscious adults.

Clothes

There is a saying that clothes make the person. In dreams, clothes present a mirror image of how we appear or our emotional state in the physical world. They represent our persona, façade, the games we play, the attitudes, emotions, and ideas we "put on" for others, or our level of awareness. Think of the fairy tale "The Emperor's New Clothes." Sometimes we're totally unaware of the public presentation we're making or that our clothes or beliefs are outdated or inappropriate. In life, clothes can hide, conceal, or help us appear to be something we're not. But in dreams, clothes reveal the naked truth.

The way we're dressed in a dream represents the image we're presenting or trying to present. If we're changing our clothes or shopping for new clothes, this may symbolize how our lives are changing or being recreated. The type of clothes we're wearing and their condition is significant. If we're wearing children's clothes, the dream may be showing that our attitudes and behaviour may be childish. If our clothing seems inappropriate and we feel embarrassed and out of place, this is often how we feel in physical life. We may be trying to fit in. If someone is lavishly dressed or their clothes seem out of place but they're still cool and confident in the dream, these people are comfortable with themselves and have no desire to fit into the status quo. If our clothes are dirty, ragged, or unkept, there are issues we've been neglecting. If clothes are worn out and old-fashioned, then our belief system and ideas may be the same. When clothes are too large, we may need time to grow into something, or we may have taken on something too big for us. If we're taking off or discarding clothes, we may be getting rid of old belief systems and becoming more in touch with who we are. If we're washing clothes, we may be cleansing or cleaning up.

Death

We may dream of a friend or relative's actual death months or even years before it takes place. This often occurs when there is a strong link or bond with this person. The dreams occur to help us prepare at a soul or emotional level so that we won't be completely traumatized when the death occurs. But most of the time dreams of death are highly symbolic. Dreams of our own death are often positive, symbolizing the end of one phase of our life and the beginning or transition to something new. We could dream of our own death when we meet a new circle of friends, change schools, change jobs, quit a team, get married, end a relationship, or retire from a long career. Dreams of death may also signify a desire to connect with a higher wisdom or may symbolize a new level of awareness, leaving behind old ideas or ways of thinking. Dreams of other people dying may indicate their influence on us is dying out or *they* may be going through real changes. Watching a person we know kill or shoot someone may help us become aware of this person's shadow or dark side. Perhaps in life they are manipulating, abusing, or killing someone's spirit.

Disease

Looking at this word closely is our first clue: *dis–ease*. If we have an illness in a dream, such as cancer or AIDS, we may ask, "What in life is eating away at me, or causing me to feel sick, toxic, or ill at *ease*?" The answers can be endless: someone constantly bullying us, a negative person at work or school, or an annoying neighbour or relative. Although there may be times when dreams of having a disease are literal—alerting us to an actual illness—in most cases, these dreams are symbolic—our soul is simply trying to make us aware of a potentially toxic situation or person in our lives.

Exams

This is one of the most common dream themes since we all attend school and experience the pressure of writing exams. The scenarios may vary: failing an exam, arriving late for an exam, realizing we haven't attended the classes we needed, or realizing with horror that we can't answer a single exam question. These dreams usually deal with feelings of inadequacy or fear of failure. We may feel we're not equipped to pass this new job, relationship, test, trial, or challenge in life. A dream of being on stage and unprepared, not knowing our lines, or having stage fright may be similar. In both cases, we feel unequipped to meet life's karmic or dharmic challenges.

Falling

This is the second most universal dream theme. Dreams of falling often symbolize fear of failure if we've climbed high in our personal or professional life, a loss of control, a steep plunge into the unknown, feeling emotionally overwhelmed, out of control, or that we have no support. We could dream of falling if our company is downsizing, if we're afraid of losing our job, or if we're afraid we won't have the marks to graduate from school. These dreams may also symbolize emotional turmoil, not feeling grounded, or a fear of falling from grace. For example, a teenage girl who was raised in a strict Catholic family had a series of falling dreams after she became sexually intimate with her boyfriend. Her dream reflected deep-seated guilt about falling from grace in her parents' eyes.

Falling often represents feelings of intense insecurity—the sense that we have nothing to hold on to and are plunging to disaster. It may be important to consider what happens at the end of the fall. What do we fall onto? Is it a safety net or a rocky abyss? Are we rescued from our fall? Are we okay in the dream despite our fall? If we fall into a safety net, our spirit is making us aware that things will turn out fine. Perhaps we just need the courage to jump. Or it may be the other way around. If we fall onto a rocky crag and break our leg, then the venture we're contemplating in life may be dangerous.

Sometimes this sensation of falling is our soul leaving or returning to our body. We may experience a jerk as we're falling asleep. This means our soul has just made a fast, jerky exit from our body like a plane leaving the runway too quickly. When our soul rejoins the body after its dimensional journeys we can experience this same jerky feeling. Or we may feel disoriented and confused if we've jumped back into our body too quickly. If we wake up and can't talk or move, we may be half in and half out of our body. Just relax and allow time to adjust to being back on earth.

Finding Valuables

If we're going through a crisis and dream of finding lost valuables, money, diamonds, precious gems, or gold this may be our soul's way of reassuring us that we possess inner resources or talents that are of value. It could also mean that what we're doing in life is valuable to the common good or to ourselves. A friend had a dream in which she was wearing expensive jewellery while she was vacationing in Rome. When she had the dream, she and her husband were on their first holiday in twenty-five years. The dream was clearly showing her this holiday was of great value to their marriage.

Flying

Flying dreams may symbolize that we're on an emotional high, soaring above the world with a clear overview. Or in physical life we may be emotionally low, and so we fly as a method of compensation (like getting on a plane and taking a holiday when we're depressed). However, most flying dreams are actually the memory of travelling in other dimensions. Since our soul has no limitations of time and space while we dream, we fly to our destination. An example of this is found in the movies *Crouching Tiger, Hidden Dragon* and *Hero*, in which the evolved characters have mastered the art of flying while they battle. In the *Harry Potter* series, the more evolved also fly or transport themselves. We all fly in dreams, whether we're consciously aware of it or not.

It's important to consider what's happening while we're flying since this mirrors our physical life. Are we able to fly freely or do we keep meeting obstacles? Is someone trying to capture us when we fly? Are we flying towards dark storm clouds or lush green valley? Are we flying too high or too low and endangering our life? Are we flying alone or with friends? In one very humbling dream I was trying to teach people to fly, but they all ended up flying backwards or they'd get caught in hydro wires! This clearly indicated my teaching methods at that time certainly weren't helping anyone move forward to enlightenment!

Houses

Jung defined the house as the "mansion of the soul." Similar to cars, houses may represent our bodies or where we're at in life. Each room represents different issues to the dreamer. Being in an attic may symbolize searching for spiritual or heightened awareness. Kitchens can represent basic needs such as eating and drinking, or nurturing and communication if we're sitting at a kitchen table with others. Food may represent what we need to nourish us, re-energize, or food for thought. The dining room is also where we take in food or new ideas; this is a social area since food is shared with others.

Bedrooms symbolize a need for rest or they may refer to sexual issues. Bathrooms are a place of privacy and also a place of release or cleansing. If we're urinating or defecating, this may symbolize emotional release. A toilet is where we get rid of emotional waste—anything toxic we no longer need. If we're taking a shower or using a bathtub, we may be cleansing ourselves of old emotions, beliefs, or relationships. Basements often represent the unconscious, things we've forgotten or packed away. Wandering in the basement or attic could mean we're exploring dreams and the unconscious. Since we keep cars in the garage, they may represent our present drive in life, or where we store old "stuff."

Losing Teeth

On a literal level, this can simply foreshadow that we will lose a tooth. The meaning, however, usually symbolizes either a karmic or dharmic change. We lose our teeth at significant points in life. Losing baby teeth means we're growing up; it's the beginning of our independence. When we make the transition from teenager to young adult, we lose our wisdom teeth. Later in life, losing teeth marks the passage to old age. So, losing teeth may represent transition, transformation, death and rebirth, passage of time, loss of power, acquiring power, growing up, or growing old. When I became ill and stopped teaching, I had several dreams where my teeth were crumbling or falling out. This represented how my life seemed to be crumbling and falling apart as I faced a huge lifestyle change.

Losing Valuable Possessions

Valuables may take many forms: good china, family heirlooms, large sums of money, a purse, wallet, credit cards, or our car. Depending on what happens in the dream, our spirit may be showing that we have great inner worth that we're prostituting or giving away. Or these dreams could come during a period of change or transition when we're afraid of losing our sense of self-worth, identity, inner resources, or belief systems.

Marriage

Dreams of marriage may represent problems or issues with an actual physical marriage. At the literal level, marriage dreams may be working through stress, anxiety, or anticipation of an upcoming marriage. If we're getting married, we may repeatedly rehearse it in our dreams until the event takes place. A dream of changes or problems in a marriage can also be taken literally.

Marriage dreams can also represent the blending of masculine and feminine energies or an energetic or spiritual marriage. If a woman dreams that the groom isn't there, this may represent the masculine parts of her personality that are missing or still developing. Perhaps she needs to develop greater independence, assertion, or drive. Similarly for men, if the bride is absent from the altar, they may need to work on integrating feminine qualities, such as warmth or nurturing of themselves and others. Or these dreams may represent real fears someone is working through before their actual marriage.

If we dream of marrying someone else, we can ask ourselves what quality we associate with this person. A dream of marrying a friend, famous person, former partner, or relative, may be suggesting a need to integrate or merge the dominant or positive qualities of this person into our psyche. For example, if we're marrying someone we perceive as extremely confident, we may need to integrate greater confidence. If we're marrying a comedian maybe we need to laugh more and lighten up. Sometimes we're just exploring these possibilities and seeing how it feels.

On a deeper symbolic level, marriage dreams may occur during times of profound transition or transformation. They symbolize the union of forces or energies of mind and spirit, masculine and feminine, or intellect and feelings. Before becoming fully enlightened we need to achieve an equal balance of both masculine and feminine qualities. Jung believed this union of opposites was necessary before individuation or enlightenment could take place. The result of this mystical inner marriage creates a whole, holy, or self-realized being.

Missing Trains or Planes

This type of dream may represent frustrations and missed opportunities similar to the phrase "missing the boat." Perhaps we've missed out on a business deal, relationship, or job we applied for. If we're travelling in a train or plane, perhaps our journey has been prearranged. We've given someone else the responsibility for getting us to our destination on time. A trip that never works out (we may forget our passport, arrive too late for our plane, arrive at the train station without our luggage, or be in a vehicle that crashes) probably corresponds to a time when life isn't moving smoothly. This may be triggered by the stress of trying too hard to control everything in life or attempting to move into karmic rather than dharmic possibilities.

Mountains, Crossroads, Bridges

Climbing a mountain symbolizes taking on a challenging task or trying to achieve a goal that may require time and hard work. If the dream ends and we're halfway up the mountain, then possibly we've achieved half of our goal. If we feel excited, revitalized, or confident as we're climbing, we have a better chance of reaching the summit. We may reach the top in a dream as we simultaneously achieve this goal in life. The emotions we're experiencing reflect the core message. If we're exhausted and it seems impossible to reach the top, this is probably how we feel in life. Are there obstacles? Do we receive help? Do we fall, get lost, or become sidetracked along the way, but still make it to the top?

Since mountains represent the meeting place between heaven and earth they also symbolize attaining new levels of insight or awareness. Biblical figures such as Moses climbed to the top of mountains to speak with God.

Crossroads symbolize a turning point in life—a time when we're trying to make an important choice or decision. In some dreams, we're standing at the crossroads not ready to make that decision. In other dreams, we actually make a choice. Bridges take us from one place to other, so they signify crossing over or making a change or transition. They may symbolize the crossing over to adolescence, parenthood, marriage, middle age, or old age. Or they may symbolize "getting over" any emotional or traumatic event. We'll look at this theme further in a discussion of "recurring dreams."

Mystical Helpers

A mystical helper may be a protection against evil or a source of strength to help us through difficult times. This may be a radiant child, angel, saint, goddess, wizard, magician, unicorn, or magical sword. Even if we don't believe in this mystical being, it may be a source of great inner power, strength, or direction. One of my students had a wizard who visited her at regular intervals. He always wore a pointy hat and long gown covered with stars and carried a torch. He started appearing in her dreams when she was going through a difficult time in grade six. He continued to appear during her teenage years whenever she needed light in her life or someone to give her emotional support or guidance.

Nude in Public

If we're naked in a dream, we may feel shock, surprise, discomfort, elation, freedom, or joy. Again, emotions are key to unlocking the meaning. We may be shopping in a crowded department store on a Saturday afternoon, look down, and discover we're not wearing clothes. We may arrive at work, take off our coat, and realize with horror we're naked. Or we may be walking in sunlit fields enjoying the freedom of being totally naked.

Dreams of nudity may represent feelings of vulnerability, fear of exposure, times when we've exposed our emotions and let down our defences, or a strong desire to break free of anything we feel is trapping us. I used to be a photojournalist and for years spent hours working alone in a darkroom. I loved photography but felt trapped and isolated. During this time, I was always having dreams in which I was in very public places and realized in shock that I'd forgotten to wear any clothes. It took me a while to figure out that my spirit was miserable in these jobs and desperately wanted to break free. We may be naked because we want to let go of people or situations that restrict us in the same way that clothes restrict our total freedom. If we're extremely embarrassed, it may suggest feelings of inadequacy or fear of exposure. Dreams of nudity may also reflect issues around sex, guilt, or embarrassment. But if we feel elated and carefree, this could symbolize we've broken free from something that previously restricted us. We've returned to that natural naked state we had as a child.

Path

This symbolizes our path, journey, or road in life. The type of path we follow may be significant. Is it smooth, well-worn, rocky, winding, or straight? A well-worn path may indicate an established or habitual route in life, while a path through a dense jungle suggests we're breaking new ground. If there are lots of obstacles, there may be many obstacles or roadblocks in life. If our path is winding, we may be taking a slower less-direct route, with twists and turns. If our path is narrow, our approach to life may be narrow and perhaps we're limiting ourselves, rather than taking a wider view of things. If our path is cluttered with lots of garbage, this may be a reflection of our life. If it's filled with sunshine, birds, and flowers, then our life journey has become dharmic and rewarding.

Past Lives

We rarely visit the past in our dreams because going backwards in time doesn't help us. I can't remember ever having a past-life dream. It doesn't help the soul to move backwards and relive times of pain and trauma. But, most importantly, we can't alter or change anything that happened in the past. That's why we most frequently go forward in time when we dream. We go into the future to observe, test out, or rehearse events that can be adapted to the present. Our present actions determine what sort of futures we have. For example, if everyone stopped littering or polluting today, our planet would be cleaner in the future.

However, if we do have a dream in which we seem to go backward in time, we can look at the overall theme or emotion. A dream from another time period can be prodding the dreamer not to make the same mistake or repeat the same pattern, or it can be indicating what may come. Look carefully at what is happening. Are we being bullied, betrayed, or otherwise attacked by others? Are we entering a war zone or a situation that is potentially dangerous? Are we searching for something that has always been elusive or unattainable? Are we reuniting with people who love and respect us? Are we fighting to help or protect others? Does the dream have any connection to events in our life?

Recurring Dreams

These dreams are often necessary for working through complex events. Depending on the complexity of the issue, they may take weeks, months, or years to resolve. In a recurring dream, our spirit chooses an appropriate dimension to work in and continues going there until everything is resolved. For example, a woman I know who lost her fiancé had recurring dreams for two years in which she was crossing different bridges. Surviving without her fiancé was a major challenge or bridge she had to cross. In the first few months, she attempted to cross treacherous rope bridges suspended over steep canyons. She was holding onto the ropes in terror and crawling on her hands and knees. By the end of the first year, the bridges had become shorter and easier to cross. The more emotional progress she made the shorter and less hazardous the bridges became. In her final dream, she drove her car across a bridge with no problems or obstacles. When this dream occurred those difficult years of grieving were behind her, just like the bridges. She had worked through her grief and reached the other side, a place where she felt confident and was ready to start dating again.

Royalty or Celebrities

If we dream we're talking with Princess Diana, Sting, Martin Luther King, Jennifer Lopez, or any famous person, consider the dominant qualities or personality characteristics of this person. What comes to mind first when we think about them or what does this person represent to us? Our dream may be encouraging us to develop the same inner qualities. Or we may be projecting positive characteristics onto this celebrity instead of becoming a star ourselves. These dreams may be a method of compensation. We may feel that our life is insignificant or boring so we befriend a celebrity to help us feel important. If we're feeling low in self-esteem, a good way to boost our ego may be to have tea with a king or queen!

Running for your Life

Running for your life or being chased or attacked is the most commonly reported dream. Similar to falling, running for your life can represent feelings of insecurity. We may feel that someone is after us. This may be a time when we don't feel in control. There are several questions that may get to the source of these dreams. We can ask, is someone after us for something we don't want to do? Is there anything in life we're running from? Are there people or situations we've been avoiding? Are circumstances in life closing in on us? Are we running from feelings or emotions we don't want to face? Are we being victimized by anyone who is more aggressive? Are we afraid to do something? Do we feel guilt over anything right now? Are we trying to get away with something? Are we in the same position we were as a child when we felt helpless or overpowered?

Sex

Sexual dreams bear some resemblance to marriage (union) dreams and can be understood literally or symbolically. They can be a common dream theme even if our sexual life is adequate because physically, sexually, and emotionally, we're always developing. A particular sexual problem can literally be mirrored in a dream. Sexual dreams can show us actual problems or lack of sexual activity. They can also represent emotional or spiritual growth. Since dreams can sometimes be compensators, if we're not sexually active, we can compensate by having sexual dreams. Sometimes we even experiment sexually when we dream. After a long period of celibacy, these dreams can prepare us for a committed relationship.

Since sex is a normal healthy form of love and self-expression, if someone denies or represses their sexuality, it can be represented as a frightening figure that haunts the dreamer. If they haven't nurtured or honoured their sexuality, they may encounter dark shadow figures in dreams. If they believe sex is wrong, dirty, or immoral, these energetic forms can become their sexual partners. These are mirrors showing the dreamer how they view sex.

Many sexual dreams are highly symbolic and have nothing to do with sex itself. For example, if we have sex with someone we know, our dream may be suggesting we integrate, blend, or merge the main qualities of this person into ourselves. We can ask what this person represents or what the first thing is we associate with this person. Often these are the qualities we can integrate to help our soul become more balanced. It may be self-esteem, strength, compassion, or a sense of humour. Having intercourse with someone of the same sex, if we're heterosexual, may indicate a need to integrate masculine or feminine energies into the personality. If we're not heterosexual, same-sex dreams may be experimentation or working through issues with partners. Since there is a strong connection between sex, creativity, and spirituality, strong sexual desire in dreams may represent a desire to reconnect with spirit. Very few dream dictionaries have entries for sex in dreams, but one of the best references to understanding sexual dreams is the chapter entitled "Erotica" in Claire Gibson's book *The Secret Life of Dreams.*

Terrorists, Explosion, Bombs, War

There are many people who actually go forward in time and witness wars, bombings and hurricanes before they happen. This type of dream can be very literal, emotionally preparing the dreamer for an actual physical event, but more frequently these dreams are symbolic. Although each of these situations may be quite different, they usually indicate some sort of potential conflict or trauma. The root word of *terrorists* is *terror*. If a terrorist is pursuing us, we may ask ourselves what we are afraid of right now. Have we avoided dealing with anything? Bombs or explosions indicate a potentially explosive situation. For example, a father may explode if a teenager misses a curfew. A wife may explode if she feels her husband has stayed out too late drinking with his buddies. War may symbolize a distressing situation in life or something in disorder. It could also be an internal conflict or a symbol of spiritual or emotional disintegration.

Dreams similar in meaning are those where we're caught in some sort of natural disaster such as earthquakes, tornadoes, floods, volcanoes, typhoons, tidal waves, rainstorms, cyclones, snowstorms, ice, or hailstorms. In our physical life, any natural disaster causes upheaval, chaos, grief, and emotional despair. Since dreams are a mirror, this can be how we're feeling in our waking life, or how we will soon feel. Dreams where we are involved in a disaster usually mean there is intense emotional stress or upheaval. The wind and water in these dreams represent our chaotic unbalanced emotions. Fire often represents anger or passionate burning emotions. Dreams with snow or ice can represent times when we're being cold hearted, when we are stuck, frozen with fear, or when we're treading thin ice in life.

Toilets

Since water can symbolize emotions, if we're urinating in a dream, it may represent release or a need to release emotions. Blocked toilets may mean we're emotionally blocked. Cleaning a toilet may indicate spiritual cleansing or washing away old attitudes and emotions. Excrement in dreams doesn't always mean dirt or filth, although it can. In some dreams it's quite the opposite. In his book *The Way of the Dream*, Jungian analyst Fraser Boa, after analyzing a client's dream about a pyramid of feces, writes, "But the light makes the hand of God visible in the shit, and if we can see the hand of God in the shit, then we can stand the shit. Otherwise we suffocate in it." It can be the fertilizer for new growth. It can symbolize the darkness of the unconscious from which new awareness grows. Excrement can also symbolize financial gain, hence the phrase, "rolling in it." If we have an excrement dream, the key is how we're feeling. If we feel awful, humiliated, upset, then we may be going through a "shitty" period in our life. If the feelings aren't negative in the dream, but more of surprise or wonder, we may be into something good. While I was doing post-graduate work, I had several excrement dreams just before I was awarded two unexpected scholarships.

Water

Depending on the individual, our bodies contain between 70% to 98% water. As we enlighten, our body becomes more water and less dense physical mass. Water is fluid, like spirit, and is able to transform, blend, and merge. Since most of our body is actually comprised of water, it often represents our present emotional state. If we're diving into water or swimming in a dream, this can mean we're diving into or exploring our emotions. If the water is calm, smooth, and peaceful, this may reflect a tranquil time in our lives. If we're swimming in rough turbulent water, but making no headway, we may be involved in a stormy unsettling time. Do we reach our destination? If so, the dream may be indicating we will be successful. Do we sink or swim? If we sink, this usually indicates we're literally over our head with demands or pressures. Does someone rescue us? This could mean we'll be rescued. Is the water frozen? If so, we may be stuck.

Hopefully, these symbols will provide a start. If you'd like to learn more, an excellent book explaining the twelve most common universal symbols is Patricia Garfield's book *The Universal Dream Key*. Garfield is considered one of the world's top dream experts. In her book, she used her own dream journals over a fifty-year period and a sample of 500 dreamers from around the world. She found the five most common dreams were:

• Being chased or attacked (reported by 80% of her participants);
• Falling or drowning (64%);
• Being lost or trapped (58%);
• Being naked or inappropriately dressed (52%); and
• Being injured, ill, or dying (48%).

It's important to know that symbols may also guide us in physical life. Spirit is working twenty-four hours a day to help us evolve. As we become aware of these symbols in dreams, we can also become aware of how they may be helping us in our day-to-day life. If a rabbit keeps crossing our path, this may be a time of dharmic possibilities—maybe things are going to multiply or grow quickly. The message could be the same if rabbits keep appearing in a dream. If we're always seeing ground-hogs running into their holes, perhaps we're hiding and keeping our emotions below the surface. If we have a flat tire two weeks in a row and we have brand new tires, we may begin to understand that something or someone in life keeps deflating us. As we become more aware of how these symbols work, they can be a source of tremendous insight.

Guided Imagery

Guided imagery is an opportunity for us to relax, meditate, and to become aware of what spirit is trying to tell us. In many ways, it's similar to a dream. The same images, scenes, and symbols may come up. Guided imagery is never an attempt to control, manipulate, or force the mind into doing or believing anything. It's the opposite; an attempt to set spirit free so that it can explore. So feel free to either follow the instructions here or allow the soul to wander in any direction it wishes. I often use this exercise in workshops and classes, but perhaps here you can become your own teacher.

Try reading this guided imagery exercise one paragraph at a time, then closing your eyes to see what surfaces. You may want to record all the experiences and insights you have. Or you may read the entire guided imagery, close your eyes, and allow your own story to emerge. Another option is to have someone you trust read this to you, and, perhaps, take turns. After you've written down your experiences, turn to the descriptions of each symbol at the beginning of this chapter to give you further insights. Keep in mind that everything is interrelated, whether this is a dream, guided imagery, a fairy tale, or your imagination wandering. The intent of spirit is always to provide insights that move us forward. Enjoy this journey wherever it takes you.

Imagine that you're leaving the room and getting into a car. It can be any car, one that you own, or one that you've never seen before. Become aware of the type of car you're driving. Become aware of your speed and pace. Is it a smooth journey or do you stop and start again?

You're driving this car to a place in the country. Perhaps you're going to a park or woods you've visited in the past and enjoyed. Or you may explore a place you've never been before. Intuitively, you know the place you're seeking.

You drive and come to a place with hiking paths. You park the car and decide to walk on the paths. As you walk, observe everything. It's a beautiful sunny day and you may see flowers, birds, butterflies, fields, and forests. Enjoy the beauty and tranquillity of this place. Feel the wind caress your body; feel the sunlight warm it. Become aware of the intelligence of nature and its ability to soothe and uplift your spirit. Now observe this path. Is it wide, narrow, straight, or winding? Are there any obstacles on the path? Can you see straight ahead? Are there lots of twists and turns? Is the path overgrown with bushes and trees? Does it travel through a forest or an open meadow? Is it hilly or flat?

After walking a few minutes you see an animal on the path ahead. This can be any animal. Spend a few minutes with this creature. You may be able to talk to it and understand what it has to say. What are the characteristics of this animal? It may be here to assist you or give you a message. You may decide to continue walking with this animal, or you may leave it on the path. Or you may encounter it later in this journey. You may even meet other animals as you walk.

Continue walking and enjoying the beauty around you. Perhaps you're enjoying the sound of birds singing or the fragrance of lilac or vanilla. Now you discover a mystical helper. This can be any number of things, an angel, fairy, elf, good wizard, goddess, magic wand, sword, unicorn, bird, apple, note, or book. Spend time with this helper to see how it can assist you. As with the animal, you may decide to take this helper with you on your journey or leave it and move on.

Gradually, you begin to hear the sound of water ahead. It's soothing and invigorating. This sound becomes clearer and clearer until you are beside an ocean, lake, stream, or waterfall. You decide to sit down beside the water. What is the water like? Is it calm, wavy, fast flowing, or slow moving? You may decide to swim, cross a bridge over this water, or take a boat to the other side and back. This seems like an enchanted place and you decide to spend some time here.

After you've been here for a while, you see a beautiful mystical helper in the form of a radiant child. This child seems angelic and glows with light. You walk toward each other and the child is smiling directly at you. You know this child has a message or information to help and guide you, so you sit, talk, and listen. Consider the possibility that this child may be part of you. Finally, the child wishes you well and tells you they must leave. You may embrace, shake their hand, or simply say goodbye.

Now it's time to go. You may sit for a few minutes and contemplate everything you've experienced, or you may begin walking. Whatever you decide, become aware that you will soon be returning to the room where you began. Your spirit has no physical boundaries of time and space. You can focus on a place and you're there. Slowly, when you're ready, return to this time and space. Open your eyes when you're ready, knowing that you can return to this place of calm and serenity whenever you wish. Smile and be grateful for this experience.

Chapter Eleven
Sample Dream Experiences

The dream world is the real world.
—Seneca Indian healer

It's often helpful to read or hear the dreams of others before attempting to understand our own. Hopefully, reading these accounts will get you started. The first dream and its meaning was written by a sixteen-year-old grade eleven student. He was a member of the first class I did dream work with in 1993. I've read and reread his dream and often use it in workshops. The intensity of this dream along with his honesty, frankness, and wisdom never cease to amaze me.

Devil Bear
— eleventh-grade male student

> *I am being dragged along the ground by my feet by what seems to be people, but I am not sure. They bring me into a village and dump me in the middle of a circle in front of a big grizzly bear standing behind a table. The bear is huge; he is standing on his hind legs, but there is a hole in his chest and the fur around it is bloodstained. The bear starts to talk, he says, "We must sacrifice." He says it over and over. I get up and he takes me to his tent where he lives. He starts to tell me of the end of the world, the darkness is coming he says. The world will be overcome with darkness and fire and ice. No sky, no birds, no life as I can see now. Just darkness, fire, and ice. I happen to look up and right into his eyes. His eyes are pure black holes. I am dragged into a deep sleep and I see the bear rip open a hole in his chest and take his heart out and wash it in water. The heart disappears right out of his hand.*
>
> *I finally awaken and the bear and I are back in the circle. A man comes up (he looks like a North American Indian) and gives me a knife and the bear a bigger knife. There are Indians all around the circle and they are chanting something but I can't hear what it is. The bear and I begin to fight. I stab him in the chest. He looks at me and laughs. I stab him again and again. Nothing happens to the bear. He does not even bleed. With a great roar the bear picks me up above him by my*

throat and sticks me with the big knife. He rips out the great knife and drops my lifeless body to the ground. At the end of this dream I was confused and sad.

This dream was a hard dream to work with, but I think that I have gotten what it was saying. The beginning, when I am being dragged into the village, represents how I was feeling this particular week. It was a real hard week for me. I just was not up to doing anything. The circle that I am put in represents three things: my house, school, and homework. They were the three things I was stuck doing that week. The bear was a hard thing to figure out but I'm pretty sure it stands for the bad side of me—my shadow. The bear mentions darkness, fire, and ice. The darkness represents the downside to the bad week I was having; the fire represents the anger I was feeling, and the ice is how I might have come across as to some people that week. The sacrifices that the bear mentions are the sacrifices I had to make personally, like staying home to get things done instead of going out with my friends.

The fight that the bear and I have at the end of the dream represents how I came out of that bad week: beat and dead tired. The bear dropped my lifeless body to the ground, and this is when I broke out of the bad week. The bear (my shadow) still lives on, waiting to show up at any time.

The Tree

— eleventh-grade male student

I'm in the kitchen looking into my backyard and I want to smell spring. As I walk onto the deck, I take a large breath, but smell nothing. I walk off the deck and towards a bare tree in an open space in my backyard, but where the grass is supposed to be, there is pavement. As I look around at the neighbouring houses, everything has a green hue to it. I walk up to the tree, shake it, and out pours a gas that swirls around the tree, and it smells of spring. To get more of this gas to come out, I shake the tree again, but instead of the gas, the tree lets go of leaves and insects; I particularly remember snail shells and a spider. Because of this downpour, I fall to the ground, rolling and hiding my face to get away, but no matter how much I think to get away from the tree, I just do not.

After about ten seconds, the leaves stop falling on me. I get up, and repeat the pattern. I shake the tree and gas comes out; I shake it again and down comes the leaves and insects. When I awoke from this dream, I was a little scared, and woke up with a jolt.

Spring usually represents renewal, or life, and wanting to smell it represents how I want to have change in my life. I have been developing bad habits lately of not doing my homework until the last minute, letting my grades slip, and not taking any steps toward accomplishing personal goals. This is represented by the green hue to everything, and the snail shell. The snail shell is a personal symbol; I have a dead snail in my aquarium that I have not taken out yet, and so I figure it represents things that I have not done.

Even though I realize what I have to change and how, I still do not because they have become habits. Bad habits are represented by the spider, and spiders spin webs that catch their prey; I have fallen into the trap of bad habits. The pavement, or concrete in the dream represents permanence and unyielding force—again, bad habits. This constant theme is further reinforced by the falling leaves, a disappointing time in my life. The act of smelling spring, then shaking the tree again but having all of those things fall on me, is reflecting how even when I try to change my life, I cannot. This is represented by my inability to roll away from the tree.

Life Choice
— eleventh-grade female student

I was in the smoking area at the back of the school. I was not by the doors; I was over by the large parking lot. The sky was grey and it looked as if it was going to storm very soon. When I looked over to the stairs, there were many students there. When I looked a second time, there was only one male student standing at the top of the stairs. Since there were no students outside, I realized that I was going to be late for religion class if I did not hurry. When I started to rush to get in, I began to feel extremely sick. I had no energy. I was so weak. I began to climb the stairs to go inside and I practically had to pull myself up because I was so weak.

When this dream began, I felt fine; this was just another day. I was filled with a feeling of panic when I realized all the students were gone. When I got sick, I felt so weak. My head was spinning and I actually felt like I was going to die. I felt as If I was going to faint. It was very scary to feel so sick.

This dream was very obvious. My dream was telling me to quit smoking. I already know this, but I guess that since I keep putting off quitting, my subconscious is trying to tell me to do it now or pay the consequences later. The reason why the dream is titled "Life Choice" was because it truly is a choice that will change my life. The fact that I was fine in the beginning of the dream, and at the end I was very weak and helpless, means that although I cannot feel the consequences of smoking at the present time, in the future I will be able to feel them and it will not be fun. The difficulty I had with climbing up the stairs symbolizes how hard it will be for me to quit, but to reach the top I will have to pull myself through it, just like how I had to pull myself up the stairs in my dream.

Sinking Fast

— *my dream*

I am in a huge pool somewhere in Brampton. I am with a man in the pool trying to hold up a large rubber lifeboat or huge rubber floatation device. We're both in the water. At first, we have it above the surface, although it's not blown up. It's totally deflated, but above the surface. The energy to keep this thing from sinking is tremendous because it's so large. Then the man lets it slip and most of it goes under the water. I'm incredulous; I can't believe he could just let go after all the effort we've been through to hold it up. I'm really upset and angry with him for giving up.

The reality of this dream was apparent; I was sinking fast. This dream occurred before my doctor told me I had to take time off work. Symbolically, in the dream I was trying to hold together my life or lifeboat. The fact that we're in a pool is also significant. A pool is an artificial container for water, not something natural like an ocean or river. Emotionally, I felt exactly like the words in the dream: totally deflated, trying to hold it together in an artificial world.

The man and woman in the dream could symbolize the masculine and feminine sides of me. The masculine side, which is usually logical, saw that this was an impossible task, this boat was already "totally deflated" so he simply let go. The feminine emotional side of me tried desperately to keep it up, even when I knew it was a losing battle. In the dream, it required tremendous energy and effort to keep this deflated boat above the surface. This paralleled my life; it required tremendous energy to go into work every day when I was really ill. I remember the feelings of anger and frustration at the end of this dream. I blamed the man for letting go rather than taking a long hard look at myself. How could he possibly just let this boat sink after years of effort? These were exactly the emotions I was feeling. The reality that I desperately needed to let go of was closing in on me, but my mind or ego didn't want to admit it. My mind wanted to be the perfect in-control teacher.

In this dream, I rehearsed and experienced all the emotions I would feel two months later, defeat, failure, anger, depression, and alienation. The dream helped me prepare for the reality I was going to experience. After this dream, I knew with absolute certainty that I needed to stop working.

Water-Skiing in Winter
— *my dream*

We're at my brother Frank's. It is January or February and my friend Ann is water-skiing behind Frank's boat. Everything on the lake is encased in ice and beautiful. I'm hoping we can go back after and take some pictures. We're going too fast now. Frank is driving. I can't believe Ann is actually doing this. She is actually breaking ice because the part we are on is frozen. I suddenly realize if she falls, she could have severe hypothermia, possibly even die. She seems oblivious to this. She perseveres for an extremely long time in her bathing suit. Her nose is frozen with ice and snow. It looks like she is going to have a severe case of frostbite.

Finally, we reach open water. She continues to ski. This was our destination, the open water across the lake. Suddenly, I see a huge hydro pole with ice built up all around it. We crash into it. Ann is smart enough to save herself. She just hops on the mound. We all have moderate scrapes and bruises, but no one is seriously injured and the boat is okay. The main emotions I feel throughout this dream are shock and amazement. I'm incredulous that Ann could be so obsessed with anything in life that she would water-ski in the middle of winter in a bikini, completely oblivious to how this could either ruin her health or kill her.

This dream took place about a year after I stopped teaching. I was still on disability and there was no real improvement in my health. My physical problems had only become more severe. I became really sick whenever a new semester began, and I felt I should go back to work. I felt it was my duty to return to teaching. I didn't see or consider any other options. I felt I had to go back out of duty, guilt, and obligation—all the wrong reasons. So I was trying to hold on to a job that was impossible for me to do. Working at that job, which was very demanding with all my physical limitations, had just about killed me. Going back was like a death sentence, although this was very hard for me to see. I felt if other people could do it, I should be able to.

In the dream, my soul presented me with a mirror of my own situation. It was showing me the insanity of what I was doing and the fact that it could be potentially fatal. I was still stuck, frozen with guilt and fear like the ice and snow in the dream. Ann was a childhood friend I had water-skied with my entire life. Ann's personality was similar to mine in the sense that she was very career-driven. She was well educated and had risen to the top of her profession. So my initial understanding of this dream was that, like Ann, I was holding onto something that would really continue to jeopardize my health. Ann was holding onto a ski rope in the winter with frostbite on her face. I was holding onto the idea of a job I couldn't do. I needed to let go, just as Ann did.

Some time later I began to understand this dream on a much deeper level. It was hard to admit what the dream was showing me. The boat represented my life—lifeboat—similar to the previous dream where I'm literally trying to hold up a lifeboat. I watched Ann ski because this was familiar to both of us. I was on thin ice—a play on words. I was hanging on the edge emotionally and spiritually. Different things were happening to us but I was walking on thin ice with the possibility of crashing. What I didn't want to admit was that I was watching Ann because I absolutely didn't have the tools or resources to help or nurture her. And I definitely didn't have the tools to help myself. The dream was trying to make me aware of my own desperately limited resources.

Sample Dreams—What Do You Think They Mean?

Dream One — *a woman in her early thirties*

Background: This woman was a gifted artist with the ability to work in several different styles. She had received a bachelor of fine arts at the University of Western Ontario, then travelled to Europe where she took part in an art exchange program. Her father owned a successful architecture business so it seemed a logical step to enrol in architecture at the University of British Columbia. But, she discovered this really wasn't her niche, possibly because it didn't allow her time for painting, drawing, sculpture, and photography—artistic pursuits she loved that can be tremendously self-healing. While at university, she suffered a complete emotional and physical breakdown. She had this dream after she had moved home to Toronto while deciding whether to pursue art full time or follow the status quo with a traditional job:

> *A couple of weeks ago, I dreamt that I was at the top of a ski hill during the spring/summer months because the grass was green. A group of people were competing for a place on the UBC (University of British Columbia) ski team. The coach was at the bottom of the hill. I wanted to be on the team and knew it wasn't possible because I got kicked out of the school. I skied down anyway, really fast and a bit out of control, but I wanted to impress the coach. When I got to the bottom, he was impressed. I told him I used to ski for UWO (University of Western Ontario). Then I was overcome with a feeling in the dream of being in the wrong place and with the wrong people. I felt unsteady emotionally, as though they would humiliate me if I screwed up. So I left.*
>
> *There was a door at the bottom of the hill behind the coach that entered into a dark room where there was a teacher instructing a class to draw Mickey Mouse. He was showing the basic shapes that made up Mickey. I grew bored and disinterested in how to draw cute little characters. I went to the back of the class and was near a door that was slightly open with bright light creeping in. Outside the door was something, or maybe God; it felt like I was being told that there is Toronto. I felt pulled by a positive and protective force to go out the door and travel back to Toronto. I went out the door and travelled back home. The light was very bright and healing.*

Dream Two — *a woman in her early forties*

Background: This woman is unhappily married, with stress-related physical problems. She is extremely popular—many people rely on her for advice and help, she has several friends, and participates in many social activities. She works full time, and is very committed and involved with her two young children.

I had a dream last night that at first I was sure was telling me how much I am feeling like my life is out of my control. But when I thought about it, I realized that although it was showing me situations where I thought I was losing control, the worst didn't happen.

I was having a dream in which Bob's two dogs (who I adore) were in my care. [Bob is the dreamer's brother.] The white husky, Arthur, has been going through a funny phase lately in which Bob is having a hard time keeping him in the yard.

Bob's dogs were in my care as I was driving a huge rented motor home. (Go figure—I've never driven one of those before!) Anyhow, I was pulling across the road from the car rental company, and I was backing into a parking space where I could clearly see there was a trailer—like a boat trailer. I got distracted by something as I was backing into the spot, and I was also conscious of the fact that people on the street were watching me back this huge thing up. (I detest being watched!) So I did what everyone was expecting: I accidentally, but gently, bumped into the trailer parked on the opposite side of the road.

I knew that I did something stupid, but I also knew I didn't cause any damage to either vehicle because of how lightly I had tapped into the trailer. A very irate, older, blonde woman shook her head and stormed across the road to report me to the rental company.

I could see what she was going to do. I bravely pulled this huge motorhome to the opposite side of the road thinking this way everyone could see if there was any damage to the trailer. I backed into a spot directly in front of the rental company. There was a lot of commotion because the dogs were barking up a storm, and I'm telling them to calm down as I do some tricky and dangerous manoeuvring of this huge oversized vehicle. I was thinking about that woman who seemed delighted to report my carelessness to this company as if I wasn't going to do it.

The woman came out just as I parked, pointing her finger angrily at me, indicating to the several rental car personnel what I did. The dogs were going crazy, and someone opened a back door on the motor home. I leaped out of the driver's seat to try to avoid a bad situation with the dogs. By this time, the back entrance of the motorhome was surrounded by people, and Arthur was trying to get out. All I could think was there was no way I could lose the dogs as I would never be forgiven and quite frankly, I felt that this would be unforgivable. Arthur is a very strong 100 lb. dog—he can pull dog sleds. So I was pulling on his collar as hard as I could, and he was pulling me as he tried to run to freedom. It was quite a scene!

I awoke thinking how this dream was showing how out-of-control I am in my life. What's with the motorhome—controlling something big—or am I carrying around my home on my back like a turtle?

Dream Three — *sequence of dreams of a teacher in her forties*

Background: This dreamer had recently taken time off work to try to clear up some serious health problems. She had been very driven and conscientious in her career and had really forgotten how to have fun. She was single, had no children, and frequently tried to assist others.

John's Dirty Laundry

I go back to a school very similar to the high school I used to teach at. I visit John, a fellow teacher. He's really stressed out because he has so much work to do. I ask him if I can help and he hands me a duffel bag of clothes that need drying. He wanted to take the laundry home to his wife at 3 p.m. when school's over. I'm home all day, so I say I can do them for him. But I start talking to people, and I get side tracked, and I forget completely. The next day I go back to the school with the intent of using the school's dryers so I can do his laundry, but I can't seem to do it. Every time I try, a young teacher has clothes in the dryer. When I walk around, none of the teachers are happy; they're all stressed out with too much work. I find an area of the school that is an amazing garden, like nothing on earth. There are huge brilliant gladiolas in rows and rows that I'm really drawn to.

Donna's Dirty Laundry

I'm running around the downtown streets of my hometown. It looks the way it was when I was a child. I meet Donna, one of my former high-school students. I talk and become friendly. I feel sorry for her. I think she's homeless or something. Then she tells me she's going away next week and asks if I will help her out by doing her laundry before she goes. I'm really taken aback by this unusual request. I absolutely don't want to do someone else's laundry. I feel it's inappropriate she even asked me, but I also feel like I can't say no.

Dirty Dishes

I go back to my childhood home to visit my brother and father. I start looking around in one of my old drawers. I find red, lycra running pants. I decide to give them to a charity. Red isn't me. Then I find a matching jacket and top. They're quite stylish but something I must have had years ago. I go into the kitchen and pull out the dishwasher. It's full of dirty dishes. On the counters are loads and loads and loads of dirty dishes waiting for me to run through the dishwasher. It looks like no one has done dishes in weeks or months; they're piled high everywhere.

What do you feel these three dreams are trying to tell the dreamer? What is the recurring theme?

Chapter Twelve
Dream Dictionaries

Every dream is a masterpiece of symbolic communication.
—Robert Johnson

Like everything else, there are excellent dream dictionaries, and others with completely fabricated meanings bordering on ridiculous. One of my students found a dictionary that implied every symbol had something to do with sex. In another dictionary, almost every symbol meant you would be receiving large sums of money. I've flipped through dictionaries where I couldn't find one symbol that was really accurate. For years, I refused to buy any of these dictionaries until one day I found myself in the book section of a second-hand store. Staring me in the face was a twenty-year-old dictionary by a well-known reputable publisher entitled *Coles Dream Guide*. Since it was around the time I was editing this chapter, I couldn't resist.

After skimming a few pages, I was incredulous—it was far worse than I expected. Nothing made logical sense, and many of the common symbols, such as *running*, were missing. It did include *falling*, which usually means insecurity or fear of falling from grace, but the explanation was scary and depressing. It states, "To dream of falling is not propitious, for sickness, failure, and disappointments in love are foretold. If one dreams of falling and actually crashes to earth, the ominous prediction is death or a prolonged illness." Furthermore, for *automobile*, we're told, "Because of their large numbers, a dream of going places in an automobile has no particular significance." Unfortunately, the entry for *sex* was very disappointing and seemed a bit contradictory: "There are few dreams that have no connection with sex, for all living things are created male and female. Therefore, as such, it has little significance."

Two or three meanings were given for every symbol, but these were always completely fabricated meanings. But most upsetting was the doom and gloom that accompanied most entries. Freud certainly wouldn't agree with this meaning for *banana*: "Eaten in a dream, this fruit betokens sickness. Seen growing, it predicts that one of your friends will prove to be a shallow individual." Many positive symbols, *firefly* for example, became quite ominous: "Young men and women who dream of seeing fireflies in a summer garden should take warning that their conduct will be severely criticized by their elders." Under the entry for *glue*, we're told, "To dream of spilling glue on your clothing is a sign that you are likely to be held up by a robber. If you dream of using glue to mend anything, you will lose money through investments. It is also an indication that your present work will not be permanent and that you do not like it." Even *goldfish*, usually a positive symbol, aren't safe in dreams: "A woman who dreams of seeing goldfish in a bowl or aquarium is warned to make sure that her shades are drawn when she retires to her room. Peeping Toms will be seeking to look in on her." Women seem to be in constant peril. I always thought wearing a *shawl* was fairly harmless, until reading, "A shawl over your shoulders is an indication that you will have difficulty in cashing a large cheque."

Many of the entries were sexist—a symbol meant one thing for a woman and quite another for a man, which is never the case. For childbirth, usually a positive symbol indicating something new in life, it said, "For a man or woman to dream of being present at the birth of a child is a warning against putting things off that should be done immediately. Wills should be made, crops should be planted, bills paid, etc. It foretells ease of body and mind for a woman to dream of giving birth to a child, but a man who has this dream has a dark outlook in both business and social affairs." This brings up another important point: a reputable dream dictionary doesn't tell the reader what they should do, or invoke fear, shame, or guilt. The entries will be interesting, providing lots of background and often the history of this symbol. Each entry will be informative, giving the reader plenty to think about. Rather than invoking fear and dread, they inspire and teach in a manner that empowers the dreamer.

If this was the first dream dictionary I'd purchased, I'd be terrified of both life and dreams. Unfortunately, a false dream dictionary keeps anyone sincerely seeking truth locked in karma and illusion. It may turn dreamwork into a negative proposition, rather than an exciting adventure leading the dreamer toward greater peace of mind and purpose. When we've read something accurate in a dream dictionary, it can be a natural high. It's exciting; that's why I'm hooked. And as we'll learn in the last chapter, with true insights, we sometimes feel the flow of energy moving through the body. This always feels good! Fortunately, there are now many excellent dream dictionaries on the market. It's worth the little bit of time and effort it takes to understand the differences. In choosing a dream dictionary, here are four things to consider:

1. Always look for a dictionary that gives several and often opposite meanings for every symbol. The better dictionaries will provide at least a paragraph or two describing symbols.

2. Look to the back to see if there's a bibliography or several references. Writing a dream dictionary is a mammoth task. It requires knowledge of symbolism, history, psychology, anthropology, mythology, history, literature, and world religions. If there is no reference list at the back, the content may be questionable. However, this is not always the case—I found one excellent dictionary with no references.

3. Check to see if there is biographical or background information on the authors. Writing a dream dictionary requires a great deal of expertise or experience. The misleading dictionary described above listed two authors on the cover but provided absolutely no biographical information.

4. There is always logic or a connection between the symbol and its meaning. Let's say "Fred" ended a lengthy relationship two years ago but emotionally he hasn't gotten over his girlfriend. He's having a series of dreams where he's walking around carrying heavy suitcases. In one dream, he tries going to a party, but has so many heavy bags he doesn't make it. Fred may look up suitcases or baggage in a dream dictionary. If it explains that this could mean he's carrying around heavy emotions or emotional baggage, this makes logical sense. But if another dictionary tells Fred that baggage means his sex life will improve or that he should buy lottery tickets, then he may question its accuracy.

We can't go wrong with the list given here. Although new dictionaries are being published all the time, this can be a starting point. They're divided into three groups: dream dictionaries, symbolic dictionaries, and pictorial symbolic dictionaries. They're all comprehensive and readable. Each is set up differently. Some are in the traditional dictionary format from A to Z, while others are divided into categories such as methods of transportation, the body, or animals. Symbolic dictionaries are definitely for anyone wanting more of a challenge. My personal favourites are Tony Crisp's *Dream Dictionary*, Wilda Tanner's *Mystical, Magical Marvelous World of Dreams*, Rosemary

Guiley's *Encyclopedia of Dreams*, Sandra Thomson's *Cloud Nine: A Dreamer's Dictionary*, Kevin Todeschi's *Dream Images and Symbols*, and Clare Gibson's *Secret Life of Dreams*.

Dream Dictionaries

Ackroyd, Eric. *A Dictionary of Dream Symbols*. Contains a section at the beginning explaining how to work with dreams, the unconscious, and describes Freudian, Jungian, and Gestalt psychology. Its setup is similar to a traditional dictionary with listings from A to Z.

Andrews, Ted. *Animal-Speak: The Spiritual and Magical Powers of Creatures Great and Small*. This is not a dream dictionary, but it's perhaps the best resource if we dream about an animal and want to understand its relationship to our lives. Detailed descriptions are given on several birds, mammals, insects, and reptiles. Each description describes the habits and habitats of these animals. It provides questions and insights about each animal, helping us understand how their behaviours may relate to our lives.

Ball, Pamela. *10,000 Dreams Interpreted*. This is one of the few good dictionaries without an extensive bibliography. It contains a 46-page introduction explaining topics such as how to gain dream insight, sleep and dream cycles, the history of dreams, archetypes, and sleep and spirituality. It contains 500 pages of A to Z dream symbols and a section at the end to record dreams.

Bethards, Betty. *Dream Book: Symbols for Self Understanding*. Excellent if you like dictionaries that are more spiritual in nature. The first section explains the relationships between dreams, karma, reincarnation, and the seven chakras. It also ties in the importance of prayer and meditation. The format is from A to Z, and often explains spiritual reasons for dreams. Although the descriptions are not always detailed, they get to the core of the meaning. It includes many entries not found in most dictionaries. Currently out of print, but worth hunting for.

Boushahla, Jo Jean and Virginia Reidel-Geubtner. *Dream Dictionary: 1,000 Dream Symbols from A to Z*. Small but mighty at 128 pages! Brief introduction includes information on dream recall, types of dreams, and working with dreams. This is followed by a brief A to Z alphabet of symbols, then several sections of dream categories: dream characters, vehicles, buildings, animals, colour, number, sex, gems and stones, and archetypes. Final chapter on archetypes is excellent, even explaining the deeper symbolic meaning behind *Snow White and the Seven Dwarfs*.

Crisp, Tony. *Dream Dictionary*. The paperback version is 420 pages and definitely a great value for the money. This is an A to Z format with lots of detail. This is really an encyclopedic dictionary. For example, if we look up the word *statistics*, we'll find five pages of charts showing statistics of how often different symbols appear in dreams. Some symbols will contain two to three pages of explanations as well as word plays and idioms to really get you thinking. For example, idioms for *wall* include: drive up the wall, go to the wall, writing on the wall, back to the wall, knock one's head against a wall. There are also examples of dreams and their meanings for many entries.

Crisp, Tony. *Dream Dictionary*. This is a revised and updated 10th anniversary edition of Tony Crisp's earlier dictionary. A bit longer than the previous edition at 455 pages. Both editions are available in paperback. This is my number one recommendation for anyone starting out; it's affordable, comprehensive, well researched, and easy to read.

Dening, Sarah. *Dreams Made Easy*. Small and inexpensive, it can be tucked into your pocket but is full of useful information. Contains themed sections on: dream people, houses, travel, your body, animals, nature, common anxiety dreams, colors, numbers, birth, and death.

Guiley, Rosemary. *The Encyclopedia of Dreams*. This is divided into two sections: part one contains 140 pages explaining the science of dreams, cross-cultural beliefs, nightmares, dreams and the paranormal, dreams and alchemy, and working with dreams. The next 217 pages contain an A to Z dream dictionary complete with illustrations. Since the author has written books on mystical experience, angels, reincarnation, and prayer, she explains the spiritual significance behind many dreams.

Linn, Denise. *The Secret Language of Signs: How to Interpret the Coincidences and Symbols in Your Life*. A great resource to start understanding how we're given signs and symbols while we're awake. The first 77 pages explain how we receive signs from our culture, heritage, religion, other people, conversations, emotions, songs, printed words, radio, television, movies, nature, illness, accidents, synchronicity, and pets. The next 200 pages make up an alphabetical dictionary of symbols that is readable and wise.

Nacson, Leon. *Interpreting Dreams A–Z.* A colourful illustrated dictionary that is adequate for younger people or beginners. Gives many meanings for every symbol in a concise fashion. Doesn't contain as many entries as most dictionaries, but the information is credible.

Tanner, Wilda B. *The Mystical, Magical Marvelous World of Dreams.* The author is an ordained minister and teacher who has worked with dreams since 1969. This is considered the Bible for some people who delve into dreams. Most descriptions are brief, but just about every possible symbol is found here. It includes some illustrations. The book is divided into three sections. The first eleven chapters deal with diverse areas, such as how dreams help you, ancient and modern dreams, goals, dream journalling, dream recall, and lucid dreaming. Part two, the largest, is divided into 32 dream categories, including animals, battles, death and dying, historical settings, names, nudity, sex, pregnancy, birth, and weather. The final section is a potpourri of A to Z definitions.

Thomson, Sandra A. *Cloud Nine: A Dreamer's Dictionary.* An excellent resource that is extremely well researched. The first 100 pages give general information on dreams along with several exercises. The remainder of the book is a dream dictionary in alphabetical format. Provides great examples of how one symbol can have multiple dream meanings.

Todeschi, Kevin J. *Dream Images and Symbols: A Dictionary.* If you can only afford one dream dictionary, this may be the most auspicious way to start. Originally published as the *Encyclopedia of Symbolism*, it was reprinted by the Association for Research and Enlightenment, which specializes in Edgar Cayce's material. The author has taught and published Cayce's material for over twenty-five years including information on akashic records, symbolism, reincarnation, karma, and soul development. His information is sound, readable, and fascinating. Several of the entries are not always found in dream dictionaries, for example: Darth Vader, Dorothy in the *Wizard of Oz*, Gandhi, *Gone with the Wind*, Mary Magdalene, and the *Book of Revelations*. There are also descriptions for most world religions and the twelve signs of the Zodiac. Another unique feature includes detailed explanations for every letter of the alphabet. Did you know there are thirteen possible meanings for the letter *A*?

Symbolic Dictionaries (more advanced content)

Chevalier, Jean and Alain Gheerbrant. *Dictionary of Symbols*. This is definitely for the more advanced or academic student. It is organized in an A to Z format. For example, if we look up *serpent*, there are 15 pages describing the religious, mythical, and cultural origins and meanings of this symbol. The book totals 1,174 pages.

Cirlot, J. E. *A Dictionary of Symbols*. This one is also for the more advanced student. It gives in-depth information in A to Z format. This book is 385 pages with illustrations.

Matthews, Boris, trans. *The Herder Dictionary of Symbols: Symbols from Art, Archaeology, Mythology, Literature, and Religion*. Great for the serious beginner of symbolism in A to Z format. Smaller and more compact at 222 pages with interesting illustrations. It explains origins of symbols from art, archaeology, mythology, literature, and religion.

Tresidder, Jack. *Dictionary of Symbols*. This is another great book to begin with. It is in an A to Z format with lots of illustrations. What makes this interesting is that interspersed in the alphabetic order are feature panels on symbolic systems such as afterworlds, the cross, beasts of fable, elements, fish, jewels, muses, numbers, planets, and the seven deadly sins.

Tresidder, Jack, ed. *The Complete Dictionary of Symbols in Myth, Art, and Literature*. The format and layout of this book is similar to Tresidder's *Dictionary of Symbols*, with an A to Z format interspersed with 61 feature panels (everything from Adam and Eve to the consorts of Zeus). It is well researched and readable with numerous pictures, paintings, and symbols. It contains completely different information from Tresidder's previous book. This is a great reference for finding most saints, sages, historical, and mythical figures. It contains 544 pages and over two thousand entries.

Pictorial Books on Symbolism

Bruce-Mitford, M. *Illustrated Book of Signs and Symbols*. An excellent cornucopia of coloured illustrations interspersed with text. It is divided into four basic sections: religions and mythologies, nature, people, and symbol systems.

Fontana, David. *Secret Language of Symbols*. David Fontana is a psychologist and university professor who has published books on dreaming and symbolism. This book is extremely comprehensive. The first three chapters cover various aspects of the power and use of symbols such as gods and myths, male and female, symbols in art, and dream symbols. The remainder of the book consists of categories in the "World of Symbols," such as shapes and colours, animals, the natural world, human and spirit symbols, and symbol systems such as alchemy, the kabbalah, the tarot, and astrology. This work is beautifully illustrated.

Gibson, Clare. *Sacred Symbols*. This provides an overview of the sacred symbols of the world's major religions and has great illustrations. It covers shamanic and tribal symbols, Mediterranean and northern European symbols, and Indian and Asian symbols including the Hindu, Chinese, Japanese, Buddhist, Jain, and Sikh faiths. The final chapter covers Jewish sacred symbols, Rastafarianism, Christianity, and Islamic symbols.

Gibson, Clare. *Signs & Symbols*. Much of this book centres on six categories: sacred symbols covering the world's major religions; symbols of identity such as national flags and emblems; symbols of magic and the occult; nature symbols; fantastic creatures; emotions; and the inner mind.

Gibson, Clare. *Secret Life of Dreams: Decoding the Messages from Your Subconscious*. There are many photographs and paintings to stimulate the imagination in this well-researched and well-written book. This is one of the best resources for a broader understanding of dream symbols. For each entry there are many questions to ask yourself, examples of possible meanings, and background information. The book is divided into 50 topics ranging from archetypes to erotica in dreams. Among these 50 topics, the book includes chapters on positive emotions, negative emotions, anxiety and frustration, conflict, the body, sports, games and entertainment, the weather, natural phenomena, time, the seasons, astral bodies, colours, shapes, numbers, magic, media, sounds, puzzles, and mysteries. This is a good investment for the true seeker.

Millidge, Judith. *Dream Symbols*. This will appeal to visual learners. It is divided into eight chapters that deal with archetypes and emotions, people, fauna, buildings, landscapes, transitions, objects, and abstractions.

Chapter Thirteen
Arriving at Truth Through Dreams

You shall know the truth, and the truth will set you free.
—Jesus (John 8:32)

Why God Doesn't Use Flashing Screens

When I first started working with my dreams, it was tough going. There were so many dreams that baffled me. It felt like I was trying to decipher a new language. I often wondered why dreams are hard to understand if they are so important. Why doesn't God just tell us? Wouldn't this be more efficient? He could have a little screen pop up while we sleep to display the appropriate messages:

> You're afraid to leave your job, but don't worry there's an opportunity waiting for you;
> You need to move to a new neighbourhood;
> Your boyfriend Jack is having an affair with your best friend Susan;
> It's your destiny to become a teacher;
> You need to start exercising—you'd have more energy;
> Your ego has gotten out of control again!
> Phone your brother, he's not feeling well.

In the beginning, the satisfaction I received from working with dreams kept me going. It can be a natural high with that rush of simply knowing. I stayed hooked because even understanding a few dreams felt amazing, and they were giving me direction. I journalled my dreams for about twenty years before I realized why God doesn't provide us with flashing television screens while we sleep.

It all has to do with free will. God doesn't intervene because He respects our free will. Dreams never try to control us; they never force or manipulate. Dreams never tell us we have to do anything. We have free will to make our own decisions. This is always the way God and spirit work. Free will gives us the option to create even more karma, or to repay our debts and live a more dharmic life of greater purpose and serenity. Dreams make us aware when something is stressful, painful, difficult, or karmic. They allow us to play with ideas or act out possibilities, but in the end, it's always up to us what we do with the awareness and insights we receive. God doesn't judge, condemn, or interfere with these decisions. Spirit just keeps guiding us until we've worked through all of our karma.

Free will is perhaps one of our greatest gifts from God. Without it we would be puppets, robots, or automatons with little human dignity. Thankfully, we're not puppets and God is not our puppet master. We were created with the potential to become enlightened. We all have the ability to be masters of our destiny or demise. Individually and collectively, we can make the world a place of great harmony or great chaos. It's a choice, and we're all responsible for our choices. Spirit never dictates what type of world we create. God never controls. He watches and waits with the patience of eternity. We have all the time in the world to clean up our karma and enact our destiny or dharma.

If God wanted, He could simply wipe out all the pollution that exists in the world. In one second, all the garbage dumps and industrial waste could disappear. But if He did, and nothing had changed inside of us, we would just keep on polluting the environment. After a few years, we'd have the same amount of garbage again. God desires us to get this right on our own. We all have access to internal wisdom. Tremendous satisfaction comes from tapping into this wisdom and working towards a personal and common good.

We see this in the movie *Oh, God!* starring George Burns as God, and John Denver as Jerry Landers the humble supermarket assistant manager who has been chosen as God's messenger. Jerry isn't happy with the state of the world, so when God first appears, he asks, "If you're so involved with us how can you permit all the suffering that goes on in the world?"

God replies, "Ah. How can I permit the suffering? I don't permit the suffering, you do. Free will. All the choices are yours."

"Choices? What choices?" Jerry asks.

God says, "You can love each other. Cherish and nurture each other. You can kill each other. Incidentally, kill is the word. It's not waste. If I meant waste, I would have written, thou shalt not waste. You're doing some very funny things with words here. You're also turning the sky to mud. I look down and I don't believe the filth. Using the rivers for toilets. Poisoning my fishes. You want a miracle? You make a fish from scratch. You can't. You think only God can make a tree. Try coming up with a mackerel. And when the last one is gone that will be that. Eighty-six on the fishes, goodbye sky, so long world, over and out."

Jerry replies, "I thought you said we were going to make it."

God answers, "I said you've got to make it work."

Perhaps the best analogy of how this works is a father-child relationship. A wise compassionate father doesn't interfere in his children's life. His children know he's always there to unconditionally love and support them. During childhood, he sets up boundaries, and codes of ethics and honour. After his children have grown, he's always concerned, but isn't overbearing or overprotective. He doesn't tell his children what to eat, where to work, whom to marry, where to buy a house, or how to raise their children. He lets his children experiment, grow, and discover all of life's mysteries on their own.

God never directly interferes or tells us what to do. We've all probably had the experience of trying to tell someone what we believed was right for them and had our words fall on deaf ears. It's the same with our Spiritual Father. He knows that, like a petulant child, we'll probably do it our way first, before we figure things out. He honours and respects our free will and ability to make choices. He knows through life's experiences—testing, trying, experimenting—we will make mistakes until we become wiser, more peaceful and compassionate. God believes that after all the trials and tribulations, we will walk a more dharmic path until we reach full enlightenment. Until we do, spirit is there twenty-four hours a day, seven days a week offering help. Even those who dismiss God from their life are still getting help on some level.

God, the perfect parent, allows us to experience consequences, frustrations, and possibilities in order to become more aware. As He watches, there is always guidance in the dream state and while we're awake. We're never deserted. Imagine a being that can simultaneously work with all six billion people on the planet in gentle unobtrusive ways. God delights in hands-on experiences. He marvels at humanity. He adores humanity because we're His children. In the physical dimension, God uses everything possible to give us help and clues. We never have to ask God for clues or signs because He knows what we want and need before we do, and He already has things in motion. We're being watched by God and a host of angels, archangels, and enlightened beings who desperately want us to clean up our karma. They can't do the work for us, but they delight in assisting whenever they can.

Let's imagine "Claire" is a real-estate agent, but she's always longed to be a pilot. For years she's been having dreams of flying planes. One afternoon, a sequence of events unfolds. She picks up a magazine and the first page has a Nike ad with the words "Just Do It." Claire turns on the radio and hears the song "I Can Fly." A client drops in and talks excitedly about their new flying lessons. Her friend sends a postcard from Brazil with a plane on the front. She picks up the newspaper and the lead story is about the expansion of the city airport. She has lunch with her boss, who comments about people getting stuck in careers they don't enjoy. Then Claire's husband phones from work to announce he's just been given a huge raise. This extra income will allow her to take time off to study. Imagine how many clues Claire would be given if she prolonged her decision for two more years?

In the world of dreams, spirit works with our emotions. We don't always need words. God doesn't stand on a cloud and say, "Hey, Claire, it's really your destiny to be a pilot." God lets us work things out in the dream state until we're comfortable with our decisions. In dreams, we may find archetypes or universal symbols energetically charged with emotion. The emotions accompanying these symbols are designed to propel us in a dharmic direction. Archetypal symbols are universally understood so that God doesn't have to hold up placards in seventy different languages. We all understand the exhilaration of climbing a mountain, the excitement of birth, the promise from a rainbow, or the ability to fly like a bird. So twenty-four hours a day, seven days a week, God and a multitude of enlightened beings guide us in our waking life and in dreams. These hints are brilliant, humourous, and insightful if we awaken to their presence. When we gain this awareness, we've found our spiritual wings.

Why God Doesn't Write Books

When I was studying to become a teacher, we were advised not to always tell students all the answers. This deprives students from the thrill of self-discovery. Learning was meant to be exciting. Good teachers don't give away the whole lesson. They ask questions, assign readings, and set up games and experiments so that students can discover the answers themselves. This is the true meaning of the Latin word for *educate*: *educare*, "to lead out, draw out, bring out." Self-discovery always feels wonderful. It's a joy, a natural high because we realize the answers are inside us and we have the capacity to be infinitely wise. This joy of self-discovery energizes and animates us, so it's only natural that we'd want to share our discoveries with others. When we do, others are energized and enlightened by our experiences and our enthusiasm. Think of the joy a six-year-old experiences when they've learned how to read their first book, ride a bike, or swim on their own. Learning and understanding in its purest form can provide a constant cyclical flow of energy, information, and insights that sustains everyone. Education or learning was originally designed by God to be an exciting joyful experience, contributing to a common good. Ever wonder why God didn't hand Moses a book and say:

> Here, Moses. I've written everything humans need to know in this book. If they follow these twelve easy steps, everyone will reach full enlightenment in just one lifetime. There will be no more suffering, wars, or disharmony. No one will die or get sick. The world will be like a Garden of Eden once again. Here it is. Have this translated into as many languages as you can. Tell everyone these are the words of the One True God. This is my truth and this truth will set everyone free.

Although there is great power in the written or spoken word, there is also great power to mistranslate, misinform, manipulate, or control. Essential parts of any written document can be left out so we don't get the entire picture. Words can be altered or substituted. The translator's own vision can replace God's. Much of the Christian Bible was first collated by the emperor Constantine while he was fusing existing pagan teachings with Christianity. Eighty gospels were possibly considered for the first New Testament, and yet only a few were chosen: Matthew, Mark, Luke, and John. What happened to the other disciples? And why is the Bible written only by men? We've seen what happened when Jerome substituted the word *witchcraft* for dreams when he was translating the Bible from Hebrew to Latin. Most of us turn to the Bible as a source of truth, but, the truth is, even Biblical scholars and theologians don't know its origins. The King James version of the Bible was written by a group of forty-seven unknown "scholars" hired by King James in 1604. Four hundred years later we still have no idea exactly who these "scholars" were. There's even speculation that William Shakespeare, who was a friend of King James, was one of these men.

Truth is different for every human being, and we each interpret things in our own way. Even history is subject to individual interpretation. Henry Ford said, "All history is bunk." And Napoleon once declared, "What is history, but a fable agreed upon." Our view of history can depend upon whether we have been conquered or whether we are the conqueror. A history book written on the 2003 war in Iraq by a Muslim scholar may give one account championing the rights of the Muslim people. If Saddam Hussein wrote this history book, he might have claimed he won the war. If an American scholar who supported George Bush wrote this book, the facts might be entirely different. Its claim could be that the Americans championed a noble cause and were clear victors. If a pacifist at a Canadian university wrote this history book, they may state that the war was unethical and there were clearly no winners.

Ten people could attend the same party and each report different experiences depending on their personalities, past experiences, how much they drank, what they ate, who they talked to, and whether they liked the music. "John" may say it was the best party he'd ever been to. He loved the food and was enthralled by this gorgeous woman he met. "Sarah" might have been counting the seconds until she could leave because she found the people boring and pretentious. "Jack" might have gotten so drunk he passed out and doesn't remember the party at all. We could say the same sentence at this party and each person would interpret it in a different way.

If we commented, "There were two deer in our backyard last night," we may get this range of ideas or responses:

- "Wow, you must really live in the boondocks!"
- "Yea, sure, I saw two bears in my backyard, and the night before there were two unicorns."
- "Were they vicious? Did they try to attack?"
- "Oh, that's great; you're so lucky to have beautiful deer around!"
- "Gee, deer always make me think of the movie *Bambi*."
- "I hope you didn't feed them, they'll be around all the time wanting more food."
- "You did! I'd love to come over sometime with my camera!"
- "That's interesting; their food supply must be depleted and they've had to move further south."
- "I wish I was with you and had my gun, I'd love to have enough venison to last the winter."
- "You know, I've never seen a deer in the wild. Just in zoos, and it's not the same."
- "Really? Did you ask if their names were Dasher and Dancer? Was Rudolph with them?"

Although books and the written word can be tremendously insightful, I believe we arrive at our greatest truths through non-physical means. I spent my entire life searching in book after book for answers or truth. The more I searched, the more I read, and sometimes the muddier my mind became. After I had completed five degrees, including a doctorate in psychology, I humbly had to admit I didn't know a whole lot, and was often frustrated in this search. A great deal of frustration ended when I finally understood that the realm of energy, spirit, dreams, and meditation was giving me answers that couldn't be found in books. Spirit has its own library; it exists within us and in many energetic sources of information on earth.

How Can We Know What's True?

It has become exceedingly difficult to know what is right or true. Even if we're completely devoted to one religion, we will probably experience doubt at times. God didn't write the Bible of any major religion. Jesus didn't write the Christian Bible. We're not sure who many of the Bible's authors really are. It's possible many of the original chapters have been completely left out. And as we've seen with St. Jerome, something is always lost in the translation. And then each Christian religion takes this third or fourth translation and reinterprets it again. Lists of religions and their Bibles could go on for pages. We have Buddhists, Muslims, Hindus, Judaism, and the Church of the Latter Day Saints with holy books written by their prophets. Included in the hundreds of existing religions, we have Anglican, Baha'i, Baptist, Buddhism, Catholicism, Christianity, Church of Christ, Church of Cyprus, Church of Greece, Church of the Latter Day Saints or Mormons, Confucianism, Episcopal Church, Hinduism, Islam, Jainism, Jehovah's Witnesses, Judaism, Lutheran Church, Methodist, Orthodox Eastern, Pentecostal Church, Presbyterian, Religious Society of Friends or Quakers, Rastafarianism, Rosicrucianism, Scientology, Seventh-Day Adventist, Shinto, Sikhism, Taoism, Unitarian, United, Unity, and Zoroastrianism. Is it any wonder we question what is truth?

To complicate matters even further, every major religion has their own morals and ideas regarding what is karma or sin. If we're a member of the Anglican Church, or the Jewish or Islamic religion, it's not a sin to divorce. However, if we're a Catholic or Hindu, divorce is a sin. Buddhists don't believe in sin or guilt the way we do in the

Western world; they believe divorce is not harmful. If we look at suicide, Anglicans believe it's not a sin. Catholics, Hindus, and members of Islam or Muslims believe suicide is a sin. If we're an Anglican, Catholic, or Muslim, cruelty to animals is not considered a grave sin. If we're Hindu, however, cruelty to animals is a sin, and animals such as the cow are revered. If we are a Buddhist, cruelty to animals is considered harmful or karmic.

Many religions believe they're the one true religion. Many religions believe they alone are the way to salvation. Many religions claim they're right and everyone else is wrong, misinformed, and misguided. If we begin exploring other religions, we can become terribly confused, misguided, lost, or cynical all in the attempt to discover truth. Many people become so disillusioned with religion, they question if God exists at all. So who is right and who is wrong? Can we find the One True God within organized religion, or must we go outside? The answer is simple: God is within every religion, but sometimes He is so hidden among interpretations, rituals, and rules that His truth can become lost. There is truth and light within every religion. If we have a sincere desire or intent to discover truth and to do the karmic and dharmic work needed to obtain it, we will. This is why nuns, monks, rabbis, hermits, priests, ministers, and imams of *every* religion have had epiphanies and mystical experiences. Truth and beauty always surround us. There is a legend in Fraser Boa's book *The Way of the Dream* about the creation of the human race:

> Legend has it that when the gods made the human race, they fell to arguing where to put the answers of life so the humans would have to search for them.
>
> One god said, "Let's put the answers on top of a mountain. They will never look for them there."
>
> "No," said the others. "They'll find them right away."
> Another god said, "Let's put them in the center of the earth. They will never look for them there."
>
> "No," said the others. "They'll find them right away."
> Then another spoke, "Let's put them in the bottom of the sea. They will never look for them there."
>
> "No," said the others. "They'll find them right away."
> Silence fell.
> After a while another god spoke, "We can put the answers

to life within them. They will never look for them there."

And so they did that.

God and truth have never been lost. Truth has always been hidden deep within our hearts. But this truth, these answers, can become buried by external non-truths. Personal truth can always be found no matter what religion we belong to. It can even be found by atheists, non-believers, and skeptics because the One True God *never* excludes any of His children.

In the movie *Oh, God!*, Jerry Landers is distraught because he's been chosen as a messenger. He feels completely inadequate to do this work. He feels there's been a mistake since he's never been part of an organized religion. But God points out that He's never been part of organized religion, either! He knew no one could misinterpret, take away, or distort what is inside us. Truth has always been there waiting to be discovered.

Ley Lines—Sources of Energetic Truth

Nothing gives rest but the sincere search for truth.
—Pascal

In ancient times, everyone understood the concept of ley lines, grid lines, or energetic highways that run through the earth. Some have always understood this wisdom, like dowsers who could find springs of water buried beneath the ground. But in this century, many have thought this practise was a little crazy, something for weirdos, not for rational sane people with a grip on reality.

We've all seen pictures of earth with multiple lines of longitude and latitude traversing the globe. They seem to form a grid system that holds the earth together. Ley lines are not physical lines that run through the earth, but they do form an *energetic* grid system. We can't see them, but this doesn't mean they don't exist. Ley lines or grids travel everywhere on earth like hydro or telephone wires. They're a source of magnetic energy and information that can be accessed by anyone. Since they're like energetic magnets, they can draw in both light and darkness. If positive activity aligned with the light is taking place at a ley line, that's what we feel. But if any type of dark karmic activity is taking place, it will draw in more dark characters because they'll be magnetically drawn to it. In life, we feel this magnetic or energetic pull to the people, places, and situations that are most like us. We can think of ley lines as energetic maps or blueprints carrying information. Since they're energetic, ley lines can move. Some are laid in stone or in permanent locations, but most are very movable and shiftable the way telephone wires can be moved or shifted.

Where two ley lines intersect or meet, there's greater energy and information, just like two hydro wires meeting in one place. In the same way that hydro wires carry the energy to run our computers, light our homes, play our CDs, the energy from ley lines carries the information to light and sustain our world. There are major and minor ley lines, just as there are major hydro wires channelling to minor electrical wires in our homes. In ancient times, we understood that many harmless snakes carried this energy and information along ley lines. They were like mail carriers or messengers. This is one of the reasons why snakes were sacred in many cultures.

Ley lines are history books of information. They can tell us what has happened at that site for millions of years if we're intuitive enough to read the energy. They hold all the wisdom needed to allow earth to run in harmony: past history, future possibilities, spiritual blueprints, destinies, and every invention that is yet to be discovered. Since they're sources of energy and information, ancient peoples gathered at these sites to pray, meditate, and receive guidance. The greatest concentrations of ley lines are often found in places where there are woods, water, and rolling hills. In the beginning, these sites were completely natural, often stone circles, hills, rivers, places of worship that our ancestors honoured and understood. Stonehenge is an example most people are familiar with. Another well-known site is the Tor in Glastonbury, a hill 520 feet above sea level dedicated to St. Michael, where pilgrims still gather. In ancient Egypt and Greece, pyramids and temples were built on these natural sites. As Christianity spread, churches were eventually built on top of the most powerful ley lines; Chartres in France with its underground spring is one example.

As churches were built, these powerful places of spiritual gathering became a different matter. When these gatherings were held at hills or circles of stones, the energy and information was accessible to everyone. We then had to belong to a specific religion to come to these sites of energy. The early stone masons who built churches knew how to trap the energy within the churches' structures. The crosses or spires at the top of churches acted like a beacon or lightning rod to draw the energy in. These steeples trapped the energy at the top of the church. The stained glass distorted the natural light from outside and prevented it from coming in. Today, most churches are places where huge amounts of energy and information are trapped. This is why many people have insights, breakthroughs, and tremendous spiritual experiences inside a church. But that energy is not freely accessible as it was in ancient times; it remains inside the church, along with all the energy and information of each person who enters the building.

What is even more enlightening is that we don't necessarily have to go to a church to have an epiphany, sudden awareness, or spiritual experience. Churches, many shopping malls, golf courses, parks, and roads are all built on ley lines. The downtown cores of many cities and towns are built on energetic ley lines. The intersections or corners often contain the greatest energy. This may explain why we suddenly have an idea or figure something out while we're driving our car, walking our dog, riding our bike, shopping, or playing golf. The original architects clearly knew what they were doing. Think of the structure of many modern shopping centres. Often there is a weather vane at the top, a church-like glass dome, and few windows letting in natural light. Why do you think shopping has become our number-one favourite activity? Why do we flock to malls on the weekends with religious fervour? There is more to this, energetically, than just getting that new pair of running shoes or jeans. This certainly doesn't mean we're drawn to shopping malls like robotic zombies just because energy is pulling us there. We'd probably go to the nearest mall when we needed to buy those running shoes anyway, but planners and developers are usually informed enough to build these malls in areas that are energetically conducive to shopping, browsing, or walking around. This is why we will never see a shopping mall built upon the former site of a tragic plane crash or near a Nazi Germany concentration camp.

Truth, energy, information can be discovered in a variety of ways, in countless places around the earth. If we're drawn to a certain bench in a park, love a particular golf course, or enjoy a certain corner in our home or garden, we may have discovered our own energetic site where we can access truth. These energy sites are everywhere since God excludes no one. It's possible there may be a ley line running through your school, backyard, home, or your favourite Tim Horton's. Before churches were built, our ancestors used natural sites but also private homes as meeting places. Is there a certain chair that everyone likes to sit in? If we watch animals carefully, we can often discover ley lines and places of energy. Cats and dogs will sleep on energy lines, and cows will walk along cow paths or ley lines.

Knowing this, if we wake up with a dream we don't quite understand, there are many places we may go to get further clarity and insight. If we have a favourite chair, a place in our garden where we like to sit, or a hiking trail we enjoy, we may choose this spot as a site to meditate on the meaning of a dream. We may go to that place, reflect on the dream, and allow insights and ideas to emerge. One of my favourite ways to meditate is by biking. There is a bike path near my home that winds along a river. It takes about two hours to bike the route from start to finish. Once I am able to clear my mind of all thoughts and just enjoy the surroundings, I always seem to get ideas and clarity. I may figure out a dream, work through an issue, understand a problem, and often I get information for the workshop manual I'm writing. It's like picking up the telephone and dialling 411 for information, except energetic information flows naturally, effortlessly, intuitively. It's a beautiful way to acquire wisdom and truth.

Truth in Dreams

Those who lose dreaming are lost.
—Australian Aboriginal Proverb

When we finally understand the meaning of a dream, there's no doubt; we just know inside. We can call it intuition, a gut feeling, a knowing, or personal truth. When we "just know," the power of intuition supercedes the mind. Although it may not seem logical or rational, we feel that it's right. An example of this inner knowing is found in the movie *The Horse Whisperer*. The movie shows the emotional traumas of fourteen-year-old Grace and her horse, Pilgrim. At the beginning of the story, Grace and her best friend are horseback riding and are involved in a horrific accident. Grace's friend doesn't survive. Pilgrim can't be ridden because he's too traumatized by the accident. Grace survives but must have one of her legs amputated. She tries returning to school, but her emotional pain is so deep that she drops out.

Annie, Grace's mother, is a magazine editor in New York. While searching for ways to help her daughter, she discovers someone on the Internet who communicates with troubled horses. When she phones this man, Tom Booker, he's far from encouraging; in fact, he's blunt and rude. But after their conversation, Annie is determined to take Grace and Pilgrim from New York to Montana to see this horse whisperer. When Annie proposes this scheme to her husband, Robert, it seems completely illogical. But she explains, "I don't care if this doesn't sound rational. Nobody is suggesting anything better. I just can't explain it, Robert. I just have this feeling. I just know it's the right thing."

Robert asks, "Why Annie?"

Her response is simply, "I just know it."

So Annie does the seemingly impossible. She takes a crazed horse and depressed daughter to Montana, guided by pure intuition. After a short time, the horse whisperer works miracles with both Grace and Pilgrim. Tom helps them retrieve the missing pieces of their spirits; they arrive broken but leave healed and capable of resuming their lives. Annie's instincts were correct. She trusted in the wisdom of her intuition rather than the often faulty logic of the mind.

Connecting to the Energy of Spirit

Why do you need a religion? Can't you just be with God? This is how God wants it.
—Anonymous

Truth comes from within. It resonates inside us. Sometimes, when we discover truth, it sends shivers through our entire body. In his book *Who Needs God,* Harold Kushner calls this "shivering before the holy." This connection, this truth, can make us weep when we don't even understand why. It allows us to "just know" when something is right, true, our path, destiny, dharma, even when others doubt or when it seems completely crazy. Inside we "just know."

If we become aware of what our soul is showing us in a dream, our body will often respond. Our body and emotions are a direct link-up to spirit and truth. If we understand a dream, at first we may experience the tiniest tingle, shiver, rush, or just the conviction, "Yes, this is right; this is it; I've got it." It feels good because it resonates inside. As time goes on, and we continue dreamwork and meditation, that tiny almost imperceptible feeling may get stronger and stronger because we're strengthening our connection to spirit.

This energy is the very pulse, the very heartbeat of the universe. It's known as *chi* in China, *ki* in Japan, *kundalini* in India. It's the energy that's activated and balanced in acupuncture. It's the energy rising up from its reservoirs of storage, the chakras in our body. It's the energy from ley lines connecting the universe.

When we get this shiver, tingle, "aha," shudder, goose bumps, or warmth, it's the energy of spirit pulsing through us. It's the current, energy, and life force of God telling us we're plugged into truth. We're alive and vibrating with no blockages. We're filled and animated with the energetic current of spirit. This current is telling us, yes, we're connected. That's right. We've got it. Remember this feeling. Remember this truth. This is who and what we are. Feel it in your body. And know that when you feel it again you're connecting to truth.

Perhaps the clearest and most important barometer in knowing whether we've understood a dream is the accompanying sense of joy and peace. Working through karma, paying our spiritual debts, or recognizing our destiny or dharma always gives us a sense of peace and joy. Anything that feels discordant isn't truth. If it's joyful, peaceful, or glowing like spirit, it's truth because spirit is truth. The One True God speaks from inside us because no one can judge, distort, or take away those unmistakable signs of energy and grace. No one can take away our shiver, vibration, gut feeling, natural high. They're all part of our spiritual inheritance from our true Father.

Final Meditation

I expect I shall be a student to the end of my days.
—Anton Chekhov

Life is a journey that can become either karmic or dharmic. If we're disconnected from spirit, we feel nothing—we're numb. But if we awaken our life force, this energy begins to surge through us. Each time we get that knowing feeling, we've connected to spirit. This is our truth. This is our spiritual path—our destiny or dharma. These are the truths that set us free and begin releasing us from lifetimes of pain and suffering. We may feel this connection more as we evolve. Energy may surge through our body when we watch a beautiful sunset, immerse ourselves in nature, show compassion to another person, make love, listen to music, play music, look at art, read poetry, write, cook, meditate, play, dance, move, or when we understand a dream. These experiences can all be direct connections to spirit. The more we engage in these experiences, the more we'll understand our place in the world. They bring us closer to our core. This is the place of natural highs.

As we dream, may any doubt, despair, or uncertainty be replaced with clarity, awareness, and conviction. May light and truth flow through us with its guiding wisdom. May you feel its warmth and joy. May this warmth extend to everyone you meet, simply by your presence. May spirit help you to feel the greatest compassion and love. In this way, person by person, we can put an end to much of the suffering that exists. May we all find our own mountaintops in life, and soar with the grace and joy that has always been inside us. As we soar, may we sweep away any shadows of karma and replace them with dharma. Enjoy this journey, for its potential for serenity, peace, exhilaration, and joy is enormous. May your destiny bring you renewed purpose and passion. May your dreams guide and inspire you to greater depths of awareness and higher mountain peaks until we're all soaring and flying as one.

References

Ackroyd, Eric. *A Dictionary of Dream Symbols*. London: Blandford, 1994.

Albert, Katherine. *Get A Good Night's Sleep*. New York: Simon & Schuster, 1996.

Anderson, Erin. "The Stuff of Dreams." *Globe and Mail*. 24 July 2004. F1, F8.

Anderson, Jane. *Sleep on It*. Sydney: Harper Collins, 1994.

Andrews, Ted. *Animal-Speak*. St. Paul: Llewellyn, 1998.

Andrews, Ted. *Dream Alchemy*. St. Paul: Llewellyn, 1991.

Bach, Richard. *Illusions*. New York: Dell, 1977.

Ball, Pamela. *10,000 Dreams Interpreted*. Great Britain: Prospero, 1997.

Ballantyne, Ned, and Stella Coeli. *Coles Dream Guide*. Toronto: Coles, 1980.

Bethards, Beth. *The Dream Book Symbols for Self-Understanding*. Boston: Element, 1995.

Boa, Fraser. *The Way of the Dream*. Boston: Shambhala, 1992.

Borysenko, Joan. *Fire in the Soul*. New York: Warner, 1993.

Boushahla, Jo Jean, and Virginia Reidel-Geubtner. *The Dream Dictionary 1000 Symbols from A to Z*. New York: Berkley, 1983.

Bradley, Marion Zimmer. *The Mists of Avalon*. New York: Random House, 1982.

Brown, Dan. *The Da Vinci Code*. New York: Doubleday, 2003.

Bruce-Mitford, Miranda. *The Illustrated Book of Signs and Symbols*. Westmount: Reader's Digest, 1996.

Budilovsky, Joan, and Eve Adamson. *The Complete Idiot's Guide to Yoga*. Indianapolis: Alpha, 2003.

Cameron, Bob, Margaret Hogan, and Patrick Lashmar. *Poetry in Focus*. Toronto: Modern Curriculum, 1983.

Cayce, Edgar. *Edgar Cayce on Atlantis*. New York: Warner, 1999.

Cayce, Edgar. *On Dreams*. New York: Warner, 1988.

Chevalier, Jean, and Alain Gheerbrant. *Dictionary of Symbols*. London: Penguin, 1996.

Cirlot, J. E. *A Dictionary of Symbols*. Trowbridge: Redwood, 1962.

Collier, Sandra. *Wake Up to Your Dreams*. Richmond Hill: Scholastic, 1996.

Coren, Stanley. *Sleep Thieves*. New York: Free Press, 1996.

Cotroneo, Christian. "While you were sleeping..." *Toronto Star*. 20 September 2002. D1, D4.

Crisp, Tony. *Dream Dictionary*. New York: Dell, 1990.

Crisp, Tony. *Dream Dictionary*. New York: Dell, 2002.

Das, Lama Surya. *Awakening the Buddha Within*. New York: Broadway, 1997.

Dean, Amy. *Night Light*. New York: Harper & Rowe.

Dee, Nurys. *Your Dreams and What They Mean How to Understand the Secret Language of Sleep*. Hammersmith: Aquarian, 1984.

Edwards, Peter. "Shrine of sacrifice." *Toronto Star*. Monday, May 6, 2002. B1 & B3.

Einstein, Alfred. *Ideas and Opinions*. New York: Three Rivers, 1982.

Emerald Tablets of Thoth the Atlantean. Translated by Doreal. Nashville: Source, 1996.

Faraday, Ann. *Dream Power*. New York: Berkley, 1972.

Faraday, Ann. *The Dream Game*. New York: AFAR, 1974.

Fontana, David. *Teach Yourself to Dream*. San Francisco: Chronicle, 1997.

Fontana, David. *The Secret Language of Dreams*. San Francisco: Chronicle, 1994.

Fontana, David. *The Secret Language of Symbols*. San Francisco: Chronicle, 1993.

Fromm, Erich. *The Forgotten Language: An Introduction to the Understanding of Dreams, Fairy Tales, and Myths*. New York: Grove Weidenfeld, 1951.

Gaarder, Jostein. *Sophie's World*. New York: Berkley, 1994.

Gannon, Sharon, and David Life. *Jivamukti Yoga*. New York: Ballentine, 2002.

Garfield, Frank, and Rhondda Stewart-Garfield. *Dreams*. Vancouver: Raincoast, 2000.

Garfield, Patricia. *Creative Dreaming*. New York: Ballentine, 1974.

Garfield, Patricia. *The Universal Dream Key*. New York: Harper Collins, 2001.

Gibson, Clare. *Signs & Symbols*. Rowayton: Saraband, 1996.

Gibson, Clare. *The Secret Life of Dreams*. Scotland: Saraband, 2003.

Gibson E. S., et al. "Sleepiness and the Health and Performance of Adolescent Students." *The Institution of Population and Public Health and the Canadian Institutes of Health Research*: November 2002.

Gillespie, Kerry. "Family bereft as abuse cases die." *Toronto Star*. 24 February 2002. A1, A6.

Goldschneider, Gary, and Joost Elffers. *The Secret Language of Destiny: A Personal Guide to Finding Your Life Purpose*. New York: Viking Studio, 1999.

Good News Bible. Toronto: Canadian Bible Society, 1979.

Greenfield, Susan, ed. *The Human Mind Explained*. Westmount: Reader's Digest, 1996.

Guiley, Rosemary Ellen. *Dreamwork for the Soul*. New York: Berkley, 1998.

Guiley, Rosemary Ellen *The Encyclopedia of Dreams*. New York: Berkley, 1993.

Harpur, Tom. "Mysteries of the cosmos dwarf those of theology." *Toronto Star*. 15 June 2003. F7.

Hazbry, Nancy, and Roy Condy. *How to Get Rid of Bad Dreams*. Richmond Hill: Scholastic, 1983.

Hauri, Peter, and Shirley Linde. *No More Sleepless Nights*. Toronto: Wiley, 1991.

Heath-Rawlings, Jordon. "Satan in a class all his own." *Toronto Star*. 18 February 2005. A3.

Holst, Wayne. "Raising religion's red flags." *Toronto Star*. 26 October 2002. L14.

Howell, Keith. "Reaching out a hand in comfort." *Toronto Star*. 6 April 2002. L14.

Ingram, Jay. "Mysteries of sleepwalkers and 'sexomaniacs'." *Toronto Star*. 2 May 2004. A14.

Johnson, Robert A. *Inner Work Using Dreams and Active Imagination for Personal Growth*. San Francisco: Harper & Row, 1986.

Jung, C. G. *Dreams*. New Jersey: Princeton UP, 1990.

Jung, C. G. *Man and His Symbols*. New York: Doubleday, 1964.

Jung, C. G. *Memories, Dreams, Reflections*. New York: Vintage, 1965.

Jung, C. G. *Modern Man in Search of a Soul*. New York: Harcourt Brace Jovanovich, 1933.

Kaplan-Williams, Strephon. *The Elements of Dreamwork*. Rockport: Element, 1990.

Kelsey, Morton. *God, Dreams and Revelation: A Christian Interpretation of Dreams*. Minneapolis: Augsburg, 1991.

Kincher, Jonni. *Dreams Can Help A Journal Guide to Understanding Your Dreams and Making Them Work For You*. Minneapolis: Free Spirit, 1988.

Kushner, Harold. *Who Needs God?* London: Simon & Schuster, 1989.

Langlois, Christine, ed. *Understanding Your Teen: Ages 13 to 19*. Mississauga: Ballantine, 1999.

Linn Denise. *The Secret Language of Signs*. New York: Ballantine, 1996.

Maas, James. *Power Sleep*. New York: Harper Collins, 1999.

MacKenzie, Norman. *Dreams and Dreaming*. London: Bloomsbury, 1965.

MacNeice, Louis. *Astrology*. London: Bloomsbury, 1989.

Matthews, Boris, trans. *The Herder Dictionary of Symbols*. Wilmette: Chiron, 1978.

Myss, Carolyn. *Sacred Contracts*. New York: Harmony, 2001.

Nesdoly, Tracy. "Evil bad luck has left me jaded." *Toronto Star*. 7 August 2004. M2.

Neville, Katherine. *The Eight*. New York: Random House, 1988.

Ostrander, Sheila, and Lynn Schroeder. *Superlearning*. New York: Dell, 1979.

Pagels, Elaine. *Beyond Belief*. New York: Vintage, 2003.

Perks, Sarah. "St. Patrick was once kidnapped by pirates." *Toronto Star*. 14 March 2004. D16.

Quinn, Jennifer. "No charges laid in fatal crash." *Toronto Star*. 8 August 2002. D3

Raffa, Jean Benedict. *Dream Theatres of the Soul*. Philadelphia: Innisfree, 1994.

Redfield, James. *The Celestine Prophecy*. New York: Warner, 1993.

Richmond, Cynthia. *Dream Power: How to Use Your Night Dreams to Change Your Life*. New York: Fireside, 2000.

Rowling, J. K. *Harry Potter and the Goblet of Fire*. Vancouver: Raincoast, 2000.

Sanford, John A. *Dreams: God's Forgotten Language*. New York: Harper Collins, 1968.

Savary, Louis M., Patricia H. Berne, and Strephon Kaplan-Williams. *Dreams and Spiritual Growth: A Judeo-Christian Way of Dreamwork*. Ramsey: Paulist, 1984.

"School Start Times: Final Report Summary." College of Education and Human Development. University of Minnesota. 1998.

Shakespeare, William. *Hamlet*. Toronto: Harcourt Brace Jovanovich, 1988.

Shapiro, Colin M., Nikola N. Trajanovic, and J. Paul Fedoroff. "Sexsomnia–A New Parasomnia?" *The Canadian Journal of Psychiatry*. (48:5) June 2003.

Shaw, Tucker. *Dreams*. New York: Alloy, 2000.

Shelley, Mary. *Frankenstein*. New York: Penguin, 1978.

Simmons, Michele, and Chris McLaughlin. *Dream Interpretation for Beginners*. London: Hodder & Stoughton, 1994.

Starbird, Margaret. *The Woman with the Alabaster Jar*. Rochester: Bear, 1993.

Tanner, Wilda B. *The Mystical Magical Marvelous World of Dreams*. Tahlequah: Sparrow Hawk, 1988.

Tart, C. T., ed. *Altered States of Consciousness*. Toronto: Wiley, 1969.

Thomson, Sandra A. *Cloud Nine: A Dreamer's Dictionary*. New York: Avon, 1994.

Todeschi, Kevin J. *Dream Images and Symbols: A Dictionary*. Virginia Beach: A.R.E., 2003.

Toye, Sue. "What Happens When We Sleep?" *University of Toronto Magazine*. (30:4) Summer 2003.

Tresidder, Jack. *Dictionary of Symbols*. San Francisco: Chronicle, 1997.

Tresidder, Jack. *The Complete Dictionary of Symbols in Myth, Art and Literature*. London: Duncan Baird, 2004.

Ullman, Montague, and Nan Zimmerman. *Working With Dreams: Self-understanding, Problem-Solving, and Enriched Creativity Through Dream Appreciation*. Los Angeles: Tarcher, 1979.

Van de Castle, R. L. *Our Dreaming Mind*. New York: Ballentine, 1994.

Vanzant, Iyanla. *Until Today*. New York: Fireside, 2000.

Weiss, Rick. "Wake up sleepy teens." *Washington Post*. 9 September 1997. Z07.

Zingrone, Frank. "Shakespeare, by god." *Toronto Star*. 16 January 2004. A21.

Index

Thank You, God, for Dreams

Thank you, God, for the gift of dreams.
A time when my body revitalizes and heals itself,
And when my soul is truly free.
Guide me in connecting to the wisdom of my spirit.
Allow my mind to recognize this grace and wisdom inside me;
Allow this grace to infuse my mind and make it holy.
Give me insight, clarity, and wisdom so that
I will awaken to my soul's journey in other dimensions.
In the darkness of night, may I journey always to dimensions of
light.
Protect me while I sleep, so that my dreams guide and inspire me.
Surround me in a pyramid of gold
That will deflect anything that is not of light.
May this protection keep away any darkness
That may prevent me from travelling in safety.
Shelter me in Your wisdom, grace, and love
Empower me while I sleep.
Help me make the connections and see the possibilities for my own
destiny.
Guide me in using this wisdom and clarity in life.
May I journey closer and closer to You
Until I truly understand the meaning of sweet dreams and blessed
peace.
Good night, dear God;
Bless this night and illuminate the path before me.

—*Marina*